Education
for the
Real
World

Henry M. Morris, Ph.D.

Master Books
A DIVISION OF CLP
San Diego, California

Education for the *Real* World

Copyright © 1977

First Edition—1st Printing 1977
              2nd Printing 1978
Second Edition—1st Printing 1983

Master Books
A Division of CLP Publishers, Inc.
P. O. Box 15908
San Diego, California 92115

ISBN 0-89051-093-8
Library of Congress Catalog Card No. 77-78017

Cataloging in Publication Data

Morris, Henry Madison, 1918-

   Education for the real world.

   1. Education. 2. Religion. I. Title.

370.114
M876e

ISBN-0-89051-093-8   77-78017

Printed in the United States of America

Foreword to the Original Edition

Is it really possible, in this twentieth century, to have a liberal arts college that is thoroughly Christian? There are many educators and educational associations that seem to feel that this is indeed an impossible combination in a technologically sophisticated society. Nor has the failure of literally hundreds of such experiments in our generation given us any encouragement to believe that it can be done. The "archaeological relics" of institutions that once enjoyed a high spiritual and academic reputation surround us on all sides.

To be perfectly honest and objective, educators in the various fields of the so-called liberal arts (fine arts, humanities, social sciences, natural sciences, etc.) who are deeply committed to the supreme authority of Holy Scripture in every area of life and thought must admit that *"with men this is impossible"* (Matt. 19:26). But hope cannot be allowed to die, for the same Lord of heaven and earth went on to say: *"but with God all things are possible."*

Thus, truly fruitful and successful Christian higher education must be carried on within the framework of divine special revelation (i.e., the Word of God) and must be sustained by Spirit-empowered faith, prayer, and obedience. The weapons of this "academic warfare" cannot be carnal, but must be "divinely powerful for the destruction of fortresses" of error on every level (cf II Cor. 10:4).

One prominent educator who is commited to this proposition is Dr. Henry M. Morris, a man whom I have known and have watched with great admiration for a quarter of a century. While it has been my experience to be closely associated with a Christian liberal arts college (Grace College, Winona Lake, Indiana) since 1948, Henry Morris has, until the 1970's, served as a professor and department head in three major secular institutions of higher learning. During those two decades, however, Dr. Morris had made a profound study of the Scriptures and hammered out a Biblical philosophy of liberal arts education which was tested in the crucible of experience at Christian Heritage College, where he served as co-founder, Academic Vice President, and President from 1970 to 1980..

It is my conviction that this volume will prove to be a significant milestone in our day. Far too much that passes for "Christian education" must be exposed for what it really it. Beginning a class with prayer and following it with a chapel service does not guarantee the Christian orientation of that class. If a study in the realm of liberal arts (whether it be literature, history, philosophy, psychology, biology, or music) does not directly or indirectly support God's special revelation to mankind in the Bible it must be either drastically revised or dropped. Such surgery in the academic body may be painful, but it is essential for the sake of its spiritual survival.

I am therefore happy to recommend this volume to Christian educators everywhere, with the prayer that God may use it to challenge all of us to a renewed determination to surrender unconditionally to His revealed plan for education that is truly Christian, even in our generation, in the light of His Great Commission to the Church (Matt. 28:18-20).

John C. Whitcomb
Winona Lake, Indiana

Foreword to the Second Edition

Dr. Henry Morris is the author of more than 40 books. He is regarded as the "dean of creation science." More than anyone else, he has made the Christian world, as well as the non-Christian world, aware of the Biblical perspective of the origin of our earth. In addition to being a qualified scientist, he is a Bible scholar uniquely qualified for the ministry God has given him.

This particular book, *Education for the Real World,* was originally published in 1977. It sold widely throughout the United States and other countries of the world. Dr. Morris has now added three additional chapters entitled, "Christian Rules for Christian Schools," "The Need for Biblical Certitude," and "The Christian and the Public School." As you read the entire book, including these new chapters, you will come to appreciate, as I did, the breadth and depth of wisdom the Lord as given Dr. Morris in a wide range of intellectual disciplines. Most of all, you will appreciate his commitment to the authority of the Scriptures and his abiding concern for the education and training of children and young people.

As a Christian school educator, I was particularly interested in his chapter, "Christian Rules for Christian Schools." He approaches this thorny topic as I knew he would—from a Biblical perspective, developing school rules that have their authority base established in Scripture. Most all of the rules that he proposes are nothing more than Biblical principles for Christian living. We all must conform to Biblical principles, and it is appropriate that we begin conforming in our early years during the educational process. Dr. Morris even includes a system of appealing decisions that adds a degree of justice and fairness for students.

Throughout all the writings of Henry Morris you discover his unique ability to communicate to his readers complex issues and topics in an understandable way. You are also impressed with his complete trust in Scriptural authority. In his chapter, "The Need for Biblical Certitude," he said, "The writer has been studying the Scripture daily and diligently for 40 years and he is more convinced today than ever before that every single word of the Bible is absolutely true and authoritative. The testimony of the psalmist in Psalm 119:97 has become more real and experiential each year: 'Oh how I love thy law! It is my meditation all the day.' "

The reading of this fine volume will give you a Biblical perspective of Christian education at all levels—elementary through college. I consider it a major contribution to America's education literature.

Dr. Paul A. Kienel
Executive Director
Association of Christian
Schools International

Introduction

As a long-time teacher, I have had the privilege of spending most of my life in the field of education. Although my original intent had been to make a career in the engineering profession, the Lord clearly led me, several years after graduation, into the ministry of teaching, and I have been there ever since.

Twenty-four years were spent teaching many different scientific subjects in secular universities, and then for eight years I taught mostly Biblical subjects in a Christian college. I have also taught regular Bible classes in various churches for over 27 years, some to junior high and senior high classes, but mostly to college-adult classes. Although an intensive travel schedule in more recent years has kept me from serving as a regular Sunday School teacher in this recent period, I have had the privilege of serving as guest teacher in many scores of church and college classrooms all over the country. In addition, I have combined the teaching with educational administrative responsibilities for over 30 years.

Many people, of course, have had even more experience in varied types of teaching. The above testimony is not meant to impress anyone, but only to express a long commitment to education and a sincere concern for its ministry to people of all ages.

The many years I spent in secular teaching, at five different universities, were marked by almost continual interaction with the evolutionary humanism being promoted in these schools, not only by faculty members and textbooks in the natural sciences but probably even more so by those in the social sciences and humanities. A similar situation prevails at practically every secular college and university in the world today. Furthermore, as I began to have more and more opportunities for contact with various Christian colleges, it became evident that most church colleges and even the interdenominational evangelical colleges had been infected by this same malady. Evolutionary cosmogonies and humanistic philosophies were often coated with a veneer of Biblical theology and Christian sentiment, but the inroads of such paganism were deep.

Although it is important to witness personally to the students on such campuses concerning their individual need of salvation (and I have had the joy of praying with many of them and seeing many accept Christ through these years), it soon became evident that this was essentially a strategy of retreat, salvaging a few here and there in the battle, but watching ungodly teachings and practices become stronger year by year, carrying greater numbers of students every year into complete unbelief.

Even the ministries of such campus Christian organizations as the Baptist Student Union, the Inter-Varsity Christian Fellowship, the Navigators, and Campus Crusade for Christ (and I have served actively as faculty advisor at one time or another for each of these) have been little more than voices in the wilderness. In spite of the many conversions resulting from the work of these organizations, the number of unsaved students increased even more rapidly, and the entrenchment of evolutionary humanism seemed to become deeper and stronger as time went on.

The real problem is that Christians have, for half a century (since the Scopes trial in particular), been concentrating on evangelism and "personal" Christianity, almost completely abandoning science and education to the evolutionary humanists. It is not enough merely to try to win individual students and teachers to Christ, important as that may be; we must win *education* to Christ! Wonderful though it is when a scientist comes to Christ, it would be still greater if we could see *science* turn to Christ.

Even though the return of the Lord Jesus may take place at any time, He did tell His followers: "Occupy till I come" (Luke 19:13). As pointed out in some detail later on, mankind is responsible for exercising dominion over the earth, and this commandment has not in any way been withdrawn. The enterprises of science and technology, and especially of education, are man's stewardship under God, to bring honor to Him. These commandments are more meaningful to the Christian than to the non-Christian, and he is under greater responsibility (because of greater knowledge) to see that they accomplish what God intended for them.

The *real* world is not the world of sin and warfare, hatred and conflict, in which we live now. This present age is only a temporary intrusion in the perfect world that God created in the beginning and which He will soon re-establish to endure forever. True education, therefore, must be education that will equip people for fruitful lives in both time and eternity.

The Christian school movement of recent decades has been a partial answer to the secularization of the public schools. Even Christian schools and colleges, however, have found it almost impossible to return to a truly Biblical system of education. In spite of their good intentions, the almost universal evolutionary bias in textbooks and the humanistic graduate schools where their faculty members have to obtain their training have prevented them from attaining or maintaining this standard.

Neither these reasons nor any others, however, can really justify any longer the common practice in Christian schools of compromising with evolution and humanism. There has been a serious revival of scientific creationism in the past twenty years and this development has eliminated any legitimate excuse for further compromise. Humanism and all other anti-Christian philosophies are based squarely on the assumption of evolution, and it has been clearly shown by creationist scientists that special creation is a much better scientific explanation for the world than evolution.[1]

There is thus bright hope and real opportunity in the days just ahead to reestablish a system of true education, based on the Biblical doctrine of education in all its fullness. God has raised up in recent years thousands of scientists, as well as many scholars in other fields, who are committed to faith in Christ and the Scriptures, and in particular to a world view founded on Biblical creationism. Such people could, if properly informed and motivated, do the necessary research, write the necessary books, and establish the necessary schools to accomplish the great ministry of bringing education and science back to God.

Or at least we ought to try! The hour is late; godless humanism has come to full flower in communism and other totalitarian systems which have already enslaved most of the world. If the Lord Jesus Christ does return soon, Christians will rejoice in His presence, but their

---

[1]See, for example, *Scientific Creationism* (ed. by Henry M. Morris, San Diego, Creation-Life Publishers, 1975, 283 pp.). This book is essentially a documented comparison of the relative effectiveness of the creation and evolution models in correlating all the scientific data relating to origins and earth history. In addition, it contains an extensive bibliography of creationist literature. A more recent book of the same type is the book *What is Creation Science?* by Henry M. Morris and Gary Parker (San Diego, Creation-Life Publishers, 1982, 318 pp.).

joy may be muted as they contemplate the billions of young people who are *not* there. And the reason they will not be there is largely because Christians have allowed those schools of an earlier day, where the youth were taught to respect God and His Word, to be replaced by schools where they are taught to reject them.

Until Christ *does* return, therefore, we must do all we can both to reclaim our public schools and, even more importantly, in view of the time factor, to establish sound Christian schools, where every teacher is God-called and properly prepared, and where all courses and textbooks completely conform to the principles of Scripture.

Although the illustrative examples in this book (reflecting my own experience) may emphasize college education, essentially the same principles and problems apply to Christian elementary and secondary schools, and, indeed to all aspects of the over-all ministry of true education at any level.

The purpose of this book is to try to place education in its true Biblical perspective, as best we can establish that perspective through sound Biblical exegesis. I believe it will be obvious that even our Christian educational enterprises have come far short of God's criteria, and we all have much work to do, as God enables, in order to build a true Biblical system of education. Furthermore, it will quickly become apparent that the opposition is strong and deeply entrenched, and a great battle must be fought and won before this goal can be reached.

Nevertheless, what God has commanded, He will enable to be accomplished. "For though we walk in the flesh, we do not war after the flesh: (For the weapons of our warfare are not carnal, but mighty through God to the pulling down of strong holds;) Casting down imaginations, and every high thing that exalteth itself against the knowledge of God, and bringing into captivity every thought [same word in the original as 'mind'] to the obedience of Christ" (II Corinthians 10:3-5).

I would like to express appreciation to a number of distinguished Christian educators who reviewed the original manuscript for this book and contributed many helpful criticisms and suggestions. These included the following:

John Whitcomb, Th.D., Director of Post-Graduate Studies, Grace Theological Seminary, Winona Lake, Indiana

Tim F. LaHaye, D.D., President, Christian Heritage College, El Cajon, California

Paul A. Kienel, M.A., Hum. D., Executive Director, Western Association of Christian Schools, Whittier, California

Vance A. Yoder, Ph.D., Academic Dean, Grace College, Winona Lake, Indiana

John N. Moore, Ed.D., Professor of Natural Science, Michigan State University, East Lansing, Michigan

Charles C. Ryrie, Th.D., Ph.D., Professor of Systematic Theology, Dallas Theological Seminary

G. Edwin Miller, Ph.D., Dean of the College, Christian Heritage College, El Cajon, California

E. William Male, Ph.D., Dean, Grace Theological Seminary, Winona Lake, Indiana

Arthur L. Peters, B.D., D.D., Executive Vice-President, Christian Heritage College, El Cajon, California

Dr. Whitcomb, a friend and colleague for many years, wrote the Foreword and this was particularly appreciated. My son, Henry M. Morris, III, assisted in various ways in research and preparation for the book, and Mrs. I. H. Morris, my mother, typed the manuscript.

Henry M. Morris
San Diego, California
June, 1977

Preface to the Second Edition

The writer has been very thankful for the fine acceptance accorded the first edition of this book. Many Christian teachers and Christian parents have testified that the Lord has used it in their lives and ministries in a much-needed way, and I hope it has contributed positively to the great cause of Christian education.

Three important topics were not treated in the first edition, however, and so three new chapters have accordingly been added to this edition. The troublesome, but necessary, matter of rules and regulations for the Christian school has been set in a Biblical context in Chapter 7. Then, since both curriculum and behavior in a Christian school must be based on Biblical standards, the need for establishing absolute confidence in the Scriptures in both students and teachers is discussed in Chapter 8. Finally, recognizing the hard fact that, even though they are unscriptural, public schools will continue to control the education of most young people for the foreseeable future, the Christian's responsibility toward these schools must also be faced, and this topic is treated in Chapter 9, stressing the urgency of restoring creationism—on at least a "two-model" basis—to these tax-supported institutions.

Dr. Paul Kienel, whom the Lord has used in such a thrilling way to lead the current renaissance of Christian education in our nation during recent years, graciously consented to write the Foreword for this second edition, and I am very grateful. In addition to Dr. Kienel, Dr. Richard Bliss, who is Director of Curriculum Development and Head of the Science Education Department at the Institute for Creation Research, has reviewed the manuscript for this new edition.

Contents

Chapter 1

Biblical Principles of Education

Christian schools are often criticized as being too idealistic, as not preparing their students for real life. "That's a jungle out there — a world of lust and politics, of struggle and survival — and young people need to be equipped to meet it. The school has to prepare them for the *real* world!"

Well, that's exactly the point. They do need to be ready to live in the real world, but the real world is not this present dying world. "The world passeth away, and the lust thereof; but he that doeth the will of God abideth forever" (I John 2:17). Christ "gave Himself for our sins that He might deliver us from this present evil world" (Galatians 1:4).

No, the *real* world is the world as God created it. "And God saw everything that He had made, and, behold, it was very good" (Genesis 1:31). That perfect created world will one day be restored and "we, according to His promise, look for new heavens and a new earth, wherein dwelleth righteousness" (II Peter 3:13).

If education is preparation for life, and life is preparation for eternity, then the schools must equip Christian young people for a life that will in turn equip them for their eternal ministries in the new earth, where "His servants shall serve Him" (Revelation 22:3), and the will of God will "be done on earth, as it is in heaven" (Matthew 6:10). Education in time must be education for eternity, if it is to be *true* education!

And true education must be grounded and governed by the Word of God, since there is nothing else in this present world which will survive in the real world. "Heaven and earth shall pass away, but my words shall not pass away" (Matthew 24:35). "Forever, O Lord, thy word is settled in heaven" (Psalm 119:89). We must therefore go to the Holy Scriptures — and only to the Scriptures — for our basic principles of real education for the real world.

The purpose of this small book is to outline the Biblical doctrine of education. Modern educators seem largely oblivious of the divine standards on this vital subject and, as a result, our present-day secular schools and colleges have become almost entirely humanistic in both curriculum and methodology. This situation has even come to characterize many religious schools, although these do attempt to ameliorate their humanistic orientation by providing a religious environment and fostering religious "experiences" for their students.

It is more than coincidental that a century of this type of education has yielded a society which is indifferent to moral and spiritual values and even to the discipline of education itself. "A good tree cannot bring forth evil fruit, neither can a corrupt tree bring forth good fruit" (Matthew 7:18).

The Bible has a great deal to say about education, a fact which is hardly surprising in light of the great importance of education. The transmission of knowledge from one generation to the next, the preparation of the young to assume their responsibilities in God's ongoing plan—such things must occupy a vital place in the divine purpose and it is quite realistic to speak of education as an actual Biblical *doctrine*. This doctrine is as important as any other doctrine of Scripture, but has been largely ignored by modern churches and even by most Christian schools, not to mention the public schools. It is high time to search the Scriptures for their teaching on this subject, to formulate them into a coherent and complete doctrine of education, and then to apply the doctrine in all of our educational systems.

THE SPECTRUM OF EDUCATION

The importance of education in the spectrum of human affairs is indicated merely by listing a representative sampling of educational activities.

I. Home
   1. Parental instruction in behavior and general living.
   2. Formal parental instruction—either directly or through employed tutors—in specific skills (reading, sewing, music, etc.).
   3. Spiritual and Biblical training, both by precept and example.

II. Church
   1. Pulpit ministry (assuming faithful teaching pastor).
   2. Formal Bible Classes (Sunday School, home study classes, etc.).
   3. Camps, retreats, summer conferences, etc.
   4. Vacation Bible Schools, youth groups, etc.

III. Elementary and Secondary Schools
   1. Public Schools.
   2. Vocational, technical, and military academies.

    3. Private non-religious schools.

    4. Parochial and denominational schools (especially Catholic, Lutheran, Reformed, Episcopalian, and Adventist).

    5. Private interdenominational or independent Christian schools.

IV. Personalized Instruction

    1. Correspondence courses, television courses, etc.

    2. Programmed-learning systems.

    3. Reading and personal research.

V. Higher Education

    1. Public colleges and universities.

    2. Private non-religious colleges and universities.

    3. Professional and vocational institutions.

    4. Denominational and sectarian colleges.

    5. Bible colleges and Bible institutes.

    6. Christian liberal arts colleges (a spectrum of institutions ranging from schools offering a predominantly secular curriculum supplemented by Bible courses and a spiritual atmosphere on the one hand, to schools attempting to structure all courses and curricula within a framework constrained by Biblical criteria on the other).

Another obvious commentary on the importance of education is the fact that every person has been a student in one way or another in the past and most people continue to be students at least intermittently throughout their lives (through Sunday School classes, personal reading, etc., if nothing else). Likewise, almost everyone is a teacher of sorts—at least as a church worker or parent, if never in a more formal sense. In fact, the education industry is so big today that a tremendous number of people actually make their living by teaching. Educational associations and teachers' unions now exert at least as much influence on our national life as does any other organized segment of society. Furthermore, it is well known that communists place great stress on teaching the young, both in their own countries and in free societies. In the latter, a major communist strategy is to infiltrate and subvert the educational system.

The potential for good or evil in the educational enterprise, depending on whether or not Biblical principles are followed in it, is obviously greater than for almost any other activity of mankind. We therefore want to make a systematic study of the Word of God to discover and understand these Biblical principles. First, however, it is necessary to take a brief look at the historical background of some of the false concepts of education that have been widely influential in modern-day school systems.

FALLACIOUS CONCEPTS OF EDUCATION

There have been many different philosophies and methodologies of education, and it is not our purpose to expound and critique all of these. There are three such concepts, however, which are of critical importance and are directly opposed to the Biblical doctrine. We shall call these systems: (1) statism; (2) rationalism; and (3) American progressivism, respectively.

(1) *Statism*. By this term we mean the system that regards the State as the ultimate authority and reality, so that all its youth should be educated by state-trained teachers with the primary goal of advancing the good of the State. Originating in antiquity, the statist philosophy of education was especially formalized and promoted by the Greek philosophers, notably Plato and Aristotle. In modern times, this system has been developed and followed to the extreme degree in Nazi Germany and in the various Communist nations.

Not a few American educators have also advocated this philosophy, which implicitly ignores the fact of a transcendent Creator and assumes that authority rests in corporate Man and his society. As far as the Bible is concerned, God has established the world's nations

(Deuteronomy 32:8; Acts 17:26), and patriotism is a noble attitude if one's country and its leaders are seeking to follow God's will. However, when such national patriotism is exploited to the point that the State—especially as personified in its leaders (whether inherent, appointed, elected, or by conquest) seeks to usurp the place or prerogatives of God, then it becomes idolatrous and blasphemous. Nations and their governments have indeed been "ordained of God" (Romans 13:1), and their future citizens should be taught to "submit to every ordinance of man for the Lord's sake" (I Peter 2:13), but when a choice between God's law and human ordinances confront them, they must be taught to "obey God rather than men" (Acts 5:29).

As we shall see, there is no Biblical authorization for government-controlled schools or teachers. Though governmental units are indeed Biblical institutions, it is the other Biblical institutions (home and church) to which God has given responsibility for teaching its citizens the truths of God's Word and the nature of God's world. While it may be argued that government schools could be appropriate if controlled locally by representatives of parents and if their teaching is in accordance with God's truth, it is assuredly *not* right when schools become a creature and tool of the State itself.

(2) *Rationalism.* The idea that human reason is autonomous and, when properly trained and utilized, is the ultimate source of truth has been strong in western civilization, especially since the Renaissance and the arrival of the "age of reason." With its roots also in Greek philosophy, it has become extremely influential since the industrial revolution and the rise of modern science, especially when combined with the powerful "scientific method." The concept that man's unfettered intellect (exercised in "academic freedom" through a "community of scholars") is potentially unlimited in

its capacity for discovering and applying "Truth" has been zealously advocated by many intellectuals in institutions of higher learning. Such scholars have argued vigorously that they should be commissioned to search for Truth as the ultimate good, without constraint or restraint from either home or church—or, for that matter, even from the State—and that they should likewise be free to teach the young whatever they think they have discovered in this search.

Such self-appointed independent seekers after truth are described by the Apostle Paul in his commentary on men of the last days—"ever learning, and never able to come to the knowledge of the truth" (II Timothy 3:7). Man's reasoning abilities and his capacity for learning the facts of God's truth (both as revealed in Scripture and as implicit in nature) are inestimably great—after all, he was created in God's image!—but they are by no means autonomous. The marvelous structure of man's brain (according to Isaac Asimov, "the most complex aggregation of matter in the universe") was created by God Himself, and it is purest arrogance for anyone to suppose his or her intellect is independent of the mind of God. Real truth can only be God's truth, and the reason so many never come to the knowledge of the truth is because they "resist the truth" and "turn away their ears from the truth" (II Timothy 3:8; 4:4). "Professing themselves to be wise, they became fools" (Romans 1:22).

Especially to be both pitied and censured in this connection are those professing Christian scholars who claim to have been born again and to believe the Bible, but who nevertheless feel it so important to maintain their acceptability to the intellectuals' "community of scholars" that they willingly yield to philosophy and scientism whenever there is apparent conflict with Scripture.

As far as the Scriptures are concerned, the idea of a community of scholars seeking and teaching truth in an atmosphere of academic freedom is presumptuous, to say the least. True teachers are divinely called and gifted, and their commission is to *transmit* the truth, as revealed in Scripture and as ascertained under the cultural mandate within the constraints of Scripture. This concept will be developed more fully in Chapters II and III.

(3) *American Progressivism.* The peculiar combination of statism and rationalism, supplemented by certain distinctively American innovations, that has been developed in the United States in the past 150 years, is here called American progressivism. The U.S. public school system has been the pride and joy of American educators ever since its beginning and has contributed significantly to American industrial leadership in the world. Nevertheless, it has also contributed to the secularization of America.

The Biblical foundations of America have been effectively summarized by Dr. Tim LaHaye;[1] originally its schools were Christian both in sponsorship and curriculum. To some degree the founding and later influence of the public school may be regarded as a divine judgment on the church because of its failure to provide Christian education for *all* Americans. In any case, for all its merits, the public school system in its present form has become perhaps the greatest of all influences *away* from God and His truth in America. To a large degree, both the form and the anti-Christian influence of the schools have been due to two remarkable men, Horace Mann and John Dewey. Mann has been called the "father of the American public school" and Dewey the "father of American progressive education." Though many other educators have had profound impact on the schools, Mann and Dewey are unquestionably the most important.

It is significant, therefore, that neither Mann nor

---

[1]Tim F. LaHaye, *The Bible's Influence on American History* (San Diego, Creation-Life Publishers, 1976) 82 pp.

Dewey were Christians in the Biblical sense (Dewey not in any sense!). Horace Mann (1796-1858) was a man who emphasized religion and morality, but he was Unitarian in church and theology. Although in those days Unitarians were not atheistic or pantheistic (as is largely true today), they did not believe in the Trinity or in the deity of Christ. Mann believed also in the unscriptural doctrine of the natural goodness of man, so that universal state-compelled education would, in his view, ultimately develop a perfect society. He stressed that every man had a basic right to full education, to enable him to reach the highest potential of his innate abilities, and that since the Christian schools were not meeting this need, the state should do it. The state should, furthermore, prepare its teachers—through its "normal" schools—so that they in turn could prepare each new generation for optimum service to society.

John Dewey (1859-1952) was born the year after Mann's death and, significantly, in the same year Charles Darwin published his history-changing book *Origin of Species*. Dewey was an early convert to Darwinism and attempted to make systematic application of evolutionary concepts to the curriculum and methodology of education. His religion was that of evolutionary pantheism. He believed that the cosmic process of evolution had finally reached a state of consciousness in man, who could therefore control future evolution. As Head of the Department of Philosophy, Psychology, and Education at the University of Chicago from 1894 to 1904, and then Professor of Philosophy and Head of Teacher's College at Columbia University from 1904 to 1930, he has profoundly influenced all other colleges of education and every generation of American teachers since his time.

Dewey was one of the founders of the American Humanist Association, the beliefs and teachings of which, for all practical purposes, constitute the state religion now fostered in his school system. His belief in the evolutionary ascendancy of man and the right of the state to guide future evolution through the training of its young is primarily responsible for modern secularism and experimentalism in the schools.

Though there is much that has been accomplished through the American educational system, it is a far cry from the type of education implied in Scripture. Even modern Christian schools have been influenced, in most cases, as much by modern secular educational philosophies as they have by Biblical principles. It is the purpose of this particular study, however, to determine and follow the latter exclusively, in so far as possible.

THE TRUE FOUNDATION
OF EDUCATION

In contrast to these false foundations of education, true education must be based on the world as it really is—not as the product of an evolutionary process but as God's Creation. Furthermore, it must be recognized that there is no dichotomy between physical truth and religious truth, as many people believe. There is one God and one universe. He is the Author of *all* Truth, and His Word is His inerrant revelation of Truth. The real foundation of education must be threefold: (1) God as Creator of all things; (2) Christ as Redeemer of all things; (3) The Holy Spirit, through the Scriptures which He inspired, as Revealer of all things. The "ontological Trinity," as it has been called, is necessarily the basis of all reality, as discussed briefly below.

(1) *God as Creator of All Truth.* If one acknowledges that God is the ultimate Creator of all things, then he should recognize that everything created was, in the beginning, *truth.* "God saw everything that He had made and, behold, it was very good" (Genesis 1:31). All reality—whether physical things, living organisms or spiritual and moral concepts—comes under the broad category of created truth and is proper

material for inclusion in the educational enterprise. *Knowledge* of the true world God created and *wisdom* in the comprehension and application of that knowledge must comprise the goals of true education. Note the testimony of Scripture concerning the foundational truth of God as the Creator of truth.

"In the beginning, God created the heavens and the earth" (Genesis 1:1).

"All things were made by Him, and without Him was not anything made that was made" (John 1:3).

"By Him were all things created, that are in heaven and that are in earth" (Colossians 1:16).

"He that planted the ear, shall He not hear? He that formed the eye, shall He not see? . . . He that teacheth man knowledge, shall not He know?" (Psalm 94:9-10).

"Thou art worthy, O Lord, to receive glory and honour and power: for thou has created all things, and for thy pleasure they are and were created?" (Revelation 4:11).

"The fear of the Lord is the beginning of knowledge" (Proverbs 1:7).

"For with thee is the fountain of life: in thy light shall we see light" (Psalm 36:9).

God is the Creator of all that is real and true and good, whether physical, biological, or spiritual. On the other hand, any distortion or dilution of the real and true and good is *not* good. It becomes untruth and, in the ideal and ultimate sense, unreal. It seems obvious that anything which is bad, false, and, finally, not real, has no proper place in education—except solely to point out to students its *true* character as *untruth*.

"God is light, and in Him is no darkness at all" (I John 1:5).

"Thou art of purer eyes than to behold evil, and canst not look on iniquity" (Habakkuk 1:13).

"But as He which hath called you is holy, so be

ye holy in all manner of conversation" (I Peter
1:15).

"Be ye therefore perfect, even as your Father
which is in heaven is perfect" (Matthew 5:48).

(2) *Christ as Sustainer and Redeemer of all
Truth.* The fact that God is the Creator, however, should
not be interpreted to mean that this present age is not,
indeed, largely characterized by evil. Physical evils
(storms, earthquakes, disintegration), biological evils
(disease, suffering, death), and spiritual evils (lying,
stealing, hatred) are all surely with us, and such things
are *not good!* Since God is completely good, however,
and since He adjudged His completed creation to be
"very good" (Genesis 1:31), sin and suffering can only
represent *temporary intruders* into His creation,
which He has allowed for a time for two reasons. First,
for man to be a responsible being in God's image, he
must be able to *choose* fellowship with his Creator. Second, for man to know God in His fulness, he must know
Him both as Creator and Redeemer.

The testimony of all human history is that man has
chosen wrongly. He desired evil rather than good and
falsehood rather than truth. Nevertheless, rather than
abandoning or destroying His creation, God is sustaining
and reconciling it. Jesus Christ, the Son of God, has
become man in order to redeem both man and the entire
creation. Because of man's sin, God's judgment had
necessarily fallen on man and all his dominion. The
redemption price is nothing less than the substitutionary death of Christ.

"And, having made peace through the blood of
His cross, by Him, to reconcile all things unto
Himself; by Him, I say, whether they be things
in earth or things in heaven" (Colossians 1:20).

"That, in the dispensation of the fulness of
times He might gather together in one all things
in Christ, both which are in heaven, and which
are on earth; even in Him" (Ephesians 1:10).

"Because the creation itself also shall be
delivered from the bondage of corruption into
the glorious liberty of the children of God"
(Romans 8:21).

Even before Christ paid the price to redeem the
world, He was "saving" it. That is, He was sustaining
and energizing its systems and processes; otherwise, it
would have collapsed into chaos under the great Curse
that was on it.

"The heavens and the earth which are now, by
the same word are kept in store, reserved unto
fire against the day of judgment and perdition of
ungodly men" (II Peter 3:7).

". . . upholding all things by the word of His
power" (Hebrews 1:3).

"For in Him we live, and move, and have our
being . . ." (Acts 17:28).

There are therefore three universal principles within
which we now must understand and teach all truth:

(1) all things as originally created were good and
were ideally and completely organized for their intended purpose, in perfect harmony with all the rest of
God's creation;

(2) all things are now under the divine Curse because
of man's sin, so that there is a universal law of decay
and death operating in all systems and processes.

(3) all things, nevertheless, are the objects of Christ's
redemptive love and are potentially reconcilable to
God on the basis of His substitutionary death and vic-
torious resurrection.

The Biblical doctrine of education must be focused on
these great themes. Whether in chemistry or sociology,
history or biology, music or literature, or whatever the
course of study, everything must be understood and
taught in the framework of God's perfect creation, the
universal effects of sin and the curse, and the saving
work of Christ. If any one or more of these are denied or
ignored, the subject is not being taught in truth.

(3) *The Holy Spirit and His Revelation of all Truth.* A legitimate question arises at this point, however. Since we ourselves are sinners, our students and their parents are sinners, and the researchers and textbook writers also are sinners, how are we now to discern the truth in order to teach it? Exactly *how* should we teach a course in geology or psychology (or even religion) so that the students learn and obey the truth rather than a lie?

The answer is by the Holy Spirit, through the Scriptures inspired by Him. As God is the Creator of truth, and Christ the Sustainer of truth, so the Spirit is the Revealer of all truth.

> "When He, the Spirit of Truth is come, He will guide you into all truth . . . for He shall not speak of Himself. . . . He shall glorify me" (John 16:13, 14).

> "The Spirit of truth . . . shall testify of me" (John 15:26).

> "Thy word is truth" (John 17:17).

There is no claim, of course, that the Bible records *every* individual item of truth. Nevertheless, such claims as in the foregoing passages do warrant the following inferences: (a) every statement of Scripture, taken in context and, properly applied, is infallibly true and authoritative; (b) the Scriptures provide the basic framework and guiding principles within which *all* truth, wherever found, must be interpreted and utilized; (c) it is the ministry of the Holy Spirit to guide men into all truth so that, wherever truth is discovered, its author and revelator must ultimately be none other than the Spirit of God; (d) since His purpose in revealing truth is to glorify the Lord Jesus Christ, all real truth must and does accomplish this purpose.

To summarize the above discussion on the foundation of education, it should be emphasized that there is no boundary or dichotomy between spiritual truth and secular truth; *all* things were created by God and are being sustained by Him. Therefore, we can learn any aspect of truth only in accordance with His will to reveal it. His written Word, as now completed (note Revelation 22:18,19) is comprehensive and definitive truth in all areas of life and study. Those aspects of truth which appear superficially to be "non-religious" are in reality fully under the authority of Biblical revelation and must be consciously and clearly taught as such in true Christian education.

THE CULTURAL MANDATE

At this point, however, we must consider a very important question. Granted that all truth is one and is under God, then to what extent can the natural man—one who, perhaps, does not believe the Bible or even believe in God—discover and apply truth? Is it valid for Christians to believe and teach data and ideas emanating from the research and reasonings of unregenerate men and, if so, to what extent is this legitimate?

The answer lies in the proper analysis and exposition of those commandments and dispensations of God that were intended to be applicable to all men, not merely to a chosen segment of mankind. The first and most significant of these is God's very first commandment—a commandment that has come to be known as the *cultural mandate*.

"So God created man in His own image, in the image of God created He him; male and female created He them. And God blessed them and God said unto them, be fruitful and multiply, and replenish [literally, 'fill'] the earth, and subdue it; and have dominion over the fish of the sea and over the fowl of the air and over every living thing that moveth upon the earth" (Genesis 1:27,28).

In order to subdue the earth and have dominion over

it, it would be necessary for mankind to occupy every region of it, so that an extensive multiplication was required, starting from the first man and woman. It is obvious also that, since man's dominion was given to him by God, it was *under* God. Man was not independent of God, but was His steward. He was to *keep* the earth (Genesis 2:15), not exploit and waste its resources. The command to "subdue" does not imply that the earth was an enemy, but rather that it was a complex and wonderful world to be ordered and controlled for man's benefit and God's glory.

The cultural mandate in this original form applied solely to the physical and biological components of the creation. The *earth* which was to be subdued was the physical globe with all its elements and components and appurtenances, possibly including even the entire solar system and conceivably, the entire physical cosmos, all of which had been "made" from the elements of the "earth" as originally created in Genesis 1:1.

The second part of the mandate had to do with the biological division of the creation, the *nephesh,* the "every living soul" of Genesis 1:21, the animals inhabiting the earth's hydrosphere and atmosphere and lithosphere.

Now, to perform the function of subduing and exercising dominion over the physical and biological creations necessarily implies the development of physical and biological sciences (physics, chemistry, hydrology, etc., as well as biology, physiology, ecology, etc.) and the concordant development of physical and biological technologies (engineering, agriculture, medicine, etc.). These assigned activities of mankind under the cultural mandate thus imply the dichotomous, yet complementary, enterprises known by the modern combinatory terms of science and technology, research and development, theory and practice, etc.

The first term in each of these pairs (science, research, theory) suggests the study and understanding of the created world or, as Newton and Kepler and other great scientists have put it, "thinking God's thoughts after Him." Such study, of course, should *now* be carried out entirely within the framework of truth as revealed in the Scriptures.

The second term (technology, development, practice) suggests the application and utilization of the physical and biological processes and systems, as learned from their scientific study, for the benefit of mankind and the glory of God.

But there were *three* great creative acts of God. Only two of them (the physical creation of Genesis 1:1 and the biological creation of Genesis 1:21) were included in the terms of the cultural mandate. The third was the spiritual creation—the creation of man and woman in God's image (Genesis 1:27). No command to subdue or to have dominion was appropriate in this case since, as originally created, man was sinless and in perfect fellowship with God. Had he remained so, there would never have been occasion for those activities of mankind now known as the social sciences. There was no need for men to study other men and their behavior (psychology, economics, etc.) or to control other men (government, criminology, etc.), for all men should have been in perfect communion with the will of God and in fellowship with one another. Those aspects of human life which were primarily physical or biological could properly have been included in the mandated physical and biological sciences, but there would have been no need for the study or dominion over man's moral or social relationships at all. Those disciplines now known as the humanities (literature, art, music, etc.) would have been devoted to glorifying God and His works, with nothing speaking of conflict or ugliness at all. All such ideal conditions, however, have been destroyed by the entrance of sin into the world.

When sin entered into the world, profound changes took place in all three of God's created domains—physical, biological, and spiritual—in response to God's curse on the creation. The "ground" itself was cursed (Genesis 3:17), as were the living creatures (Genesis 3:14), but the curse fell most heavily upon mankind (Genesis 3:19). The principle of decay and disintegration began to operate in physical systems; mutations, disease, and death began to function in biological systems (including man's body); and, most importantly, separation and alienation from God became man's tragic experience in the spiritual realm from then on. Alienation from God, of course, immediately produced alienation between man and man, soon leading to fratricide (Genesis 4:8) and eventually to universal violence and anarchy (Genesis 6:5-13).

After the great Flood, there was a new start for the world and mankind, but it is still under the curse and will be so until the establishment of the new earth (Revelation 22:3). According to the Apostle Paul, "we know that the whole creation groaneth and travaileth in pain together until now" (Romans 8:22).

In spite of the universal curse, however, God has not destroyed the world. To the contrary, He has undertaken to redeem it and to reconcile it once again to His will and fellowship. Even the physical and biological aspects of the curse were "for man's sake" (Genesis 3:17), and God promised a coming Redeemer at the same time that He pronounced the curse (Genesis 3:15).

Furthermore, the cultural mandate is still in effect, as is evident from its restatement to Noah after the Flood (Genesis 9:1,2). In fact it was now broadened to include human inter-relationships; man was now given the responsibility to govern mankind as well as the animals (Genesis 9:6). This broadened mandate is now incorporated in the Noahic covenant (Genesis 9:12), which was established with all men and is still in effect to this very day.

Therefore, the physical and biological sciences, both

pure and applied, are still needed and warranted. In addition, in this present world, there has now arisen a great need for the social sciences (psychology, sociology, etc.) and their technologies for implementation in organized human societies (economics, government, politics, etc.), so that these fields now also come within the terms of the cultural mandate and thus are proper disciplines for inclusion in education.

There is a problem, however—a very serious problem. Man's sin has so corrupted his moral and spiritual nature that he is said to be "dead in trespasses and sins" (Ephesians 2:1). He is not capable of reasoning correctly in the realm of intrinsic meanings, moral choices, spiritual relationships or anything related to his unique creation in God's image, until he is "born again" (John 3:3). Therefore, all educational activities—textbooks, schools, courses, research studies, etc.—must be examined very critically in light of God's Word to discern whether they are true or false and whether their use will be good or bad. This subject will be examined in greater depth in Chapter III. In general, we can merely point out here that factual and quantitative data in all areas of study are accessible to all men and thus are appropriate to incorporate in courses and curricula. The interpretive and philosophical treatments that may be applied to such data, however, strongly depend on one's spiritual condition and may be false and dangerous if not carefully constrained by Scripture. Such dangers are especially present in the social sciences (and even more in the so-called humanities and fine arts), because these fields are more closely related to man's spiritual nature, which is dominated completely by sin (Romans 3:10-19) until he receives the new birth. These important implications of the Adamic mandate, the Edenic curse, and the Noahic covenant will be discussed in greater detail in Chapter IV.

THE TRANSMISSION OF TRUTH
(The Ministry of Teaching)

It is important that true knowledge and wisdom, once known, not be either lost or corrupted. It is, therefore, the responsibility of each generation to transmit its knowledge of truth, undiluted and undistorted, to the succeeding generation. This is the ministry of teaching. Formal educational programs may be conducted either in the home, the church, or the school, and we shall discuss these institutions in that order.

(1) *Primary Responsibility in the Home*. The home is the first and most fundamental of all human institutions. It was established directly by God when He made the first man and woman (Genesis 2:18,24). In the original creation—indeed, up until the time of the Noahic Flood—there was apparently no other institution at all for either governmental or educational purposes. It was evidently the responsibility of the parents, especially the father, to maintain order in the household and to teach the children.

After the Flood, as we have noted, God did establish the institution of human government, but there is no intimation of any formal divinely established educational institution. In fact, the first actual mention of teaching in any form is found in Genesis 18:19. Speaking of Abraham, God said: "For I know him, that he will command his children and his household after him, and they shall keep the way of the Lord to do justice and judgment." It is significant that this first mention of teaching in the Bible not only speaks of a father teaching his children but also suggests that the primary purpose of that teaching was moral and spiritual, rather than vocational or cultural.

The same themes are stressed in the Mosaic laws:

"And these words, which I command thee this day, shall be in thine heart: And thou shalt teach them diligently unto thy children, and shalt talk

of them when thou sittest in thine house, and
when thou walkest by the way, and when thou
liest down, and when thou risest up"
(Deuteronomy 6:6,7).

The first priority in education, therefore, is clearly
the revealed Word of God. The importance of teaching
the Scriptures to children is further confirmed in the
New Testament.

"And that from a child thou hast known the
holy scriptures, which are able to make thee
wise unto salvation through faith which is in
Christ Jesus" (II Timothy 3:15).

"And ye fathers, provoke not your children to
wrath: but bring them up in the nurture and admonition of the Lord" (Ephesians 6:4).

It is clear that, in God's economy, the primary
responsibility for educating the young lies in the home.
The foundation of this education is in recognition of God
and His purposes, as revealed in the Scriptures. For
most of the world's history and in most of its cultures,
all other education has likewise been centered in the
home. Formal schools are characteristic only of more
complex societies.

(2) *The Church and the Great Commission.* Sadly, the parents in most of the homes throughout history
have not measured up to their teaching responsibilities,
especially in transmitting the true knowledge of God
and His Word. In any case, in this present age, one of
the primary ministries of the church is that of teaching.

The Great Commission was given by Christ to all His
disciples, especially as organized in the church. His
command was not only to make disciples and baptize
them, but also to "teach them to observe all things
whatsoever I have commanded you" (Matthew 28:20).
In view of the tremendous breadth and depth of Jesus'
life and teachings (John says "if they should be written
every one . . . even the world itself could not contain the
books that should be written" John 21:25), this commandment is exceedingly comprehensive. Since Jesus

taught that all the Old Testament was inspired and authoritative, everything contained therein is certainly also included in His commandment. Furthermore, all the implications in Scripture relative to the physical universe in all its aspects are a legitimate extension of the command.

It becomes obvious that education in *all* truth is the responsibility of Christians—both individually in their homes and corporately in the church. Individual fathers no doubt found it impossible to assimilate and transmit the entire body of truth to their children, especially as more and more divine revelation was given to men through the ages and as more and more knowledge of the creation was accumulated. In the church, on the other hand, God is able to call and equip teachers as needed for all aspects of its educational ministries. The teaching function of the church would in no way replace or usurp that of the home, but would complement and extend it.

The church, with the Holy Scriptures to guide it, and the Holy Spirit to empower it, is therefore established by God to guard and transmit the full truth of God's written revelation and natural revelation, ". . . the church of the living God, the pillar and ground of the truth" (I Timothy 3:15). It should be stressed that the term "church" in this connection refers to what is known as the "local church" as an institution. Each local church is responsible for guarding and teaching God's truth to its own members and community.

(3) *The School as an Extension of the Home and Church.* It is significant that there is no reference in the Scriptures to the school as a separate institution established by God. In spite of the great importance of the teaching ministry, God has not seen fit to ordain schools as such. Even the implications of the cultural mandate and the Noahic covenant, with the establishment of the institution of human government, do not suggest the parallel establishment of schools as instruments of such

human governments. As far as the Bible is concerned, the function of transmitting truth and educating the young belongs to the home and church.

This fact does not necessarily mean that parents and pastors have to do all the actual work of teaching. It is certainly appropriate for them to employ qualified tutors and trainers, but the control of the educational process should remain primarily with the home and secondarily with the church.

As with so many other divine ordinances, however, man has sadly corrupted God's plan, especially in these latter days, until finally the educational activities of mankind—as formalized in vast systems of public education—have become a chief instrument for turning men *away* from the truth, insofar as God's purposes are concerned.

The methods and institutions for teaching and child training have varied from nation to nation and century to century. Archaeology has revealed that even the most ancient civilizations had high technologies, and that literacy may have been the rule rather than the exception. In Egypt and Mesopotamia, there were schools associated both with the temples and the government. Advanced training for scholars and scientists was probably a function of religious priesthoods in most cases.

This seems to have been true also in Greece and Rome, especially after the advent of the great philosophers. With the latter, formal schools began to be developed, organized especially around training in grammar and rhetoric, training in music and poetry, and training in gymnastics, respectively. Such schools were designed to perpetuate the Greek and Roman culture and tended to glorify the state.

Regardless of the methods of education employed in various times and places, our real concern is to determine what the Bible says on the subject. As already shown, the Scriptures indicate that teaching was originally the province primarily of the home. As time went on, some teaching functions seem also to have been assumed by the religious leaders of Israel.

For example, what was tantamount to a "school for prophets" seems to have been established in Israel in the days of Samuel and again under Elijah and Elisha. This is evident from the several references to an organized group called "the sons of the prophets" (I Samuel 10:5,10; II Kings 2:3,5,7,15). Likewise, there are incidental references to the teaching of scholars in the tabernacle (I Chronicles 25:8 mentions "the teacher and the scholar," as does Malachi 2:12). One of the functions of the priests and Levites was to teach God's law to the people (Leviticus 10:11; Deuteronomy 33:10; II Chronicles 17:7,9; Ezra 7:10). II Chronicles 15:3 mentions the ministry of the "teaching priest".

More formal schools developed with the rise of the synagogue and other post-exile institutions. According to the Talmud and Hebrew tradition, boys were trained in regular classes at the local synagogue school (the title "Rabbi" meant, essentially, "teacher"). Emphasis was on the teaching of the Scriptures, but in the process, the students were also taught reading, writing, and mathematics. The teaching of foreign languages and of physical education were specifically prohibited because of their close associations with pagan philosophy and culture.

The early Christians were able to utilize to a limited extent the Jewish synagogues (Matthew 13:52; Acts 13:5; etc.) as opportunities for evangelistic teaching, but soon had to develop in their churches means for more formal instruction of their own members. Although all Christians were exhorted to "teach and admonish one another" (Colossians 3:16), the Holy Spirit also prepared and called special teachers for the church (I Corinthians 12:28). This ministry of teaching continues to this present day and is vital for our understanding of the Biblical doctrine of education.

(4) *The Gift and Calling of Teaching.* There are three main New Testament passages dealing with the different "gifts" possessed by individual Christians for use in the service of Christ and the church (Romans 12:1-8; I Corinthians 12:1-31; and Ephesians 4:7-16). Each of these utilizes the analogy of the various members of a human body, applying it to the role of individual believers in serving the entire Christian community (Romans 12:4,5; I Corinthians 12:12-27; Ephesians 4:12,15,16). In one case, the gifts are said to be from God (Romans 12:3); in another, from the Spirit (I Corinthians 12:7-11); and in the other, from Christ (Ephesians 4:7).

All three lists are different, which indicates that no complete specific enumeration is possible or necessary. Some gifts, including that of the apostle and probably others as well, were only to apply until their purpose had been served. No doubt, other gifts not specifically included in any one of the three lists would be added as needed in the future, so that all necessary provisions for the carrying out of the Great Commission in all ages would be available.

In view of this variable nature of the gifts, it is significant that the gifts of teaching and prophecy are the only ones included in all three lists (Romans 12:6,7; I Corinthians 12:28; Ephesians 4:11). Since the gift of prophecy (the supernatural conveyance of divine revelation to man—note II Peter 1:21) would cease (I Corinthians 13:8) when there was no further need for it (evidently when God's revelation had been completed—note Revelation 22:18), it is evident that the gift of teaching is the one gift absolutely essential in every church in every age!

The gift and ministry of teaching, of course, focus primarily on the teaching of the Scriptures. It must not be forgotten, however, that the Scriptures provide the framework for *all* teaching. All truth—physical, biological, and spiritual—is created and sustained by

God in Christ and revealed by the Spirit. Furthermore, the ministry of teaching is the responsibility of the home and the church—not of the state. Consequently, this vital gift of teaching applies to all true God-called teachers—teachers of science and grammar as well as teachers of the Bible and theology.

Having the gift of teaching is not simply equivalent to having a talent for teaching, of course. There are many ungodly men and women who are excellent teachers as far as natural abilities are concerned. As a matter of fact, the more effective such a person is in the art of teaching, the more dangerous he is. This is true not only for those in secular schools but also for those in Christian schools and even in Sunday schools. The Apostle Peter gave sober warning against false teachers, no matter how winsome and eloquent they might be.

> ". . . there shall be false teachers among you,
> who privily shall bring in damnable heresies . . .
> and many shall follow their pernicious ways . . .
> they speak great swelling words of vanity, they
> allure through the lusts of the flesh . . ." (II
> Peter 2:1,2,18).

All teaching—no matter how profound, attractive, or eloquent, must be tested by its fidelity to the Word of God (Isaiah 8:20; Acts 17:11). Those who are teachers or who desire to be teachers should continually examine themselves on this basis, to be sure they are teaching by virtue of God's calling them to such a ministry, and for no other reason. There is, in fact, a serious warning to all who aspire to the teaching profession.

> "My brethren, be not many masters [literally,
> 'don't many of you become teachers'], knowing
> that we shall receive the greater condemnation"
> (James 3:1).

That is, a teacher's influence for good or bad is so great that failure to exercise it for good will result in greater punishment than would failure in other ministries. On the other hand, a good teacher receives great rewards.

"Let the elders that rule well be counted worthy of double honor, especially they who labor in the word and doctrine" (I Timothy 5:17).

"I have no greater joy than to hear that my children walk in truth" (III John 4).

"Whosoever therefore shall break one of these least commandments, and shall teach men so, he shall be called the least in the kingdom of heaven: but whosoever shall do and teach them the same shall be called great in the kingdom of heaven" (Matthew 5:19).

There will be further discussion on teacher qualifications in Chapter V. At this point we merely wish to stress the importance of being sure that one is truly called to the ministry of teaching, and thus has been given the gift of teaching by the Holy Spirit. This is only the beginning, of course. Even the Apostles had to have three years of training under Christ (perhaps corresponding, in the modern setting, to a three-year Bible Institute), and the highly educated Paul still had to undergo three years of special study in the desert and in Damascus (Galatians 1:11-24—possibly analogous to a three-year Seminary training) before they were ready to go forth as teachers of the Word.

It is obvious that adequate training is necessary before one can effectively teach mathematics or biology, but too often people attempt to teach the Bible with only a minimum of background study. The following admonitions are salutary in this connection.

"Study to show thyself approved unto God, a workman that needeth not to be ashamed, rightly dividing the word of truth" (II Timothy 2:15).

"My son, if thou wilt receive my words, and hide my commandments with thee: So that thou incline thine ear unto wisdom, and apply thine heart to understanding; Yea, if thou criest after knowledge, and liftest up thy voice for understanding; If thou seekest her as silver, and

searchest for her as for hid treasures; Then
shalt thou understand the fear of the Lord, and
find the knowledge of God" (Proverbs 2:1-5).

"Oh how love I thy law! it is my meditation all
the day. . . . I have more understanding than all
my teachers: for thy testimonies are my
meditation" (Psalm 119:97,99).

THE GOALS OF TRUE EDUCATION

True Christian education, as set forth in the Bible,
embraces all truth, whether "secular" or "spiritual."
It is not narrow and restricted education, as some
might assume, but extremely comprehensive—in fact
universal—in its scope. Nothing is to be excluded except
false knowledge and harmful philosophy, but, unfortunately, these constitute a large component of modern
educational curricula. They must be removed from a
Christian curriculum, but there is far more than enough
genuine and valuable truth to incorporate in their
stead.[1]

The main goals of such an education are threefold:
the transmission of the truth; the training of individual
students for productive lives in the will of God; and the
development of corporate completeness in Christ. Each
of these goals is discussed briefly below:

(1) *Indoctrination in the Truth.* All of God's
revelation is "forever settled in heaven" (Psalm
119:89). However, through the ages, He has been
gradually transmitting it into the minds and hearts of
men. "God . . . at sundry times and in divers manners
spake in time past unto the fathers by the prophets"
(Hebrews 1:1). Although these prophetic revelations
have now ceased (I Corinthians 13:8; Revelation 22:18)
and the written Word is complete, in one sense God is

---

[1]For criteria justifying an exception to this rule, see Chapter IV, p. 140 and
Chapter V, p. 149.

still transmitting His truth to men. That is, God-called teachers continue to expound the written Word and new truth is continually being discovered therein.

> ". . . every scribe which is instructed unto the kingdom of heaven is like unto a man that is an householder, which bringeth forth out of his treasure things new and old" (Matthew 13:52).

Also, under the cultural mandate, researchers continually are discovering truth concerning God's creation and then applying it in many technologies.

All of this is truth which must be transmitted from each generation to the next. Though it is desirable that none should be lost or corrupted at all, it is absolutely necessary that God's written Word especially be maintained and transmitted uncorrupted. This, of course, is a main reason for Bible-centered education.

> "One generation shall praise thy works to another, and shall declare thy mighty acts" (Psalm 145:4).

> "A seed shall serve him; it shall be accounted to [of] the Lord for a generation. They shall come and declare His righteousness unto a people that shall be born, that He hath done this" (Psalm 22:30,31).

> "Thou, therefore, my son, be strong in the grace that is in Christ Jesus. And the things that thou hast heard of me [from me] among [attested by] many witnesses, the same commit thou to faithful men, who shall be able to teach others also" (II Timothy 2:1,2).

The teacher, of course, must both know and believe the truth if he is going to transmit it effectively.

The actual process of transmission is nothing less than *indoctrination*. It is significant that, in the New Testament, the word "doctrine" is the same noun as "teaching" (Greek, *didaskalia*). That is, the process of true teaching is nothing more nor less than indoctrinating. Teaching is not the discovery of truth, nor sharing the truth; it is indoctrinating the truth!

Such indoctrination, with no distortion or dilution, is absolutely vital in true education. Otherwise, the truth will be either corrupted or lost altogether.

"I . . . write unto you, and exhort you that ye should earnestly contend for the faith which was once delivered unto the saints" (Jude 3).

"Whosoever transgresseth and abideth not in the doctrine of Christ, hath not God. . . . If there come any unto you, and bring not this doctrine, receive him not unto your house, neither bid him God speed" (II John 9,10).

The "doctrine of Christ" in this passage is, literally, "Christ's teachings." The command is, in effect, not to allow anyone who does not abide in His teachings—that is, teach them all, without addition or deletion—to teach in your house, or church, or school. In fact, such a false teacher is not even to be pleasantly sent on his way. Rather, he must be exposed and opposed as "a deceiver and an antichrist" (II John 7) because he is effectively rejecting either the deity or humanity of Christ.

Such Scriptures point up the extreme importance of this aspect of the teaching ministry. No doubt the above warning applies specifically to those false teachers who willfully and knowingly distort the teachings of Christ. At the same time, those who take on the ministry of teaching without proper preparation and understanding on their own part may innocently distort those teachings and the effect on their students and in the preservation of the faith may well be as bad as though they did it deliberately.

(2) *Training of Students.* A second major goal of education is that of preparing students for productive, Christ-honoring lives. Every believer has been "saved and called with an holy calling" (II Timothy 1:9), and it is the privilege of the teacher to help that student find God's will for his life and to help prepare him for a fruitful ministry in his field of service.

The familiar proverb is relevant here. "Train up a child in the way he should go: and when he is old, he will not depart from it" (Proverbs 22:6). The original language does not refer primarily to moral behavior. Rather, the phrase "the way he should go" should be understood in the sense of "the way he was ordained to go." God has called each Christian and provided basic talents for that child or young person to enable him to fill a very specific role in the kingdom of God. The teacher needs to help him find and follow God's will in this calling. Then, his life will not be squandered in an occupation or activities which are *not* "the way he should go."

The teacher (or the parent—remember that the primary teaching responsibility is still in the home) may well, by virtue of his own experience and knowledge of the Word, be better able to recognize God's will for that student than the student himself. Hence the command—"Train up . . . ." This word actually means "dedicate;" the same word as is used in connection with the dedication of the holy temple. It is important to note that the command to dedicate the child in the way God had planned for him was not given to the child but to his teacher. What an important ministry, and what a sober responsibility! The teacher is not only to teach the truth, but also to teach the child!

(3) *Completeness in Christ.* Traditionally there has been a division among teachers in the public schools as to whether their responsibility was to teach history (or algebra or art or whatever their subject was), or to teach and develop the child into a good citizen. In the one case, they felt no responsibility for discipline or extra-curricular duties; in the other, they felt that specific course content was relatively unimportant if the child was becoming "well-adjusted."

As we have pointed out, however, the Biblical doctrine of education stresses that both are vitally important. Solid truth, complete and unmixed with error, must be taught, but teachers must also do all in their power to help all their students find and follow God's will for their individual lives.

Now, all of this is ultimately directed toward a third and even greater goal, the glory of God through Jesus Christ. This is beautifully expressed by Paul to the Ephesians in his discussion of the "gifts (including that of the teacher).

"But unto everyone of us is given grace according to the measure of the gift of Christ. . . . For the perfecting of the saints, for the work of the ministry, for the edifying of the body of Christ: Till we all come in the unity of the faith, and of the knowledge of the Son of God, unto a perfect man, unto the measure of the stature of the fulness of Christ" (Ephesians 4:7,12,13).

The eventual goal of education—as well as that of evangelism, the pastoral ministry, and all the other callings of God—is that all His creation shall be in harmony with Him and shall honor His name (see the testimony of universal praise in Psalm 148:1-14; Psalm 150:1-6; Ephesians 3:21; Revelation 4:9-11; 5:8-14; etc.). The teacher must help his students fulfill God's will in their lives because they are to "grow up into Him in all things," with each member of the body functioning in its own necessary contribution to the whole, "the whole body fitly joined together and compacted by that which every joint supplieth, according to the effectual working in the measure of every part" (Ephesians 4:15,16).

The teacher must likewise be careful to teach the truth, as it really is in Christ, to his students. The body can only be effectively unified in "the unity of the faith and of the knowledge of the Son of God" (Ephesians 4:13). The teacher, in other words, must manifest both love and truth in his teaching, "speaking the truth in love" (Ephesians 4:15).

Thus, the wonderful three-fold goal of teaching must be to transmit the truth in fulness and purity, to train the student with love and wisdom, and to glorify Christ, in whom perfect love and absolute truth will be united forever.

Chapter 2

The Creationist Framework of True Education

The material taught in the educational system is much more than a set of facts to be memorized and utilized. The facts must be analyzed and interpreted; they must be placed in a coherent framework, so that men can understand how individual bits of truth relate to each other and to the whole body of truth. Such a framework, if sufficiently comprehensive to embrace *all* facts, becomes a world view.

The foundation of any world view must necessarily be its concept of origins. The way in which a person views life and its meaning, as well as its ultimate goals, inevitably depends on what he believes about ultimate beginnings. Intentional or not, the teacher and textbook are certain to deal with origins, implicitly or explicitly, in every subject which they teach. One's world view is thus bound to affect everything he believes and teaches, one way or another. It is important that public school teachers and textbook writers recognize this fact and attempt to deal with their respective subjects as objectively as possible in relation to the different concepts of origins. In a Christian school, however, the Christian world view is vital and must be convincingly presented as qualitatively superior to all others.

THE TWO COSMOGONIES

As a matter of fact, there are really just two basic world views, those of evolution and creation. The Biblical cosmogony is the only true creationist cosmogony, all others are evolutionary. To appreciate the significance of this fact, it is important to understand first the meaning of these two terms.

Evolutionism is the philosophy that purports to explain the origin and development of all things in terms of continuing natural processes in a self-existing universe. Creationism, on the other hand, explains the origin and development of all things by completed supernatural processes in a universe created and sustained by a transcendent, self-existing Creator.

By these definitions, the two concepts are mutually exclusive, and it is meaningless to talk about believing in *both* evolution and creation, as many have tried to do. Some try to think of evolution as "God's method of creation," but this concept is merely a special form of evolution known as *theistic evolution* and is certainly not creationism as above defined. Similarly, there is a special form of creation known as *progressive creation,* in which certain acts of supernatural creation are supposedly inserted into various stages of the naturalistic evolutionary process, but this inevitably becomes either theistic evolutionism or true creationism when examined critically as to the specific acts of creation which are postulated. These compromise concepts will be examined in more detail later, but for the present our discussion will center on the basic evolution and creation models as defined above.

Both of these basic concepts of origins may be considered as axiomatic in their respective systems. There is no way to test either of them scientifically; they are questions of history rather than science. As axioms, however, they can be compared in terms of their respective abilities to correlate the scientific data. Just as each axiom is the opposite of the other, each has two corollaries which are opposite to those of its rival.

In the evolution model, the present order necessarily involves changes amounting to innovation and integration, bringing new systems into existence and developing them "vertically" toward higher degrees of complexity (or "order," or "information"). The creation model, on the other hand, indicates that the present order must be characterized by conservational (i.e., "horizontal") changes within limits, supplemented perhaps by *downward* vertical changes, leading toward decreased complexity and perhaps complete disintegration. Such a model is supported by such Scriptures as Genesis 1:31 and 2:3 (speaking of the completed, perfect creation) and Genesis 3:17-19 and Romans 8:20-22 (telling of God's curse on all creation because of man's sin).

Another corollary of the evolution model is that earth history has been dominated by uniformitarianism (uniform operation of natural laws and processes). In contrast, the creation model suggests that the geological and other records of earth history should be interpreted in terms of catastrophism (highly accelerated process rates operating within uniform laws). Peter confirms this model by pointing out that the original world order was cataclysmically destroyed in the Genesis flood (II Peter 3:3-6).

It should be stressed that there exist only these two basic models of origins, creation and evolution, and that they must be defined essentially as above. It is significant that all cosmogonies, whether in ancient paganism or modern scientism, are really evolutionary cosmogonies, with the sole exception of the Genesis record. All such systems start with the universe in some form, with the various forces of nature, perhaps as personified by different gods and goddesses, gradually changing it into its present form. Only in the book of Genesis is there an account of the actual creation of the universe itself, with all its basic systems brought into existence and organization by a transcendent personal God in the beginning.

As stressed above, neither of these basic cosmogonies can be proved, or even tested, scientifically. Either one must be accepted on faith, and so both are fundamentally religious in nature. It should be obvious, therefore, that both should be taught in the public schools, on as nearly an equal and objective basis as possible. If there are parents and teachers who desire only creation to be taught, they should form a private Christian school for this purpose. If there are those who desire only evolution to be taught, they should form a private humanistic school for this purpose. In the *public* school, however, both should be taught. An anomalous situation exists today, however, in which evolution is considered the only acceptable cosmogony for the public schools. This fact will be documented in the next section.

EVOLUTIONISM IN
MODERN EDUCATION

The dominance of evolutionary teaching in modern biology is such a well-known fact that it hardly needs documentation. However, it is not as well known that evolutionary thinking is also basic in most other disciplines. In fact, its influence is more powerful in the social sciences and humanities than in the natural sciences.

To illustrate this state of affairs, consider the following comments from authorities in the various fields. These are typical and could be multiplied many times over if needed.

(1) Natural Sciences (Biology, Geology, Astronomy, Physics, etc.). James D. Watson, one of the co-discoverers of the structure of the D.N.A. molecule, universally recognized as one of the world's leading molecular biologists says:

> "Today, the theory of evolution is an accepted fact for everyone but a fundamentalist minority, whose objections are based not on reasoning but on doctrinaire adherence to religious principles."[1]

Similarly the prominent evolutionary ecologist, Rene Dubos, has said:

> "Most enlightened persons now accept as a fact that everything in the cosmos . . . from heavenly bodies to human beings . . . has developed and continues to develop through evolutionary processes."[2]

(2) Social Sciences and Humanities (History, Psychology, Sociology, Literature, etc.). The man who was probably the most influential evolutionist of our present generation, until his recent death, was Sir Julian Huxley. Selected as the first Director-General of UNESCO, and also as the keynote speaker at the great Darwinian Centennial Convocation at the University of Chicago in 1959, Sir Julian was probably the man more responsible than any other one person for the modern acceptance of the neo-Darwinian concept of evolution. Although he was a biologist, he was wide-ranging in his cultural interests and, among other things, was one of the founders of the American Humanist Association. Concerning the influence of evolution in non-biological fields, he said:

> "The concept of evolution was soon extended into other than biological fields. . . . subjects like linguistics, social anthropology, comparative

---

[1] James D. Watson, *Molecular Biology of the Gene* (New York; W. A. Benjamin, Inc., 1970), p. 2.

[2] Rene Dubos, "Humanistic Biology," *American Scientist,* Vol. 53, March 1965, p. 6.

law and religion . . . today we are enabled to see
evolution as a universal and all-pervading
process."[1]

In the same vein, Rene Dubos pointed out:

"Evolutionary concepts are applied also to
social institutions and to the arts. Indeed, most
political parties, as well as schools of theology,
sociology, history, or arts, teach these concepts
and make them the basis of their doctrines."[2]

(3) Morals, Ethics, and Religion. It is bad enough
that the teaching of those subjects involving human
social and economic activities (government,
economics, history, sociology, etc.) and those involving
personal and cultural relationships (psychology, art,
literature, philosophy, etc.) should be dominated by a
naturalistic evolutionary perspective, as the foregoing
quotations indicate. But it is still worse when this
philosophy takes over in the spiritual realm—ethics,
morality, religion. That, however, is what has happened. If evolution is the ultimate reality, then those actions are moral and ethical—even religious—which contribute to the further advance of the evolutionary
process.

Ernst Mayr, one of the nation's foremost current
leaders of evolutionary thought and a professor at Harvard, says:

". . . the Darwinian revolution of 1859 [was]
perhaps the most fundamental of all intellectual
revolutions in the history of mankind. It not only
eliminated man's anthropocentrism, but
affected every metaphysical and ethical concept, if consistently applied."[3]

Dr. Theodosius Dobzhansky, Russian immigrant,
professor at Columbia, Stanford, Rockefeller, and

---

[1] Julian Huxley, "Evolution and Genetics," Chapter 8 in *What Is Science?*
(Ed. by J. R. Newman; New York: Simon and Schuster, 1955), p. 272.

[2] Rene Dubos, *ibid.*

[3] Ernst Mayr, "The Nature of the Darwinian Revolution," *Science,* Vol. 176,
June 2, 1972, p. 981.

University of California (Davis), was one of the world's leading evolutionary geneticists until his recent death. Such a doctrinaire evolutionist that he refused to read anything written by a creationist, Dobzhansky discussed evolutionary ethics as follows:

"Natural selection can favor egotism, hedonism, cowardice, . . . cheating and exploitation. . . . Ethics are human ethics. They are products of cultural evolution."[1]

Another significant evaluation of the moral implications of evolution comes from a professor at Emory University:

"Unbridled self-indulgence on the part of one generation without regard to future ones is the *modus operandi* of biological evolution and may be regarded as rational behavior."[2]

(4) *Education Theory and Method.* The content of practically every discipline taught in modern schools and colleges is thus based on the evolutionary premise. More documentation to this effect is available if needed.[3]

But this is not all. Not only the content, but the methodology itself—the very curriculum and structure—of modern education is based on evolution. This fact is illustrated best in the writings of the architect of modern education, John Dewey himself. Of his philosophy, biographer and historian Will Durant says:

"The starting point of his system of thought is biological: he sees man as an organism in environment, remaking as well as made. Things are to be understood through their origins and their functions, without the intrusion of supernatural considerations."[4]

---

[1] Theodosius Dobzhansky, "Ethics and Values in Biological and Cultural Evolution," *Zygon, the Journal of Religion and Science,* 1974.

[2] W. H. Murdy, "Anthropocentrism - a Modern Version," *Science,* Vol. VII, 187, March 28, 1975, p. 1172.

[3] Henry M. Morris, *The Troubled Waters of Evolution* (San Diego, Creation-Life Publishers, 1974), pp. 25-48; 145-194).

[4] Will Durant, "John Dewey," in *Encyclopedia Britannica,* 1956, p. 297.

His antipathy to the Bible and Christianity is indicated by the following:

"I cannot understand how any realization of the democratic ideal as a vital moral and spiritual ideal in human affairs is possible without surrender of the conception of the basic division to which supernatural Christianity is committed." [1]

In other words, there is no difference in Dewey's philosophy between Christian and non-Christian, believer or unbeliever, saved or lost. All are products of the same naturalistic process and animal ancestry.

"Man is a social animal . . . the heart of the sociality of man is in education." [2]

Education, in Dewey's view, was the means to the end of attaining an ideal humanistic society, in which man, as personified in the democratic state, would be the ultimate reality. His followers have led the public schools farther and farther toward this goal. One of these, John S. Brubacher, discussing one of Dewey's articles on "Education as a Religion," interpreted its meaning as follows:

"Education would then become at once the symbol of humanity's as-yet-unrealized potentialities and the means of its salvation. . . . It would not be in conflict with science! On the contrary, it would be based on science." [3]

By "science," of course, Brubacher means *evolution*. Modern educationalists believe that application of the same principles of evolutionary progress that supposedly produced man in the past will thereby lead man's society onward and upward to perfection in the future. Our nation's public schools and the colleges of education which produce their teachers are indeed

[1] John Dewey, *A Common Faith* (New Haven, Yale University Press, 1934), p. 84.
[2] John Dewey, *Intelligence in the Modern World* (New York, Modern Library, 1939), p. 629.
[3] John S. Brubacher, *Modern Philosophies of Education* (New York, McGraw-Hill Publ. Co., 1939), p. 321.

seeking diligently to apply those principles today, and the schools have become, in effect, religious centers for the indoctrination and propagation of the gospel of evolutionary humanism.

HISTORY OF THE
EVOLUTIONARY WORLD-VIEW

John Dewey, of course, was not the originator of the theory of evolution, which he adopted and implemented so vigorously. But neither, for that matter, was Charles Darwin, who is usually given credit for it. Evolution was a belief held by many long before Darwin. As a matter of fact, Darwin did not even originate the idea of natural selection, although this was his claim and the theme of his famous book. The perceptive historian, Jacques Barzun, Professor of History at Columbia University, has been only one of many to call attention to this fact.

"Darwin was not a thinker, and he did not originate the ideas that he used." [1]

The long pre-Darwinian history of evolutionary thought and influence has been outlined by the writer in another book [2] and it will only be mentioned here. The Genesis record of special creation is unique and only those religions which have accepted its authenticity have been creationist religions. People of all other beliefs in all ages have been evolutionists of one sort or another.

This was especially true of the Greek and Roman philosophies on which so much of modern educational theory is based. Ancient paganism was completely evolutionist in its cosmogony, so that modern Darwinism is not a new "scientific" discovery at all but

---

[1] Jacques Barzun, *Darwin, Marx, Wagner* (2nd Ed., Garden City, N.Y., Doubleday, 1959), p. 84.
[2] Henry M. Morris, *The Troubled Waters of Evolution*, (San Diego, Creation-Life Publishers, 1974), p. 50-76.

merely a revival of pagan philosophy. Note the following description of the philosophical systems of Miletus,
from which later Greek philosophy developed
(Socrates, Plato, Aristotle, etc.), as expounded by the
Professor of Philosophy of Science at New York University.

"The type of thinking initiated by the Milesian
school of pre-Socratic thinkers—Thales, Anax-
imander and Anaximenes—in the sixth century
B.C. was carried forward in many directions.
One of the most remarkable of such
speculations, representing a culmination of
their materialistic thought, was to be found in
the Atomist school. Originally worked out in its
main features by Leucippus and Democritus in
the fifth century B.C., the teachings of atomism
were later adopted as a basis for the primarily
ethical philosophy of Epicureanism. . . . It
elaborates the conception of a universe whose
order arises out of a blind interplay of atoms
rather than as a product of deliberate design; of
a universe boundless in spatial extent, infinite
in its duration and containing innumerable
worlds in various stages of development or
decay. . . . It was the same conception, however,
which once more came into the foreground of
attention at the dawn of modern thought and has
remained up to the present time an inspiration
for those modes of scientific thinking that
renounce any appeal to teleology in the interpretation of physical phenomena."[1]

This is very similar, if not quite identical, to modern
evolutionary cosmogonies. The remarkable fact,
however, is that these ideas did not really "originate"
even at Miletus. Very similar constructs will be found
in the writings of ancient Chinese and Hindu

---

[1] Milton K. Munitz, *Theories of the Universe* (Glencoe, Illinois, The Free
Press, 1957), pp. 63-64.

philosophies, as well as those of Egypt, Assyria, and other ancient nations.

Such evolutionary ideas of cosmogony universally coincided with pantheistic concepts of cosmology. The cosmos itself was the ultimate reality. God was everywhere and in everything. As the universe evolved, so God was evolving. God and nature were synonymous.

Although pantheism was a satisfying concept to the intellectuals, however, it was not satisfying to the common man or woman. If God was everywhere, He could not actually be *seen* anywhere! People needed someone concrete to whom they could pray and from whom they could expect answers to personal needs they had. Consequently pantheism to the philosopher was polytheism to the layman. Though the great World Spirit was everywhere, this pantheistic god could be locally worshipped as the god of the river, the goddess of the forest, etc. Thus a great pantheon of gods and goddesses emerged, all actually mere personifications of the various forces and systems of nature.

This pantheon was essentially the same in all ancient nations, though different names were given to individual deities in different nations and languages. Furthermore, all were associated with two other systems, spiritism (or animism) and astrology. The idols which were constructed to represent the gods were believed to have actual powers, effected through the "spirit" operating through the image. From the perspective of the Bible, of course, these spirits in some cases were quite real, being identified as demons, part of the Satanic hierarchy of fallen angels.

> "What say I then? that the idol is any thing, or that which is offered in sacrifice to idols is any thing? But I say, that the things which the Gentiles sacrifice, they sacrifice to devils [literally, 'demons'], and not to God: and I would not that ye should have fellowship with devils" (I Corinthians 10:19,20).

In addition, the greatest of these gods and goddesses were identified with the very stars in the heavens, and ancient pagan polytheistic pantheism everywhere involved worship of the "host of heaven"—a term applied throughout the Bible both to stars and to angels, including the fallen angels (note especially the symbolic representation of Satan's angels by "stars" in Revelation 12:3-9).

The influence of the stars on human lives was thus closely associated with the influence of the spirits on human lives, and the resulting systems of astrology, spiritism, and idolatry were all really one. These, in turn, were part of the complex emanating from the pantheistic evolutionary philosophy of the intellectual and religious leaders of ancient times. The spirits were quite real, and their power and influence quite real (though always, in ancient times as well as modern times, much fraud and deception was also associated with these occult systems).

It should be emphasized that none of these "gods" were believed to be self-existent or eternal. They were all mere personifications of natural forces, aspects of the great "all-god" of pantheism. They were said to have emerged in various ways out of the primeval water or fire or air which constituted the original Chaos from which all things had been formed. Matter—in some form —was the sole eternal entity (exactly as it is in modern evolutionary thought), in conjunction with Space and Time, and everything else—gods as well as man—had come from this by processes innate to Nature.

Once we recognize the one-ness of all the ancient religions and philosophies (comprising a common complex of pantheism, polytheism, astrology, idolatry, and demonism) and that all were founded on essentially the same evolutionary cosmogony being taught in our schools today, we are able to see why it is so urgent to reestablish a truly Christian educational system, and to expunge from it all influences of this monstrous philosophy of evolutionary pantheistic humanism.

Where did it all come from in the first place? As far as the ancient civilizations are concerned, it is generally agreed by archaeologists that the earliest was that of Sumeria, founded in the Tigris-Euphrates region by the first Babylonians. The founding and nature of this first nation have, as yet, been only dimly clarified through either ancient tradition or modern archaeology. The true account is found only in the Bible, in Genesis 10 and 11.

> "And Cush begat Nimrod: he began to be a mighty one in the earth. . . . And the beginning of his kingdom was Babel, and Erech, and Accad, and Calneh, in the land of Shinar" (Genesis 10:8,10).

As the founder and king of Babel, Nimrod beyond question was the leader of the first great post-Flood rebellion against God, described in Genesis 11:1-9. This rebellion culminated in the confusion of tongues and dispersion of the nations.

> "So the Lord scattered them abroad from thence upon the face of all the earth. . . . the Lord did there confound the language of all the earth" (Genesis 11:8,9).

In view of these facts, it is all but certain that this worldwide religious system originated at Babel under Nimrod. At the dispersion, the family units which scattered carried the system with them wherever they settled. Their languages were changed, so that the gods and goddesses acquired different names in each new nation, but they were all the same. As time went on, of course, the religions became more and more divergent, and intellectual leaders in each nation developed more and more sophisticated philosophies by which to rationalize their beliefs, and especially by which to justify their continuing rebellion against the true God of creation.

But it all began at Babylon. No wonder that the

Apostle John, in the closing book of the Bible, speaks of Babylon in such harsh terms:

". . . the inhabitants of the earth have been made drunk with the wine of her fornication . . . . Mystery, Babylon the great, the mother of harlots and abominations of the earth . . . . come out of her, my people, that ye be not partaker of her sins, and that ye receive not of her plagues" (Revelation 17:2,5; 18:4).

There is here clear incentive for Christians to divest themselves completely of the Babylonian philosophy which has been transmitted to modern educational systems in a direct line from Babel to the Greek philosophers to modern Darwinian and humanist philosophy. The system has contaminated even our Christian schools to an alarming, though largely unrecognized, degree.

THE ORIGIN OF EVOLUTIONARY PHILOSOPHY

Furthermore, this age-long, worldwide rebellious philosophy could hardly have originated solely in the mind of Nimrod, or of any other human being. It involves also the "host of heaven," the demonic spirits of idolatry, astrology, and spiritism, and therefore ultimately Satan himself. The almost inevitable conclusion (though such an idea, of course, will be ridiculed by modern naturalistic evolutionists) is that Satan was the first evolutionist, and that he in some way, either directly or indirectly, implanted these concepts in the mind of Nimrod and whatever other ancient philosophers were involved in the great rebellion at Babel. After all, evolutionary pantheism *is* the world's religious system, and such a worldwide effect requires an adequate cause.

". . . and Satan, which deceiveth the whole world" (Revelation 12:9).

". . . and the whole world lieth in the wicked one" (I John 5:19).

". . . In whom the god of this world hath blinded the minds of them which believe not . . ." (II
Corinthians 4:4).

". . . for he is a liar, and the father of it" (John
8:44).

Though modern evolutionism is essentially synonymous
with humanism, which deifies man, its real goal (and
even this is coming more clearly into focus today, with
the resurgence of astrology and other forms of occultism) is nothing less than Satanism, which exalts
Satan as god.

The sin of Satan, who originally was created as God's
"anointed cherub" (Ezekiel 28:14) is just this—that he
desires to replace God on the throne of the universe. He
wants to be God and apparently believes that he can do
this.

"For thou hast said in thine heart, I will as-
cend into heaven, I will exalt my throne above
the stars of God: . . . I will be like the most
High" (Isaiah 14:13,14).

He is not only the "deceiver of the whole world"
(Revelation 12:9), he has evidently deceived himself,
believing that a mere creature could ever displace the
Creator.

It is significant that he recognizes this same desire in
man and has used it through the ages to good advantage, persuading men that God does not really exist independently of the cosmos, and that, therefore, man
can assume the place of ruler of the world. Whenever
men can be persuaded to worship someone or
something apart from the true God, they are engaging
in creature worship, rather than worship of the Creator,
and thus in effect are worshipping themselves. Note the
testimony of Scripture:

"And the serpent said . . . then your eyes shall
be opened, and ye shall be as gods . . ." (Genesis
3:4,5).

"And the king shall do according to his will:
and he shall exalt himself, and magnify himself

above every god, and he shall speak marvelous
things against the God of gods, . . . Neither shall
he regard the God of his fathers, nor the desire
of women, nor regard any god: for he shall
magnify himself above all. But in his estate
shall he honor the god of forces: and a god whom
his fathers knew not shall he honor . . ." (Daniel
11:36-38).

"Because that, when they knew God, they
glorified Him not as God; neither were
thankful; but became vain in their imaginations,
and their foolish heart was darkened. Professing
themselves to be wise, they became fools, and
changed the glory of the uncorruptible God into
an image made like unto corruptible man, and to
birds, and four-footed beasts, and creeping
things. Wherefore God also gave them up to un-
cleanness through the lusts of their own hearts,
to dishonor their own bodies between
themselves: who changed the truth of God into a
lie, and worshipped and served the creature
more than the Creator, who is blessed for ever.
Amen" (Romans 1:21-25).

". . . and that man of sin be revealed, the son
of perdition; who opposeth and exalteth himself
above all that is called God, or that is
worshipped; so that he as God sitteth in the temple of God, shewing himself that he is God. . . .
And for this cause, God shall send them strong
delusion, that they should believe a lie" (II
Thessalonians 2:3,4,11).

"And he opened his mouth in blasphemy
against God, . . . And all that dwell upon the
earth shall worship him, whose names are not
written in the book of Life of the Lamb slain
from the foundation of the world" (Revelation
13:6,8).

There are many other Scriptures to the same effect,

documenting man's desire to do away with the true God and to worship himself or some other creature as God, thus reflecting Satan's own rebellion against God. Eventually, this continuing warfare will culminate in the worldwide reign of a great Man, claiming to be God.

It is obvious that present trends in human societies could be rapidly leading toward this situation, and there is no stronger influence that could facilitate its establishment than that of indoctrinating children and young people in its philosophic rationale—namely, that evolutionary humanism (or even evolutionary spiritism, for those to whom the occult has a stronger appeal than naturalism) is the true doctrine of the world. Of course, humanism is only the stepping-stone on the road to Satanism. Man will never be satisfied with worshipping another man, no matter how great, for he knows that all men, like himself, are mortal and very fallible. Pure atheism is not adequate, either, for all experience and reason assure him that a complex universe must somehow have an adequate cause to explain it. He must worship something beyond himself and his own environment, and yet he rejects the true God of creation. It is logical and necessary, under such conditions, that he will eventually put his faith in the one who is leading all rebellion against God.

"And they worshipped the dragon which gave
power unto the beast" (Revelation 13:4).

It is utterly absurd for men to believe there could be any other god of this universe than its Creator, or that it could come into existence in any other way than by special creation. Yet such foolishness is at least understandable in light of the tremendous power of the great Dragon who has deceived the whole world. But how is it possible to rationalize *his* rebellion? Surely a creature so wise and powerful as Satan would be intelligent enough to know that he could have no hope of dethroning his own Maker!

Yet it must be recognized that the only means by

which Satan could come to know God had created him would be for God to tell him so. He had not existed eternally; God had created him (Ezekiel 28:15). All sin begins in doubting the Word of God, and this must likewise have been how Satan fell. He refused to believe that God was his Creator, and therefore rationalized his pride and rebellion.

But if God was not the Creator, then where did the cosmos come from and how did God and the angels come into being? The only possible answer would have to be that the universe had always existed in some form, but that it was continually changing with time, and that these processes of change had in some unknown and marvelous way generated living spirits along with everything else! Thus the idea of evolutionism, along with pantheism, must originally have been born in the mind of Satan himself.

Such a conclusion may seem capricious—or even shocking—at first, but how else can we explain Satan's rebellion? Apart from the true record of creation as given in Genesis, the only other possibility (that is, if Satan did not originate the idea of evolution) is that neither God nor Satan exists, and thus man is alone and solely responsible not only for discovering the evolutionary idea but also for directing evolution in the future. The latter, of course, represents the consensus of modern scientism and educationalism.

For the Bible-believing Christian, however, the conclusion that Satan was the first evolutionist seems inescapable. It is no wonder, then, that this type of philosophy and cosmogony has permeated every extra-Biblical system, ancient or modern, throughout history.

It may have been providential that what is apparently the world's oldest cosmogony was found recorded on a tablet excavated in Babylonia a number of years ago. This is the famous Babylonian cosmogony, known as the *Enuma Elish*. It is remarkable that this original evolutionary system describes the universe in its initial stages as being exactly how it would have appeared to Satan at the moment of his creation, when he first came into consciousness. It is clear from the Bible that the angels are a part of the creation, and that they could not have existed prior to the creation of the physical universe—the space-mass-time cosmos—on the first day of creation week. According to God's testimony in Exodus 20:11, everything in heaven and in earth was made in the six days of that first week, and this must have included the angels. Since they were present when the foundations of the earth were laid, as stated in Job 38: 4-7, (which event probably corresponds to the calling-forth of the solid earth from its primeval watery matrix on the third day) they must have been created either on the first or the second day. Most likely they were created on the first day, perhaps even as the first divine act after the initial creation of the elemental universe. In any case, it is significant that the earth as initially created was "unformed," with all its components suspended, as it were, in a vast matrix of waters (note both Genesis 1:2 and II Peter 3:5 in this connection).

This, then, would be the first thing Satan would observe at the moment of his creation. If he later decided to reject God's Word, then it would have to be this vast universe of waters to which he must ascribe his first beginnings. With this in mind, it is fascinating to study the *Enuma Elish*.

"Specifically, *Enuma Elish* assumes that all things have evolved out of water. This description presents the earliest stage of the universe as one of watery chaos. The chaos consisted of three intermingled elements: Apsu, who represents the sweet waters; Ti'amat, who represents the sea; and Mumnu, who cannot as yet be identified with certainty but may represent cloud banks and mist. These three types of

waters were mingled in a large undefined mass.
. . . Then, in the midst of this watery chaos two
gods came into existence." [1]

It does not seem too far-fetched to see in this first
evolutionary cosmogony the explanation of Satan
himself, to his first disciples there in the temple-shrine
atop the Tower of Babel, concerning the beginning of
the world.

Whether this is completely correct or not, there can
be no doubt that the evolutionary philosophy has been
the basis of all anti-Biblical systems down through the
ages. The tragedy is that it has been accepted and
believed, in one form or another, by unnumbered multitudes of people, in the name of intellectualism or
science or philosophy, in preference to the true and simple and reasonable account of creation given in Genesis.

THE EVIDENCE FOR CREATION

In view of the foregoing facts and analysis, even in
view of the range of uncertainty that necessarily exists
in any discussion of primeval history, it should be
crystal clear that true education must be built on a solid
base of creationism. Evolution in any form must be rejected and repudiated, along with all aspects of the
humanistic and occultistic philosophies which stem
from it. If any of these systems are introduced into the
curriculum or other programs at all, it must only be for
the purpose of providing Biblical and scientific am-
munition against them.

In public schools, of course, it may be necessary to
teach *both* creation and evolution, both humanism and
theism, allowing the students to make their own choice
as to which to believe. In Christian schools, however,
there is no justification at all for teaching falsehood

---

[1] Thorkild Jacobsen, "Enuma Elish - The Babylonian Genesis" in *Theories
of the Universe* (Ed. by M. K. Munitz, Glencoe, Illinois: The Free Press,
1957), p. 9.

along with truth. In teaching this truth, it is essential that students not only know what the truth is, but also *why* we know it to be the truth. This means, obviously, that they should be instructed thoroughly (in every class where the question has any bearing at all, and this includes practically all of them) as to why creation and Biblical Christianity are true and why evolution and humanism are false. It is vital for students not only to know what they believe, but why they believe it, and also how to defend and propagate the truth among those who don't believe it. The following discussion gives, in a very abbreviated form, some of the abundant evidence, from both Scripture and science, for believing in special creation.

Biblical Evidence

(1) God's work of both calling things into existence and building them into completed and functioning form was finished at the end of the six days of creation.

"Thus the heavens and the earth were finished, and all the host of them. And on the seventh day God ended His work which He had made; and He rested on the seventh day from all His work which He had made. And God blessed the seventh day, and sanctified it; because that in it He had rested from all His work which God created and made" (Genesis 2:1-3).

". . . the works were finished from the foundation of the world. For He spake in a certain place of the seventh day on this wise. And God did rest the seventh day from all His works" (Hebrews 4:3-4).

These verses make it very emphatic that God is no longer "creating" or making anything. Thus, no process of *vertical* evolution is possible now at all.

(2) God made the various entities in His creation the way He wanted them to be, and therefore imposed a principle of permanency, or conservation, on them

when He was through. Although "horizontal" changes could take place within the created range of variability of these systems, never could a "vertical" change convert one kind into a different kind.

"And God made the beast of the earth after his kind, and cattle after their kind, and everything that creepeth upon the earth after his kind: and God saw that it was good" (Genesis 1:25, et al). (The phrase "after its kind" occurs ten times in Genesis 1.)

"But God giveth it a body as it hath pleased Him, and to every seed his own body. All flesh is not the same flesh: but there is one kind of flesh of men, another flesh of beasts, another of fishes, and another of birds. There are also celestial bodies, and bodies terrestrial: but the glory of the celestial is one, and the glory of the terrestrial is another. There is one glory of the sun, and another glory of the moon, and another glory of the stars: for one star differeth from another star in glory" (I Corinthians 15:38-41).

"Can the fig tree, my brethren, bear olive berries? either a vine figs? so can no fountain both yield salt water and fresh" (James 3:12).

Every kind of organism, and even every type of inorganic system, was created with its own structure for its own functions. The world is not in a continuous state of evolutionary flux at all.

(3) All things were made in six literal days. In the Genesis account, each day (Hebrew yom) was numbered in sequence ("first day," "second day," etc.) and had a beginning and ending ("evening and morning"), both of which constructions *always* indicate literal days, in the Old Testament. Furthermore, God Himself made it indelibly clear in the Ten Commandments that man's six work days corresponded precisely to His own six work days.

"Remember the sabbath day, to keep it holy.

Six days shalt thou labor, and do all thy work. . . .
For in six days the Lord made heaven and
earth, the sea, and all that in them is, and rested
the seventh day . . .'' (Exodus 20:8,9,11).

Evolution of all things, obviously, would be quite impossible in six literal days.

(4) Everything in all the universe was still good, in
God's omniscient judgment, at the end of the six days of
creation. There was no disorder or suffering or death or
anything *bad* anywhere.

"And God saw every thing that He had made,
and behold, it was very good" (Genesis 1:31).

The very essence of evolution, on the other hand, is
natural selection and the survival of the fittest. The
evolutionary ages of geology are identified by the fossils
of dead animals which clearly speak of suffering and
death all over the world throughout the entire history of
evolution, an obvious contradiction.

(5) The philosophy of evolutionary uniformitarianism
was predicted and repudiated by the Apostle Peter 1900
years ago.

". . . there shall come in the last days scoffers,
. . . saying . . . all things continue as they were
from the beginning of the creation. For this they
willingly are ignorant of, that by the word of
God the heavens were of old, and the earth stand-
ing out of the water and in the water: whereby
the world that then was, being overflowed with
water, perished" (II Peter 3:3-6).

The belief that all things can be understood in terms of
processes that have continued unchanged since the very
beginning of creation is nothing less than evolutionary
naturalism. Peter says that those who hold such a view
are guilty of willful ignorance. The evidence is all
against such a belief, the evidence both of special creation by God's Word in the beginning, and a global
cataclysm later.

For these and many other reasons, it is clear that an

omnipotent, omniscient, holy, loving God did not and
could not use such an inefficient, foolish, wasteful, cruel
process as evolution as His method of creation. Both
theistic evolution and its tongue-in-cheek equivalent,
progressive creation, must be completely repudiated by
Biblical Christians.

Scientific Evidence

Although evolution is often claimed to be based on
scientific evidence, whereas creation is supposedly only
based on Biblical evidence, the fact is that the scientific
evidence supports creationism much better than
evolutionism. Actually, neither concept of origins can
be firmly proved or disproved by the scientific method,
so that either one of them must ultimately be accepted
on faith. The essence of the scientific method is experimental observation of repeatable phenomena, but
this is quite impossible in the case of events of the
prehistoric past. In fact, it is possible to interpret every
phenomenon of the present in terms of either an
evolutionary or creationist origin in the past.
Nevertheless, these presently observable scientific
data will always be found to correlate more directly and
simply with the creation model than with the evolution
model. That is, the facts can be made to fit the evolution
model by continually expanding and modifying the
model, but they will fit the creation model directly
without such modification.

A number of basic fallacies in the evolution model are
briefly discussed below, each with documentation from
evolutionist writers. In each case, the facts provide
negative evidence against evolution while, at the same
time, fitting exactly what would be expected on the
basis of creation.

(1) No *vertical* evolution (that is, change from one
kind of organism to a higher, more complex kind of
organism) has ever been observed taking place.

Horizontal changes (different varieties of dogs, shift in coloration of the peppered moth, etc.) are frequently observed, of course, and this type of change fits the creation model very well, but the vertical changes required by evolution are never seen. Evolutionists believe they do take place, but so slowly as to be unobservable.

> "Evolution, at least in the sense that Darwin speaks of it, cannot be detected within the lifetime of a single observer."[1]

Since real science is based on observation, it should be obvious that evolution is altogether unscientific. On the other hand, these horizontal changes within the kinds, with no vertical changes and with clear-cut gaps between the kinds, are precisely what would be predicted from the creation model.

(2) No transitional series from one kind of organism to a higher kind of organism has ever been found in the fossil record of the past. If evolution ever really happened, there must have been a tremendous number of such transitional series and literally billions of animals representing these intermediate forms, but no one has ever yet found a single true intermediate fossil form anywhere in the fossils.

> "Despite the bright promise that paleontology provides a means of 'seeing' evolution, it has presented some nasty difficulties for evolutionists, the most notorious of which is the presence of 'gaps' in the fossil record. Evolution requires intermediate forms between species and paleontology does not provide them."[2]

Once again, on the other hand, these gaps in the fossil record, which pose such "nasty difficulties" for evolutionists, are exactly what would be expected on the basis of creation.

---

[1] David G. Kitts, "Paleontology and Evolutionary Theory," *Evolution*, Volume 28, September 1974, p. 466.
[2] *Ibid*, p. 467.

(3) Evolution in the vertical sense seems to be completely impossible in terms of the basic laws of science, especially the law of increasing entropy, the second law of thermodynamics. Evolution requires some kind of basic principle operating in nature which impels organisms and other systems to proceed uphill toward higher, more complex systems, all the way from primeval random particles to simple one-celled organisms to higher animals and man. The entropy law, however, states the observed fact that all systems tend naturally to go downhill toward lower degrees of order. The evolutionist has no answer to this conflict except to insist that, since evolution is true and systems do proceed upward toward greater "information" content and higher order, there must be some way by which the natural downhill tendency is offset in open systems to enable evolution to happen anyhow.

"As far as we know, all changes are in the direction of increasing entropy, of increasing disorder, of increasing randomness, of running down." [1]

"In the complex course of its evolution, life exhibits a remarkable contrast to the tendency expressed in the Second Law of Thermodynamics. Where the Second Law expresses an irreversible progression toward increased entropy and disorder, life evolves continually higher levels of order." [2]

". . . the relation between irreversible thermodynamics and information theory [is] one of the most fundamental unsolved problems in biology." [3]

Under certain very special conditions, either in artificial systems or living systems, order can be made to increase temporarily. These conditions require both a

---

[1] Isaac Asimov, "Can Decreasing Entropy Exist in the Universe?" *Science Digest,* May 1973, p. 76.

[2] J. H. Rush, *The Dawn of Life* (New York: Signet, 1962), p. 35.

[3] Charles J. Smith, "Problems with Entropy in Biology," *Biosystems,* V. T., 1975, p. 259.

pre-existing program to specify how the organization is to proceed and also a specific energy conversion system by which the external energy is assimilated and converted into the specific work required to increase the complexity of the system. The evolutionary process, however, has neither of these, and so seems precluded by the entropy principle. On the other hand, the entropy law fits the creation model perfectly. By creationism, all things were created in perfect order in the beginning, and have since been running down. This principle is a fact of empirical science, but it was also recorded in the Bible, in the form of the great Curse of decay and death placed by the Creator on His creation because of man's sin.

(4) There has not been enough time in earth history for evolution to be feasible, even if it were possible. Evolutionists acknowledge that at least a billion years would be required, but there is no firm evidence that the earth is more than a few thousand years old.

> "This date of 3100 B.C. thus sets the limit of recorded history. No earlier dates can be obtained by calendrical means, and indeed the dates cannot be regarded as reliable before 2000 B.C." [1]

> "The rocks do date the fossils, but the fossils date the rocks more accurately. Stratigraphy cannot avoid this kind of reasoning, if it insists on using only temporal concepts, because circularity is inherent in the derivation of time scales." [2]

Before the beginning of written history, there is no way to date anything by provable scientific means. The geological ages actually are identified by their contained fossils, arranged according to their assumed stage of evolution. The geological time scale is based on

[1] Colin Renfrew, *Before Civilization* (New York, Alfred A. Knoff, 1974), p. 28. Dr. Renfrew is Professor of Archaeology at Southampton University.

[2] J. C. O'Rourke, "Pragmatism versus Materialism in Stratigraphy," *American Journal of Science,* Vol. 276, January 1976, p. 53.

the assumption and requirements of evolution. There is no other objective proof that the earth is much older than the actual dates of written history, which in turn accord perfectly with the short chronology inferred from the Biblical record.

Thus there is no evidence that: (1) evolution in the "vertical" sense is occurring at present; (2) evolution from one kind of organism to a different kind ever took place in the past; (3) evolution from one kind to a more complex kind is possible at all, regardless of how much time might be available; (4) there has been enough time for evolution even if it were possible.

This discussion has, of course, been very brief and incomplete. There is a great deal of literature on scientific creationism now available, however, including several book by the present writer.[1,2,3] In the past ten years (1973-1983), at least 150 formal debates have been held on university campuses between evolutionist scientists and creationist scientists (especially those of the staff of the Institute for Creation Research). These debates have made it obvious that the scientific case for creation is much more convincing than that for evolution. In the Creation Research Society, there are more than 700 scientists, each with a post-graduate degree in science, who are strict creationists. There is no justification any more, if there ever was, for teachers in Christian schools to attempt to accommodate evolutionary philosophy in their teaching.

IMPORTANCE OF CREATION EMPHASIS IN TEACHING

It is important that teachers recognize how important it is to emphasize the truth of creationism in all their

[1] *Scientific Creationism* (San Diego: Creation-Life Publishers, 1974) 277 pp. An extensive bibliography on scientific creationism is included.
[2] *The Genesis Flood* (Co-author, John C. Whitcomb. Philadelphia, Presbyterian and Reformed Publishing Co. 1961), 518 pp.
[3] *What is Creation Science?* (Co-author, Gary E. Parker. San Diego: Creation-Life Publishers, 1982), 318 pp.

teaching. This is not merely a peripheral subject, of concern only to, say, biologists and theologians. It is vital in every field and should continually be implicit, if not explicit, throughout the curriculum, in the Christian school or college. Several reasons for this emphasis are outlined below.

(1) *Integral Part of the Gospel.* Every Christian is commanded in the Great Commission to "preach the gospel to every creature" (Mark 16:15), and this involves "teaching them to observe all things whatsoever I have commanded you" (Matthew 28:20). More particularly, the "everlasting gospel" (thus the true gospel has never been any different) includes a strong command to acknowledge God as Creator—"worship Him that made heaven and earth, the sea, and the fountains of waters" (Revelation 14:6,7).

(2) *Honoring to God.* Since Christians are commanded to do everything "to the glory of God" (I Corinthians 10:31), it is appropriate frequently to acknowledge His wisdom, power, and love in creation, as well as in redemption. Even the entire creation is exhorted in Scripture to praise God for His great work of creation.

"Let them praise the name of the Lord for He commanded, and they were created. He hath also stablished them for ever and ever: He hath made a decree which shall not pass" (Psalm 148:5,6).

"Thou art worthy, O Lord, to receive glory and honour and power: for thou hast created all things, and for thy pleasure they are and were created" (Revelation 4:11).

No matter what the subject matter of the course may be, there are always in the data of that field complex systems and relationships which give evidence for God as Creator and against any process of random, cruel evolution. It is up to the teacher to discern these evidences and then to share them with the class, thus honoring God and edifying the students.

(3) *Necessary for Real Understanding.* If the student is ever really to *understand* any phenomenon or system, he must appreciate its origin and purpose. Obviously, the meaning and purpose and future of any system depend first of all on the origin of that system. For true comprehension, we need to know the teleological "why" as well as the technological "what." Since God is the Creator of all things, that fact is the priority essential to the true understanding of anything.

(4) *Corrective to Evolutionary Teachings.* As stressed previously, the evolutionary philosophy is present in one way or another in practically every textbook and in the training of practically every teacher. Evolution, furthermore, is continually impressed on the minds of young people through television and many other means. Unless positive teaching is directed against it, most of them will automatically be conditioned to evolutionary thinking regardless of whether the teachers themselves are evolutionists. In fact, sinful human nature itself makes everyone naturally inclined to escape from God's will if possible, so the idea of long ages of slow random changes has a basic attraction to all people just by itself. The lie of evolution has an instinctive appeal, and this requires the truth of creation to be taught all the more vigorously and clearly.

(5) *Acknowledgment of Man's Stewardship under God.* Many of the problems in today's world, such as environmental pollution, increasing crime, and others, are rooted in evolutionary thinking. If people would honestly acknowledge the Creator, and their resulting position as stewards of the creation under God, it could not help but go a long way toward solving these problems. All men are responsible to their Creator, under the terms of the Adamic cultural mandate, as included and extended in the Noahic covenant, but they are unaware of this fact and therefore live as though there would never be an accounting of their stewardship.

A solid emphasis on God as Creator and Sovereign, in every sphere of the natural world and in human life, would condition men to think and behave with their eternal responsibilities and coming judgment in view.

"God that made the world and all things therein, seeing that He is Lord of heaven and earth . . . hath made of one blood all nations of men for to dwell on all the face of the earth, and hath determined the times before appointed, and the bounds of their habitation; . . . but now commandeth all men everywhere to repent: because He hath appointed a day, in the which He will judge the world in righteousness by that man whom He hath ordained . . ." (Acts 17:24,26,30,31).

Furthermore, genuine recognition of God as Creator and man as responsible steward leads directly to the necessary acknowledgment of man's failure and need of salvation. Thus a response to Christ as Saviour is first elicited through confession of Him as Creator, Sustainer, and righteous Judge. No doubt this is why the final reference in Scripture to the one true and eternal Gospel (Revelation 14:6) stresses acknowledgment of God's work in creation.

In concluding and summarizing this chapter, we must stress once again that this question of creation or evolution is not merely a peripheral scientific issue, but rather is nothing less than the age-long conflict between God and Satan. There are only two basic world-views. One is a God-centered view of life and meaning and purpose—the other is a creature-centered view. Any educational system for the training of the coming generation must and will seek to inculcate one or the other. Any attempt to mediate or compromise between these two world-views will thus inevitably result in eventual capitulation of one of them, and this almost always will be in favor of the humanistic evolutionary system.

Historically speaking, past experience has confirmed

over and over again that schools or other institutions which either compromise on this issue, or consider it unimportant (which amounts to the same thing) have eventually been taken over by evolutionism and finally by one or another of its correlative philosophies (humanism, socialism, existentialism, etc.). It is of vital and primary importance, therefore, that the truth of special creation be emphasized in every curriculum—in fact every course and by every teacher—in any Christian school which seeks to be true to its divine calling, and that all students be armed with an adequate array of both Biblical and scientific evidences for defending and propagating it.

Chapter 3

Humanistic and Super- Humanistic Education

In this chapter we wish to examine more closely the two systems, both built on the foundation and framework of evolution, that have dominated educational theory and practice in every non-Christian society of the past or present. These systems are humanism and what might be called "superhumanism." Other possible terms are naturalism and supernaturalism, rationalism and irrationalism, materialism and immaterialism. One system views man as the pinnacle of the evolutionary process and as the ultimate arbiter of meaning; the other considers the spirit world beyond the physical as a higher order of existence toward which all things evolve. The first system is man-centered, the second is ultimately Satan-centered. Modern man, having rejected Biblical theism, must turn either to naturalistic humanism or supernaturalistic occultism.

In the western world the humanistic system has

dominated education for centuries; in the East, superhumanism has permeated most thinking. In recent decades, however, humanism has been making great inroads in the East, and superhumanism in the West, so that the two most likely will eventually merge in a vast system of religion and education which exalts both man and Satan (as per Revelation 13:4).

Although Christians need to be alert to the influence of both of these anti-Christian philosophies, the system of naturalistic evolutionary humanism still dominates the schools and colleges of America and of western civilization in general.

HUMANISTIC EMPHASES
IN MODERN EDUCATION

In this section we will document briefly the nature and premises of humanism and its current influence in education. Though not all educators would admit, or even recognize, that they are indoctrinating students in a religion of evolutionary humanism, this is unquestionably the net effect of modern curricula in the nation's public schools and secular universities. The following quotations will illustrate the thrust of this type of teaching.

(1) *Man — the Highest Attainment of Evolution.* John Dewey, the man more responsible than any other single individual for the curriculum and methodology of modern American public education, understood human nature in this way:

". . . the cosmic process . . . and the forces bound up with the cosmic have come to consciousness in man."[1]

Similarly, the prolific evolutionary researcher and writer, Theodosius Dobzhansky, comments in the same vein.

---

[1] John Dewey, "Evolution and Ethics," Scientific Monthly, Volume 78, February 1954, p. 66.

". . . the evolutionary process has, apparently,
for the first and only time in the history of the
Cosmos, become conscious of itself."[1]

The pantheistic, and even mystical, overtones in such
statements somehow seem incongruous with the
naturalistic and materialistic premises of these men.

(2) *Man Now Able to Control Future Evolution.*
Humanistically-oriented scientists and philosophers are
quite proud of the fact that man now "understands" his
past evolution and they believe that he will soon be able
to direct and control his future evolution.

"We no longer need be subject to blind external forces but can manipulate the environment and eventually may be able to manipulate
our genes. Thus, unlike any other species, we
may be able to interfere with our biologic
evolution."[2]

One of the leading evolutionary geneticists was also a
leading advocate of controlled evolution. Dr. H. J.
Muller even regarded such a procedure as essentially
equivalent to universal salvation.

"Through the unprecedented faculty of long-
range foresight, jointly serviced and exercised
by us, we can, in securing and advancing our
position, increasingly avoid the missteps of
blind nature, circumvent its cruelties, reform
our own natures, and enhance our own values."[3]

Evolutionists differ among themselves as to just *how*
future evolution should be controlled. By DNA
modification, cloning, or other imminent techniques of
genetic engineering, as planned and implemented by an
academic elite, or by application of principles of population genetics through controlled environments, or by

---

[1]Theodosius Dobzhansky, "Changing Man," *Science,* Volume 155, January
27, 1967, p. 409.
[2]A. G. Motulsky, "Brave New World?", *Science,* Vol. 185, August 23, 1974, p.
653.
[3]H. J. Muller, "Human Values in Relation to Evolution," *Science,* Volume
127, March 21, 1958, p. 629.

as yet unsettled mechanisms, most evolutionists are nevertheless urging some such broad plan of action for future progress.

(3) *Man Responsible Only to Himself.* In humanism, since there is no external Creator and since man is the highest achievement of the evolutionary process, man himself becomes the only god there is. Evolutionary humanism either generates anarchism, in which each man is in effect his own god and does his own thing, or else leads to collectivism, in which the state becomes god, represented by a man at its helm who receives its worship.

One of the founders of the American Humanist Association, Sir Julian Huxley, defined humanism as follows:

> "I use the word 'humanist' to mean someone who believes that man is just as much a natural phenomenon as an animal or plant; that his body, mind and soul were not supernaturally created but are products of evolution, and that he is not under the control or guidance of any supernatural being or beings, but has to rely on himself and his own powers."[1]

The humanist belief that man must be his own Savior was reaffirmed in the 1974 Manifesto of the Association:

> "No deity will save us; we must save ourselves."[2]

(4) *Humanism as Religion.* Evolutionists commonly object to the teaching of creation in public schools on the grounds that creation requires the existence of God and His creative power, and that this is a religious belief. The real fact, of course, is that it requires a much higher order of faith to believe there is no God and that all things have been produced by random evolutionary processes than it does to believe in a real

---

[1] American Humanist Association promotional brochure.
[2] Manifesto of A.H.A., as widely reported in the news media. This new 1974 Manifesto was signed by such leaders in modern education as B. F. Skinner, Isaac Asimov, Sidney Hook, Rabbi Kaplan, Corliss Lamont, and others.

God and real creation.

Doctrinaire humanists, of course, do recognize and even insist that humanism is a religious faith.

"Humanism is the belief that man shapes his own destiny. It is a constructive philosophy, a non-theistic religion, a way of life."[1]

"The American Humanist Association is a non-profit tax-exempt organization, incorporated in the early 1940's in Illinois for educational and religious purposes. Humanist counsellors can solemnize weddings, conduct memorial services, and assist in individual value counselling."[2]

The Humanist Association was founded by John Dewey and Julian Huxley, along with such leaders of modern thought as Linus Pauling, Erich Fromm, Benjamin Spock, Margaret Sanger, Buckminster Fuller, Brock Chisholm, Carl Rogers, Hudson Hoagland, and others. Although its formal membership has never been large, its influence has been far out of proportion to its numbers.

The aim of Dewey and his disciples was, for all practical purposes, to establish their own humanistic religion as the religion of the state, taught in the schools of the state. Of course, they would never say it this way, but the effect is the same, especially since the banning of prayer and Bible reading from the school. Courses are nearly always taught today strictly in a secular, humanistic frame of reference, with emphasis always upon man and his ability to solve the world's problems, especially as society evolves to a man-centered world politico-economic system.

In spite of this almost universal educational commitment to evolutionary humanism, however, humanism is altogether false. As seen in the previous chapter, the

---

[1] A. H. A. Promotional Brochure.
[2] *Ibid.*

evolutionary system is completely repudiated by Scripture and all true science. Since humanism is based on evolution, this humanistic bias and basis in modern education is false and very harmful. Even Christian schools and colleges have been inadvertently influenced by humanism, either through textbooks or the secular training and associations of their faculties.

True Biblical education, which should be the deliberate goal of every Christian educational enterprise, must positively renounce and oppose all such man-centered emphases, removing them completely from its curriculum and methodology. True education should be controlled by the home and church and must be founded on God as Creator, centered in Christ as Redeemer, and guided by the Spirit-inspired Scriptures as Revealer of all truth. Modern education, in opposition to true education, has been perverted to state control, and has been founded on evolution, centered on man, and guided by the prophets of humanism such as Dewey and Darwin.

REVIVAL OF OCCULTISM AMONG STUDENTS

Although humanism still dominates western educational institutions today, there has in recent years been a significant rise of student interest in "superhuman-ism." Multitudes of young people have been waking up to the fact that naturalistic humanism and evolutionary scientism are barren in themselves. Modern science has led to television and the automobile, but it has also been used to produce nuclear bombs, water pollution, and an energy crisis. Man has proven to be a very fallible deity. One by one, latter-day idols have fallen; Hitler, Stalin, Mao, and many others have been literally worshipped by multitudes even in our own day, but they all had feet of clay and are now in their graves.

But if man himself is not going to prove out as the ultimate savior of the universe, and if he will not have God to rule over him, where will he turn? The tremendous current upsurge of interest in the supernatural suggests that many today are finding their answer in mystical, emotional, or "religious" experiences. These experiences supposedly place them in touch with superhuman knowledge and power, but they often lead instead to demonism and Satanism.

The number of these occult movements today is almost endless. Although most of them are still rejected by the scientific and educational establishments, on the basis of their own naturalistic and humanistic premises, tremendous numbers of college students and other young people have become involved in them.

The so-called drug culture, with its influence over millions, is in large part religious in motivation. The psychedelic "trips" induced by drugs are said to impart profound religious experiences to their users, involving a sense of superhuman knowledge and oneness with the cosmos. It is not surprising that such drug users frequently become involved in witchcraft cults, and even formal Satanism, with its black masses, sexual perversions, masochism, and even ritual murders.

Demonism—often called spiritualism—has, of course, long been practiced in one form or another throughout the world. Largely driven underground as a result of the Biblical revivals of the periods of the Reformation and Great Awakening, it began a great comeback in the western world about a century ago (largely coincident with the rise of Darwinism, incidentally) and now has tremendous influence over unknown millions around the world. Whether in the crude form of animism, where demonic spirits are placated by various sacrifices and frequently possess and control the bodies of people, or in the more sophisticated form of spiritualism, where the spirits assume the identities of dead friends or relatives in seances, or in the still

more scientific garb of psychic research, where spirits
operate through what are taken to be unusual mental
powers of living people (extra-sensory perception,
prophesying, multiple identities, mind-reading, etc.), it
is obvious that a vast complex of what seem to be
superhuman activities do take place in this world, and
that these are believed by millions of their practitioners
to be associated with actual spirit beings.

But this is not all. It was pointed out in the previous
chapter that spiritism in the ancient world was always
closely associated with astrology. It is no coincidence,
therefore, that there has been a great modern revival of
astrology also. Scientists, of course, almost unanimous-
ly condemn what seems to be the grossly unscientific
notion that the positions and motions of stars and
planets can have influences on individual human lives.
Yet over a million copies of astrology magazines are
sold annually in the United States, and almost every
daily newspaper carries astrological horoscopes.
Astrology is even more influential in other countries
than in America, and its influence is especially
widespread among young people.

And then, what about the various mystical Eastern
religious movements that have been sweeping over this
country? Beginning with the Zen Buddhism of the
"Beatnik" generation of the fifties, then the hippie
movement and its drug culture of the sixties, with the
introduction of various other cults from the East, we
now have a tremendous wave of mystical "meditation"
movements sweeping the nation, most involving repeti-
tion of supposedly meaningless words or phrases (which
in many cases have been found upon translation to be
prayers to a Hindu god or goddess) as their principle of
"meditation". The most visible of these are the
Transcendental Meditation and Hare Krishna cults, but
there are also the cults of yoga, zen, the divine light
mission, scientology, "Moonism," and numerous
others. Even traditional Hinduism and Buddhism, especially their themes of reincarnation and ultimate nir-

vana (submergence in the universal all-spirit of philosophical pantheism), have been winning hosts of adherents in the West.

To all of these trends, we should add the strange fascination people have for the para-normal. The recurrent furor over flying saucers and other U.F.O.'s, the strange disappearances in the Bermuda Triangle, the "chariots of the gods" cult, the searches for Bigfoot and the Abominable Snowman, the pyramid-power craze, and other current fads provide a sad commentary on the fact that multitudes desire to have faith in the supernatural, but that they will believe almost anything before they will believe the Bible.

Various pseudo-Christian cults with their millions of adherents also appeal to this human longing. For example, Mormonism, with its divine revelations and mysterious quasi-histories, many mind-healing and mental peace movements (Christian Science, Unity, Divine Science, etc.), and numerous others have had profound effects.

This great complex of superhumanistic movements, all more or less interrelated with each other, has been making tremendous strides in the western world in recent decades. Although traditional naturalistic humanism still dominates the educational systems, superhumanism is beginning to look like a serious rival in the imminent future. Already more than a hundred universities offer courses in parapsychology, and many offer courses in the eastern religions, some even in witchcraft. Student chapters of the meditation movements are active on practically every campus.

Although to a degree this growing interest in the supernatural and para-normal might be regarded by Christians as an encouraging reaction against the sterile humanism and materialism of modern education, it should be realized that this may be even more inimical to true Christianity in the long run. It is bad enough to worship man as god, but it is still worse to bow down to Satan!

SPIRITUAL IMPLICATIONS
OF OCCULT REVIVAL

Before Christian educators are impressed too favorably by the rising interest in the supernatural, it is well to get a sound Biblical perspective on the subject. Consider the following Biblical and prophetic warnings:

"Now the Spirit speaketh expressly, that in the latter times some shall depart from the faith, giving heed to seducing spirits and doctrines of devils [i.e., 'demons']" (I Timothy 4:1).

"Now as Jannes and Jambres [that is, the Egyptian sorcerers] withstood Moses, so do these also resist the truth: men of corrupt minds, reprobate concerning the faith . . . . But evil men and seducers [that is 'spiritual seducers,' 'conjurers'] shall wax worse and worse, deceiving and being deceived" (II Timothy 3:8,13).

"And many false prophets shall rise, and shall deceive many. And because iniquity shall abound, the love of many shall wax cold . . . . For there shall arise false Christs and false prophets, and shall shew great signs and wonders, insomuch that, if it were possible, they shall deceive the very elect" (Matthew 24:11,12,24).

"And when they shall say unto you, Seek unto them that have familiar spirits, and unto wizards that peep, and that mutter: should not a people seek unto their God? for the living to the dead? To the law and to the testimony: if they speak not according to this word, it is because there is no light in them" (Isaiah 8:19,20).

"But when ye pray, use not vain repetitions, as the heathen do: for they think that they shall be heard for their much speaking" (Matthew 6:7).

"And the rest of the men which were not killed
by these plagues yet repented not of the works of
their hands, that they should not worship devils
and idols of gold, and silver, and brass, and
stone, and of wood: which neither can see, nor
hear, nor walk: neither repented they of their
murders, nor of their sorceries, nor of their fornication, nor of their thefts" (Revelation
9:20,21).

It is worth noting that the word "sorceries" in the
Scripture quoted above is actually the word from which
we get our English word "pharmacology." The iden-
tification of "drugs" and "sorceries" in this manner
derives from the fact that, in ancient times, sorcerers
and soothsayers used drugs to induce the visions which
enabled them to commune with the spirits and to perform their feats of magic or prophecy. The modern connection of drugs and witchcraft is, thus, no accident.

It is also noteworthy that all these superhuman
phenomena are associated in the Scriptures not only
with sin and immorality in general, but with deception
in particular. Note II Timothy 3:13, cited
above—"deceiving and being deceived." Occult practitioners deceive others, either intentionally or uninten-
tionally, but they also deceive themselves. It is possible
even for a Christian to deceive himself.

"If we say that we have no sin, we deceive
ourselves and the truth is not in us" (I John 1:8).

This self-deception, it should be noted, has to do with a
person thinking that he has arrived at a state of perfection. This is the typical goal of the superhumanists,
whether they believe in attaining a state of nirvana by
perfect obedience, or a state of perfect peace and pure
holiness through meditation, or perhaps even an instant
state of complete sanctification through some religious
experience, or a state of perfect knowledge through
mental awareness or spirit-communication, or
whatever. The besetting sin of the superhumanists is
that of pride—thinking they have no sin, because of the

supernatural experiences they have undergone or the
supernatural insights they have acquired.

As pointed out in the preceding chapter, pride is the
very sin of Satan himself. He is not only the deceiver of
the whole world, he has deceived himself into thinking
he can be as great as God and eventually even replace
God. He used the same lie to deceive Eve and has been
using it ever since. His demonic hosts are likewise
deceivers, and his work through his human emissaries
as well is carried out by deception. There are frequent
warnings in Scripture against such deception.

"Let no man deceive you by any means . . . (II
Thessalonians 2:3).

"Now I beseech you, brethren, mark them
which cause divisions and offenses contrary to
the doctrine which ye have learned; and avoid
them. For they . . . by good words and fair
speeches deceive the hearts of the simple"
(Romans 16:17,18).

". . . be no more children, tossed to and fro,
and carried about with every wind of doctrine,
by the sleight of men, and cunning craftiness,
whereby they lie in wait to deceive" (Ephesians
4:14).

"And with all deceivableness of un-
righteousness in them that perish; because they
received not the love of the truth, that they
might be saved. And for this cause God shall
send them strong delusion, that they should
believe a lie" (II Thessalonians 2:10,11).

"But I fear, lest by any means, as the serpent
beguiled Eve through his subtlety, so your minds
should be corrupted from the simplicity that is
in Christ . . . . For such are false apostles,
deceitful workers, transforming themselves
into the apostles of Christ. And no marvel; for
Satan himself is transformed into an angel of
light. Therefore it is no great thing if his
ministers also be transformed into the ministers

of righteousness; whose end shall be according to their works" (II Corinthians 11:3,13-15).

It is obvious from these and other Scriptures that occultism in its various manifestations, including even its supernatural aspects, is based on deception. Therefore it should certainly not be incorporated in educational curricula, regardless of the barrenness of naturalistic humanism. It is significant that the deception may be either human or demonic, and that often the deceivers are themselves deceived by their own deceptions.

It is interesting that the naturalistic humanists vigorously oppose the supernaturalistic super-humanists, even though both agree in opposing the true God of creation. Most scientists and educators are agreed that all the phenomena discussed in this section—demon possession, astrological prophecies, flying saucers, extra-sensory perception, witchcraft, spiritistic phenomena, psycho-kinesis, mind reading, and all the rest—have strictly naturalistic explanations. It is significant that professional magicians have been among the most insistent that *all* supposedly supernatural occurrences are actually purely natural and are often produced fraudulently.[1] They maintain that all such phenomena can be, and have been, duplicated by professional illusionists and mentalists, and there is nothing supernatural about any of it.

Similarly, there is no doubt that many of the evidences cited by von Däniken and others for interplanetary astronauts and U.F.O.'s, for the occult character of the Bermuda Triangle, the great pyramid, etc., for the existence of Sasquatch monsters and the like, and similar remarkable phenomena have been explained by perfectly natural means. A great many of these have even been proved to be hoaxes or frauds. Again, it seems there is a close association of human

---

[1]See, for example, Milbourne Christopher: *Mediums, Mystics, and the Occult* (New York, Thomas Crowell Co., 1975, 275 pp.). The author is considered "America's foremost professional illusionist" and is former president of the Society of American Magicians.

deceivers with such para-normal phenomena.

On the other hand, there does seem to be always a small residuum of U.F.O. sightings, of E.S.P. phenomena, of demonic possessions, of Jeane Dixon prophecies, and all the rest of these strange phenomena—not to mention the volumes of testimonies of people brought to peace and fulfillment by transcendental meditation and the like—which cannot be explained (or at least have not yet been explained) in terms of either naturalistic causes or hoaxes.

From the Biblical viewpoint, of course, there is no question that demonic spirits actually do exist and that they do have certain abilities to affect physical and mental phenomena. Consequently, the Christian does not necessarily attribute all such superhuman occurrences to either hoaxes or natural causes; some may indeed have supernatural causes. Unless they can be shown clearly to be caused by the power of God or His angels, however (that is, unless they conform fully to Biblical principles and bring honor to Christ and His Word), they must in such cases be explained as demonic miracles, accomplished for the *precise purpose of deception!* It is not surprising to find demonic deception so intertwined with human deceivers and charlatans in these phenomena, since both are bent on resistance to the great truth of God's Creation and Redeeming Purpose for the world. Dr. Clifford Wilson, competent as a Biblical theologian, archaeologist, and psycho-linguist, has tried to maintain a good balance in evaluating these things, [1,2] for those who wish to read further on the subject.

It should not be forgotten that superhumanism, no less than humanism, is based ultimately on evolutionism. Like the pantheism and polytheism of the ancient pagans, they constitute the two sides of the

---

[1] *East Meets West in the Occult Explosion* (San Diego, Master Books, 1976), 176 pp.
[2] *Crash Go the Chariots* (Revised Edition, San Diego, Master Books, 1976), 161 pp.

coin. In fact, it is really the same old coin, brightened up with a new gloss to appear modern. The ancient philosophers were materialistic pantheists, just as are modern evolutionary humanists, both regarding the material universe as self-existent, with man as the highest entity yet evolved in the universe. They were quite skeptical with regard to anything supposedly miraculous. The polytheists, however, believed in the supernatural, exactly as do the modern superhumanists; they believed in astrology, in superhuman spirits, in miracles, and other phenomena in very much the same way as do present-day supernaturalists. In any case, both systems presuppose—just as do pantheism and humanism—the eternity of matter and the continuing evolution of all things. The supernaturalists, however, believe that evolution applies not only to the physical world but also to the spiritual world as well. The gods and goddesses evolved from primordial matter, and through reincarnation human spirits evolve into other human spirits and then into superhuman spirits. The world itself continues to evolve from one cycle to another, age after age. In none of these systems is there any recognition of the one true eternal God who created all things in the beginning and who controls all things, judges all things, and has undertaken to redeem all things.

NATURALISM, OCCULTISM, AND HUMAN NATURE

There is another interesting insight into human nature provided by this age-long rivalry between naturalism and supernaturalism, an insight which is very important for Christian teachers to keep in mind. It seems that some people are inclined to be very skeptical, examining and interpreting all phenomena from a rationalistic point of view. Such people become the scientists, the philosophers, the technologists, the lawyers. They are dominated, as it were, by the mind, the mental component of human nature.

Others are dominated more by the heart, the emotional component of human nature. These tend to become the artists, the poets, the priests, the missionaries. They are inclined more to feelings, to credulity, to irrationalism. These in the former age would have tended to be the polytheists, in the modern age to be the superhumanists. The other group would be the pantheists in one era, the humanists today.

This dichotomy is over-simplified, of course, but does point out the fact that man is both soul and spirit, a creature influenced both by "experience" and "reason," by "emotion" and "mind," by "feeling" and "thinking." Some people are dominated by the one, some by the other. Similarly, some nations in the world and some periods in history are characterized mainly by pragmatism, others by idealism.

Satan is a highly intelligent and utterly malevolent spirit, and he knows when to use rationalism and when to use irrationalism to deceive men of varying times and places. And, of course, *most* people of all times and places are primarily governed by *neither* soul nor spirit; they are people of *bodily* interests primarily, and he appeals to them neither through reason nor through emotion, but through their physical natures (food, drink, sport, sex, comfort, money, etc.).

In any case, every person is a composite of body, soul, and spirit, and Satan and his angels will utilize whatever attack bears the greatest promise of victory in a given time and place. In every case, however, the underlying premise is that of evolution over infinite ages of all aspects of the eternal cosmos, into higher and higher orders of existence.

In contrast to these ubiquitous deceptions of men and devils, we do have the complete Truth in the self-existing triune Creator of all things, and in the Holy Scriptures which constitute His Word to man. The

Truth, as it is in Christ, satisfies every human need—physical, mental, emotional—both now and in all future ages. There is no need to compromise with falsehood at any point, whether that deception takes the form of an evolutionary humanism or of an evolutionary superhumanism, of naturalism or supernaturalism. The one leads to man worship, the other ultimately to Satan worship, and both are under God's condemnation, since both objects of worship are creatures rather than the Creator.

BIBLICAL EVALUATION OF HUMAN REASONING

"Wherefore God also gave them up . . . who changed the truth of God into a lie, and worshipped and served the creature more than the Creator, who is blessed for ever. Amen" (Romans 1:24,25).

Men and women in their natural state are sinners and their minds are blinded (II Corinthians 4:4) with regard to God's eternal truths of creation, redemption, and consummation. Therefore, it is essential that one submit his mind to the revelation of God through Scripture if he would learn real truth. It is obvious that true Christian education must proceed from this premise.

Secular educational systems seek to impart knowledge (awareness of facts) and wisdom (organized and applied knowledge, based on experience and/or reasonings), and this goal would be appropriate and commendable if based on the true knowledge and wisdom found only in Jesus Christ (Colossians 2:3). If the knowledge is wrong, not based on real facts, and if the wisdom sought is based solely on human reasonings as an end in themselves (that is, if it becomes the *"love* of wisdom"), then the education provided is false and harmful. Consider briefly the implications associated with false knowledge and false wisdom.

(1) *Knowledge Falsely So-Called.* The word "knowledge" means essentially the same thing as "science"; and both English words are translations of the same Hebrew and Greek words in the Bible. True knowledge is, of course, valid and good, but false knowledge is bad. All real facts, rightly recorded and analyzed, will glorify God; thus they constitute proper materials for possible inclusion in a Christian curriculum.

On the other hand, it should be remembered that eating of the fruit of the tree of knowledge of good and evil was the occasion of man's primeval fall and God's curse on the earth. At that time, man already had the knowledge of good; everything he knew, and everything God had created, was good (Genesis 1:31). He did not *need* the knowledge of evil and would have been better off had he never acquired it, through eating the forbidden fruit.

The question is whether students today should be given in their schools training in those areas of knowledge associated with evil, or in only those areas of positive good. This problem will be discussed more in depth later but it may be mentioned at this point that, although evil is now an accomplished fact, it is still better to teach only those facts that at least *lead* to good. Facts associated with evil must be taught, when necessary to teach them at all, in such a way as to stress the nature of the evil, as well as its remedy, so that even these will then directly lead to God's glory and man's good.

Of course, there is a great amount of knowledge abroad in the land today which is not real knowledge at all. Evolution, for example, is often said to be a *fact* of science. Similarly, the Bible is *known* to contain many scientific mistakes. Such "facts" as these are not facts at all. They are what Paul has called "science falsely so called" (I Timothy 6:20).

As a matter of fact, this passage (I Timothy 6:20) is an incisive condemnation of evolutionary philosophy in general and of Greek philosophy in particular. The Greek word is *gnosis* (knowledge) and is often equated with gnosticism. It really refers, in context, to any philosophy contrary to the Christian faith.

The *"gnosis* falsely-so-called," like all other philosophical systems not grounded in Scripture, was based on an evolutionary cosmogony, and Paul's warning against such false knowledge or (literally) "pseudo-science" is just as valid in the twentieth century as it was in the first.

"O Timothy, keep that which is committed to
thy trust, avoiding profane and vain babblings,
and oppositions of science falsely so-called: . . ."
(I Timothy 6:20).

Note that this false science is described also as "profane and vain babblings," a graphic phrase meaning essentially "ungodly and pointless speculations." The command to "avoid" such things does not suggest retreating from them, but rather is a command not to be influenced by them.

Unfortunately, this is exactly what has happened over and over again in the history of the Christian church. Christian teachers and leaders have allowed pagan philosophical fads to influence their exegesis of the Word, in order to relieve the tension between the world and the gospel. Compromise with worldly philosophies, however, is always a prelude to disintegration of the church or school that engages in it. The Apostle Paul, therefore, commands Christians *not* to compromise with evolutionary pseudo-science or ungodly speculative humanistic philosophies, but rather to guard and maintain the Biblical truths committed to our trust, "contending earnestly for the faith which was once for all delivered unto the saints" (Jude 3).

We emphasize again that such warnings against false science do not apply to true science. Real science, or real knowledge, has to do with observable, testable, factual data. The real facts of biology and geology and history and other fields are proper objects of study for

Christians under appropriate conditions and, when correctly integrated and interpreted, are bound to be God-honoring in the long run. The Scripture says concerning even those facts resulting from man's sinfulness:

"Surely the wrath of man shall praise thee:
the remainder of wrath shalt thou restrain"
(Psalm 76:10).

The appropriate conditions for such study, of course, vary considerably with the particular type of facts dealt with, and this problem will be discussed more later on. The important point here is that the Christian teacher needs to be very cautious and critical concerning real facts, on the one hand, and interpretations or opinions concerning those facts, on the other. It is dangerous to teach "science falsely so-called" as real science.

The sad truth is that even normally-careful scientists and scholars tend to confuse their own opinions with facts whenever these begin to affect the questions of origins or purposes or destinies, because "they did not like to retain God in their knowledge" (Romans 1:28). Of one thing we can be sure, however. Real facts will always agree with the testimony of the Scriptures. Even when situations arise where there seems to be a conflict between science and the Bible, we know the conflict cannot be real and will be resolved on further study.

With this confidence we can proceed to study all the factual data available, interpreting them in conformity with the framework of history and meaning given in Scripture.

"Casting down imaginations, and every high
thing that exalteth itself against the knowledge
of God, and bringing into captivity every thought
to the obedience of Christ" (II Corinthians 10:5).

(2) *The Love of Human Wisdom (Philosophy)*. In addition to warning against false knowledge, the Scriptures give strong warning against false wisdom. The Bible does distinguish between knowledge and

wisdom, but insists that the "fear of the Lord" is both "the beginning of knowledge" and "the beginning of wisdom" (Proverbs 1:7; 9:10). True wisdom is in Christ (I Corinthians 1:30), and men are exhorted to acquire and love true wisdom (Proverbs 4:5-7).

Whereas knowledge has to do with factual information, wisdom involves the interpretive correlation and application of knowledge. In fact, wisdom becomes character, the use of one's knowledge and understanding in ordering one's own life and in dealing with others. If based on Scripture and on true facts, centered in Christ, wisdom is a priceless jewel. But if one bases his wisdom on mere human reasonings—and especially if he becomes so enamored of his own reasonings or the reasonings of other men, that he places these on a level equal to or greater than the Scriptures themselves—then such wisdom is both false and dangerous, and should be altogether rejected by the Christian.

The fact is that, throughout history, intellectual leaders in every nation have yielded to this very temptation, placing human wisdom on a pedestal and rejecting or ignoring God's wisdom as inscripturated in the Bible. The result is *philosophy,* the "love of wisdom." This English word is derived from two Greek words, both used frequently in the New Testament and meaning, respectively, "love" and "wisdom." As such, it is regarded in the Bible as utterly wrong, to be completely rejected by Christian believers.

Actually the word itself is used only twice in any form in the Bible, but both of these passages are very important and instructive. Colossians 2:8 contains the following warning:

> "Beware lest any man spoil you through philosophy and vain deceit, after the tradition of men, after the rudiments of the world, and not after Christ" (Colossians 2:8).

In this unique occurrence of "philosophy," believers

are warned to beware of it! It is humanistic ("the tradition of men"), worldly, deceitful, and futile ("vain deceit"), rejecting the true wisdom in Jesus Christ.

The same theme is found in Acts 17, where "philosophers" are gathered at the Areopagus to indulge in their speculations.

> "Then certain philosophers of the Epicureans, and the Stoicks, encountered him. And some said, What will this babbler say? other some, He seemeth to be a setter forth of strange gods: because he preached unto them Jesus, and the resurrection. . . . (For all the Athenians and strangers which were there spent their time in nothing else, but either to tell, or to hear some new thing)" (Acts 17:18,21).

The naturalistic bias of these philosophers, like that of modern philosophers, was seen in their response to Paul's preaching of creation, judgment to come, and the victory of Christ over man's greatest enemy, death. The creationist emphasis in this important passage (Acts 17:29) was discussed in the previous chapter. It was climaxed by an exhortation to repent and return to the true God, who, since He had created them, would one day judge them. The assurance of this fact was guaranteed, even to those unfamiliar with the Old Testament Scriptures, by the miraculous resurrection of Christ from the dead. The evidence for the reality of this miracle was overwhelming, and it was of such a character as to testify of the presence and power of the Creator Himself. This was not something that could be accomplished either by the human magicians or the demonic spirits with which they were acquainted. Nevertheless, the attitude of the philosophers was typical—they either scoffed at the whole story or indicated they would just keep a neutral attitude.

> "And when they heard of the resurrection of the dead, some mocked: and others said, We will hear thee again of this matter. So Paul

departed from among them" (Acts 17:32,33).

There were, of course, a few who were converted (Acts 17:34), as is always true when God's truth is proclaimed, but the great majority of these rationalistic philosophers were so enamored of their own learning and reasoning, that they were unable to see the true wisdom of God when it was shown them.

It is significant that, although the New Testament was written in the period when Greek and Roman philosophy was most highly esteemed by people everywhere, the New Testament writers have *nothing good to say about it whatever!* The only times the word was used ("philosophy" in one case, "philosophers" in the other), in the entire New Testament, it was used in a completely negative context. Those Christian intellectuals in every age of the church who have labored to accommodate the Scriptures to philosophy have caused untold harm to the true gospel by such temporizing and compromising. Our modern school systems—even most Christian schools—are so infected with these humanistic and evolutionary philosophies that the only way ever to get back to true Christian education is to make a clean break with human philosophy in any guise, both its roots and its fruits.

We recognize, of course, that the word "philosophy" is today often used in a more innocuous sense. People use it to mean simply one's perspective, or system of thought, with respect to a certain field. Thus, we talk of our "educational philosophy" or "athletic philosophy" or "political philosophy."Many Christians even try to develop a "Christian philosophy" or "Biblical philosophy." The word has come to be sort of an "in" word, a cliche. Even in these usages, however, the implicit emphasis is on human reasoning. It would be far better simply to study the Word of God for one's system of thought, with respect to education or politics or anything else. Instead of trying to reason out a "philosophy of economics," say, the Christian should develop a system of "Christian economics" from Scripture, and the same is true in every field.

In any case, if we are ever to develop a truly Biblical system of education, our legacy of humanistic philosophy from Babylon and Greece, through Mann and Darwin and Dewey, must be completely renounced. Man's wisdom is simply not capable of attaining the knowledge of the truth (II Timothy 3:7), no matter how diligently he studies and labors, until he submits himself unreservedly to the authority of Christ and the Scriptures. This fact is strongly emphasized in the New Testament, as discussed in the following section.

THE FOLLY OF HUMAN WISDOM

Man-centered reasonings are anathema to God. Note the following themes in Scripture:

(1) Human wisdom always leads away from God, if not founded on, guided by, and subject to, Biblical revelation.

> "For it is written, I will destroy the wisdom of the wise, and will bring to nothing the understanding of the prudent. Where is the wise? where is the scribe? where is the disputer of this world? hath not God made foolish the wisdom of this world? For after that in the wisdom of God the world by wisdom knew not God, it pleased God by the foolishness of preaching to save them that believe" (I Corinthians 1:19-21).

(2) Human wisdom, in the long run, will come to absolutely nothing.

> "Howbeit we speak wisdom among them that are perfect: yet not the wisdom of this world, nor of the princes of this world, that come to nought" (I Corinthians 2:6).

And if that is true, then why should a Christian educational curriculum waste time and money on such a futile enterprise as the teaching of human philosophies?

(3) Human wisdom is actually at war with God, so that the history of philosophy is nothing more nor less than the history of the rebellion of man and Satan against God.

> "Because the carnal mind is enmity against God: for it is not subject to the law of God, neither indeed can be" (Romans 8:7).

(4) Human wisdom is utter foolishness, as far as God is concerned.

> "For the wisdom of this world is foolishness with God. For it is written, He taketh the wise in their own craftiness. And again, The Lord knoweth the thoughts of the wise, that they are vain" (I Corinthians 3:19-20).

(5) Human wisdom is not searching for truth or for God. Many Christians have tended to regard these ancient and modern philosophers as sincere seekers who attained much truth in their thinking but who fell somewhat short. In this view, the truth which they did acquire should be combined and integrated with the revelatory truth of Scripture to get a harmonious whole. The Bible, on the other hand, makes it plain that human reasoning is not seeking God but is rebelling against God.

> "As it is written, There is none righteous, no not one: There is none that understandeth, there is none that seeketh after God" (Romans 3:10,11).

> "Because that, when they knew God, they glorified Him not as God, neither were thankful; but became vain in their imaginations [literally 'reasonings'], and their foolish heart was darkened" (Romans 1:21).

If they were really seeking God and the true wisdom, they would find it. The fact that these humanistic philosophers did *not* find God proves they were *not* seeking real truth.

> "Because that which may be known of God is manifest in them: for God hath shewed it unto

them" (Romans 1:19).

"I love them that love me; and those that seek me early shall find me" (Proverbs 8:17).

"But without faith it is impossible to please Him: for he that cometh to God must believe that He is, and that He is a rewarder of them that diligently seek Him" (Hebrews 11:6).

(6) Apparent truths in philosophy are false because they are incomplete. Many authors have called attention to concepts or moral laws in the writings of the philosophers which are very similar to teachings in the Bible, regarding this as something commendable. These very similarities, however, make them the more dangerous. The essence of Satan's attack is deception, the counterfeiting of that which is genuine by something which appears to be genuine, or that which is part genuine, part false.

"And no marvel; for Satan himself is transformed into an angel of light. Therefore it is no great thing if his ministers also be transformed as the ministers of righteousness" (II Corinthians 11:14,15).

(7) The natural mind of man is, because of his fallen nature, incapable of attaining real truth even if he desired it. His is a mind of vanity and darkness, corruption and blindness.

". . . Walk not as other Gentiles walk, in the vanity of their mind, Having the understanding darkened, being alienated from the life of God through the ignorance that is in them, because of the blindness of their heart" (Ephesians 4:17,18).

". . . unto them that are defiled and unbelieving is nothing pure; but even their mind and conscience is defiled" (Titus 1:15).

"Ever learning and never able to come to the knowledge of the truth" (II Timothy 3:7).

"But if our gospel be hid, it is hid to them that

are lost: In whom the god of this world hath blinded the minds of them which believe not, lest the light of the glorious gospel of Christ, who is the image of God, should shine unto them" (II Corinthians 4:3,4).

In view of all these clear analyses and warnings from the Bible, it is evident that humanistic reasonings have no value or justification in God's sight; the same is true of superhumanistic reasonings. All "creature-centered" philosophy is false and harmful, and the same must be true of any works of men or spirits that may be based on such philosophy—in fact, so is "every high thing that exalteth itself against the knowledge of God" (II Corinthians 10:5).

We are forced to conclude, therefore, that—difficult as such a choice and position may be in the eyes of men—a true Christian educational system, whether in church or university or elementary school or anything else, must completely divorce itself from all philosophy of either human or superhuman origin or content. Teachings or practices based on such philosophies, if they are necessary to be discussed at all, must be clearly delineated as anti-Christian in their entirety, with cogent reasons given for repudiating them. While such a stand is different from that of most Christian institutions, and is bound to be unpopular and misunderstood, it would seem that concern for Biblical integrity demands that we return to it.

Chapter 4

Christ-Centered Education

Having shown that all man-centered (or superman-centered) philosophy must be expunged from educational systems if they are to provide true education, the immediate question is what to put in its place. Practically every course in the curriculum and almost every textbook now in use are structured around these humanistic and evolutionistic premises. If we cannot use information and materials from non-Christian sources, then what can we use? There are very few Christian textbooks available of any sort and few if any Christian graduate schools for training teachers in any of the sciences or humanities.

And does this position mean we cannot use the scientific discoveries of non-Christians like Einstein or Freud? How about the literature of Byron or Poe, and the political theories of Jefferson and Ben Franklin and Tom Paine? Exactly what is the true Biblical and Christian doctrine of education in relation to the data and analyses developed from the work of men who do not believe the Bible and the gospel of Christ?

It follows from our previous discussion, of course, that evolutionism as the basic premise in all research and teaching should be replaced by creationism and that education should be God-centered rather than man-centered, theistic rather than humanistic. But how do we apply these principles in developing specific courses, especially courses like grammar and mathematics, as well as physics and history and many others?

THE EDENIC MANDATE
AND ITS IMPLICATIONS

To answer such questions, it is necessary first to remember that God is concerned with all men and the entire world. He created all things and governs all things. He is not involved merely in saving souls out of the world but in redeeming the world itself. He had a holy purpose in every thing he did in creation, and we can be sure His purposes will not fail, despite the interruption occasioned by sin and the curse.

The creation of man and woman, of course, was the climax of creation. All things created previously were for the purpose of preparing the world for these beings made in God's image. Even the angels had been created for the purpose of serving man (Hebrews 1:14).

The first commandment given to Adam and Eve is very comprehensive and significant.

"And God blessed them, and God said unto them, Be fruitful, and multiply, and replenish [or 'fill'] the earth, and subdue it: and have dominion over the fish of the sea, and over the fowl of the air, and over every living thing that moveth upon the earth" (Genesis 1:28).

This commandment obviously was not for Adam and Eve only, but for all those descendants of theirs who would fill the earth as they obeyed the instruction of fruitfulness and multiplication.

Now the significant thing as far as education is concerned is that this commandment was not withdrawn at the time of man's fall. In fact, it was specifically continued and even expanded at the time of Noah, and its provisions are referred to recurrently throughout the Bible, in various ways.

Therefore, this primeval instruction is still in force and is still applicable to all men. Whether men believe in God's Word or not, whether they are aware of this all-embracing commandment or not, is irrelevant. It is still there.

Now look more closely at its implications. Man was: (1) to "subdue the earth"; (2) "to govern all lower creatures on the earth." The first provision has to do with physical systems, the second with biological systems. To do either of these would require men and women filling the entire earth—hence, the command to multiply.

The earth and all things thereon had been prepared by God for man's home. In delegating its control to man, there is no suggestion that God was no longer concerned with it. Man was merely a steward under God's over-all ownership, and all of this arrangement was to be for man's good and God's glory. It was, in a sense, a probational arrangement, with man destined ultimately, should he prove faithful, for much larger responsibilities throughout God's infinite creation.

The first pair, of course, could not directly exercise dominion over the physical and biological systems of the whole planet. Therefore, God gave them immediate responsibilities in a small and choice part of it, the beautiful garden in Eden. There, Adam was to "dress it and to keep it" (Genesis 2:15). He also was made acquainted with all the animals there, through actually examining and naming them (Genesis 2:19,20). As their family multiplied, had not sin come in to disrupt these plans, these activities would have eventually become worldwide.

Before Adam or his descendants could effectively subdue the earth—or even that portion of it in the garden—they would have to learn enough about its processes to know *how* to "till the ground" (Genesis 2:5) and enough about the animals to know how to provide for their needs too. There is no indication that God gave Adam any lessons in agronomy or horticulture or animal husbandry. It was Adam's responsibility to acquire the necessary information himself and then to utilize it properly in accord with the terms of his stewardship.

Thus, this first great commission to mankind, to all intents and purposes, was a commission for both research and development, justification for the broad enterprises of science and technology. As the population multiplied, more and more parts and processes of the earth could be studied, and more and more applications could be implemented for its most effective development in accord with God's over-all plans. All of this, if faithfully and wisely carried out, would have brought glory to God and enrichment to human life.

(1) *The Natural Sciences.* It should also be noted that this two-fold division of man's responsibility (studying and caring for both physical systems and living creatures) would correspond, in modern terminology, to the physical sciences with the technologies based on them and the biological sciences with their corresponding technologies. These two categories today comprise what are known as the natural sciences (physics, chemistry, biology, geology, physiology, etc.). The various technologies for making the resulting information useful to man include such professions as engineering, medicine, agriculture, architecture, and others.

Man has the unique capacity, among all living creatures, of transmitting information thus acquired through research and development to other people, so that the information becomes their possession also. Animals do not have this ability—it is one of the attributes associated with man's creation in God's image. Animals possess many remarkable instinctive abilities, but these were specially created and are transmitted genetically. Animals can also be taught many "tricks" by man, but information learned in this way is never transmitted by them to other animals. Man alone can accumulate knowledge and convey it to other people. This necessary activity leads, of course, directly to the institution of education and, eventually, to the profession of teaching.

All of this marvelous complex of activities—research and development and then the widespread transmission of the knowledge and experience gained by such research and development—or in other words, the broad categories of science, technology, and education—stem directly from this primeval commission of God to man.

This is what is known as the *cultural mandate*. In a sense, this threefold division embraces all the original categories of legitimate human occupations, and to some extent all people still engage in all three types of activities—that is, they learn new things, they develop new methods, and they teach others. With growing populations, of course, there would be both need and justification for more and more specializations, but all would relate in some way to these three broad, basic categories. With this development, another overlapping category of activities would arise—that of implementing the actual utilization and enjoyment of the contributions of research and technology in the life of mankind. This would include a host of so-called vocational activities—banking, merchandising, transportation, journalism, manufacturing, building, and many others. The skills and knowledge associated with all such occupations would, of course, originally also have to come through research and development and then be transmitted through teaching.

(2) *The Humanities and Social Sciences.* Related to this group, and yet with distinctive characteristics of its own, would be a category which might broadly be designated as the fine arts, or humanities. This group of specialists would also serve to implement the enjoyment of human life through music, literature, art, and theology. In the original purpose of God, man was created for fellowship with Himself, and for a brief time Adam and Eve did enjoy that direct communion with God. Had sin not intervened, no doubt those who would have become specialists in these fine arts would have dedicated their talents to the praises of God and His glorious creation. All music and literature and art would have been designed and practiced with this motivation, and, with an infinite universe before them and an infinite God to love, there would never have been a dearth of themes. There would probably also have been full-time theologians, although all men would have studied to learn about God in great measure, because all would have had a heart of thankfulness and love desiring to know Him in His fulness.

The cultural mandate, in its original expression, clearly implies all such activities as listed above. There is one group of activities not included however: the so-called social sciences, with their associated technologies and service occupations. The social sciences include such fields as psychology, sociology, and political science. The related professional technologies include law, government, military, police, welfare, psychiatry, and others designed to regulate and control human behavior and interpersonal and social relationships.

These social sciences were not included in the original cultural mandate because there was no need for them. There was a need for man to govern the animals, but no need to govern other men. All men and women were created in God's image, so that all human behavior should have been completely unselfish and loving; all people would have been in perfect fellowship

with God and with one another. Such governmental
authority as may have been exercised would have been
patriarchal only, with the father responsible, and the
mother as helpmeet, in the teaching of their children.
There would have been no crime or war, so no need for
police or soldiers. No laws were in force (except the
restriction on eating the forbidden fruit), so no gover-
nors or lawyers were necessary. There was ample
wealth for everyone and all would be content and fulfilled, so social workers and psychologists were also unnecessary. But this idyllic world that might have been
all changed when sin came into the world.

THE BONDAGE OF CORRUPTION

When man sinned, God cursed the ground for man's
sake (Genesis 3:17). Profound changes ensued in both
the physical and biological realms, both of which had
been entrusted to man as his dominion. The very
elements of the earth were subjected to a principle of
disintegration and decay, so that all natural physical
systems ever since have tended to go toward a state of
disorder. All animals, as well as man, began to age and
finally would die.

The most significant effect of man's sin and God's
curse, however, was the immediate loss of fellowship
between them. Sin had entered into the world, and death
by sin (Romans 5:12). Adam and Eve tried to hide from
God, and so have all men and women ever since. They
are no longer in fellowship with their Creator and
therefore no longer in fellowship with each other, "Having the understanding darkened, being alienated from
the life of God" (Ephesians 4:18). All mankind is now
under "the bondage of corruption," with "the whole
creation groaning and travailing in pain together"
(Romans 8:21,22).

The physical creation is now under the domain of the
law of entropy, in which order always tends to

CHRIST—CENTERED EDUCATION

decrease. The organic creation is now under the law of death, in which all creatures tend both to disintegrate physically and finally to die biologically. But the spiritual creation—namely mankind—endures a threefold curse, not only decaying physically and dying biologically, but in bondage to sin and Satan spiritually.

> "I find then a law, that, when I would do good, evil is present with me. For I delight in the law of God after the inward man: But I see another law in my members, warring against the law of my mind, and bringing me into captivity to the law of sin which is in my members" (Romans 7:21-23).

The Apostle Paul wrote these words as a Christian believer, with access to the liberating and restoring power of Christ. If the law of sin was a present problem even to such a man as Paul, how much more must it dominate the life and thought of the natural man.

As a matter of fact, sin so completely controls the unsaved man that he is enslaved to it.

> "Jesus answered them, "Whosoever committeth sin is the servant of sin" (John 8:34).

> "Know ye not, that to whom ye yield yourselves servants to obey, his servants ye are to whom ye obey; whether of sin unto death, or of obedience unto righteousness?" (Romans 6:16).

> "What then? are we better than they? No, in no wise, for we have before proved both Jews and Gentiles, that they are all under sin. . . . They are all gone out of the way, they are together become unprofitable; there is none that doeth good, no, not one. . . . Destruction and misery are in their ways: And the way of peace have they not known: There is no fear of God before their eyes" (Romans 3:9,12,16-18).

In many cases, this sinful nature leads to gross sins of the flesh, such as murder and fornication. Even more universally, it produces sins of the mind and heart. The terrible catalog of sins in the first chapter of Romans lists both types of sins together (note "fornication," "maliciousness," "murder," "deceit," etc. in verse 29; "haters of God," "proud," "without understanding," etc. in verses 30 and 31). In the eternal lake of fire will be found those who are "the fearful, and unbelieving," as well as "the abominable, and murderers, and whoremongers, and sorcerers, and idolators, and all liars" (Revelation 21:8).

Thus, man's rejection of the Word of God in the beginning, and his continued rebellion against it throughout history, has led to every manner of evil in the moral and spiritual realms. The prevalence of all kinds of problems in the human personality, in the body politic, and in society in general, characterizes this present world.

As far as education is concerned, this factor must continuously be recognized if the curriculum is to be meaningful and effective. Problems between peoples and nations exist only because of the existence of sin in the heart.

> "From whence come wars and fightings among you? come they not hence, even of your lusts that war in your members? Ye lust, and have not: ye kill, and desire to have, and cannot obtain. ye fight and war, yet ye have not, because ye ask not. Ye ask, and receive not, because ye ask amiss, that ye may consume it upon your lusts. Ye adulterers and adulteresses, know ye not that the friendship of the world is enmity with God? whosoever therefore will be a friend of the world is the enemy of God?" (James 4:1-4).

As already discussed, there would have been no need for what we now call the social sciences in the world of mankind as God originally created it. But with the entrance of sin and death, a multitude of personal neuroses and social tensions quickly developed.

The further tragedy was that mankind was now not equipped to cope with such things. Being "alienated from the life of God" (Ephesians 4:18), the "god of this world" having "blinded the minds of them which believe not" (II Corinthians 4:4), there was no way that natural men and women could solve their problems in the social, moral, personal, spiritual areas of life. They were now "dead in trespasses and sins," walking "according to the prince of the power of the air, the spirit that now worketh in the children of disobedience," "fulfilling the desires of the flesh and of the mind; and were by nature the children of wrath" (Ephesians 2:1,2,3).

God in the beginning had given no instructions concerning social orders or governments or legal regulations or any such thing, because they were not needed. Consequently, when sin came in, conditions among people rapidly deteriorated morally and socially, until eventually a state of virtual anarchy prevailed.

"And God saw that the wickedness of man was great in the earth, and that every imagination of the thoughts of his heart was only evil continually" (Genesis 6:5).

Whether men in the ungodly antediluvian society tried to develop any formal legal systems or behavioral clinics to control the proliferating wickedness and violence is not known. Even if they did, however, they utterly failed, because soon "the earth was filled with violence" (Genesis 6:11). The only remedy, finally, was complete destruction in the great Flood.

In spite of the fall, however, man was still in the image of God. The image had been seriously marred, as it were, but not annihilated. It is mentioned as still a present reality after the Flood and even in the Apostolic period (Genesis 9:6; James 3:9). Therefore, although man was spiritually dead in trespasses and sins, he could still be made to realize his need of forgiveness and salvation. He would have to be "born again," but God Himself would make this possible through His great work of substitution and redemption. In symbolic token of the coming death of His own Son for the sin of the world, God instituted the principle of animal sacrifice as an atonement (or "covering") for sin. Adam and Eve believed God's promise, as did Noah and occasional others, but the great masses of the antediluvians completely rejected God and His gift of salvation, finally perishing in the waters of the Flood.

THE NOAHIC COVENANT

It might have seemed reasonable, in view of man's complete failure in his stewardship, for God to have withdrawn his commission and completely removed man's authority over the creation. The remarkable fact is, however, that the cultural mandate to man was not only renewed, but enlarged. Noah and his descendants were not only to control the animals, but now also to govern themselves. A condition of anarchy, such as had developed in the antediluvian world, was not to be permitted to recur. The wording of the commission was similar to that given Adam in the beginning, but with differences necessitated by the long prevalence of sin and the curse in the world.

> "And God blessed Noah and his sons, and said unto them, Be fruitful, and multiply, and replenish the earth. And the fear of you and the dread of you shall be upon every beast of the earth, and upon every fowl of the air, upon all that moveth upon the earth, and upon all the fishes of the sea; unto your hand are they delivered. . . . "Whoso sheddeth man's blood, by man shall his blood be shed: for in the image of God made He man" (Genesis 9:1-2,6).

It is evident that the command to be fruitful and multiply and the command to have dominion over the animals, both of which had been given to Adam, were now reiterated to Noah. These were the essential elements of the Edenic mandate which, as we have seen, provide the basis for the practice and teaching of science and technology, as well as their implementation in human affairs. As noted, the original mandate embraced the physical sciences and the biological sciences, so its renewal continues to warrant these sciences in the post-diluvian world, and this would include teaching them to succeeding generations.

A very significant command was now added, however. To man was also given the institution of human government, as epitomized in the authority to impose capital punishment as penalty for murder. This ultimate in governmental authority, of course, implies also that human government was now responsible to regulate other human interrelationships as well, since uncontrolled self-centered activities could otherwise quickly lead to violence and murder, and even anarchy.

Apparently God did not, at the time of Noah, institute a particular legal system or a particular form of government, although this would come later. It was only the responsibility to establish laws and government that was given, and it is interesting to note that a number of different ancient legal codes have been unearthed by archaeologists.

In any case, it is obvious that the existence of sin in human life, combined with the responsibility of regulating human behavior, required the development of the whole complex of activities now known as the social sciences and their related technologies and services. These also, at least in principle, would then become appropriate subjects for incorporation in educational curricula.

The great problem in this connection, however, is that man's heart and mind have been so blinded by sin that he cannot be depended on to reason correctly nor to judge and act equitably when dealing with personal, social, or spiritual relationships. The facts of the natural sciences are the same whether observed and analyzed by believers or unbelievers, because they are controlled by fixed natural laws established by God. Human behavior, on the other hand, involves a third factor (in addition to the physical and biological)—namely, that of the moral and spiritual freedom of choices resulting from creation in the image of God.

As already mentioned, men and women in their fallen condition are spiritually dead in sins, their minds blinded by the wicked one, and therefore cannot even think rationally in these realms. The social sciences developed on the basis of their humanistic and evolutionary premises are bound to be wrong because of these facts, and they certainly should not be taught in this context to young people.

And yet God's commandment to Noah concerning human government undoubtedly was intended to apply to all men, so that God recognized some capacity even in sinful man to organize an effective social and political structure for the maintaining of order in an ungodly world. This cannot be a contradiction, of course, and evidently must be harmonized with the concurrent incapacity of man in moral and spiritual decisions by drawing a line between empirical facts and the use of human reasonings to interpret and apply those facts.

Even in the realm of the natural sciences, this distinction is important. However, moral and spiritual factors are not usually involved in interpreting and applying the empirical facts of the natural sciences (except in questions of origin and purpose), and so do not affect them in the same way they do in the social sciences.

The extension of the primeval cultural mandate to incorporate responsibility for human government along with dominion in the inorganic and organic realms of the earth has been called the Noahic covenant. On God's side, the covenant entailed a promise never to send the Flood again and never to destroy all life again as long as the earth remained. The token of the covenant was to be the beautiful rainbow in the sky after every rain (Genesis 8:21-22; 9:9-16).

PRESENT STATUS OF THE
NOAHIC COVENANT

The cultural mandate, or Noahic covenant, was applicable to all men and, as far as God is concerned, it is still in effect today. The basic human dominion over the natural world is confirmed in Psalm 8:

"Thou madest him to have dominion over the works of thy hands; thou hast put all things under his feet: All sheep and oxen, yea, and the beasts of the field; The fowl of the air, and the fish of the sea, and whatsoever passeth through the paths of the seas" (Psalm 8:6-8).

This passage is quoted and affirmed in Hebrews 2:6-9, where it is extended and applied not only to man in general, but in its ultimate accomplishment to the Son of Man in particular. That man, though still responsible for the earth, has failed in his responsibility is indicated by Hebrews 2:8. ". . . we see not *yet* all things subjected unto him." Note also the statement in Psalm 115:16 that ". . . the earth hath He given to the children of men." That God still holds mankind in general responsible for his stewardship over the earth is also noted in the prophetic warning concerning the coming great tribulation that God will "destroy them which destroy the earth" (Revelation 11:18).

With respect to that part of the mandate concerning human government, the classic New Testament confirmation is in Romans 13.

"Let every soul be subject unto the higher powers. For there is no power but of God: the powers that be are ordained of God. . . . For he is the minister of God to thee for good. But if thou do that which is evil, be afraid, for he beareth not the sword in vain: for he is the minister of God, a revenger to execute wrath upon him that doeth evil. . . . Render therefore to all their dues: tribute to whom tribute is due; custom to whom custom; fear to whom fear; honor to whom honor" (Romans 13:1,4,7).

As has often been pointed out, the government to which Christians were commanded here to give obedience was a pagan dictatorship, very far removed from God's ideal theocratic form of government. Yet Paul insisted that even this government was ordained by God and had the divine authority to inflict capital punishment or to wage warfare if necessary to avenge evil.

The perennial question in this regard has to do with conditions under which men are justified in refusing obedience to a particular government and perhaps even in replacing it with another government. The answer, of course, is found in the words of the Apostle Peter: "We ought to obey God rather than men" (Acts 5:29). The government is a divine institution, in a generic sense, but this does not *necessarily* mean that a *particular government* or a *particular ruler* is heaven-sent.[1] Mankind in general is responsible for human government, and the men and women in each nation are responsible for the government of that nation. As long as it is serving effectively in fulfilling God's purpose for human government—that of maintaining order and justice, in accord with Biblical guidelines—then obedience and honor should be accorded it. Furthermore, believers should pray for it and for the men currently ministering in that government.

"I exhort therefore, that, first of all, supplications, prayers, intercessions, and giving of thanks, be made for all men; For kings, and

---

[1] In one sense, it is true that God often has raised up and used ungodly kings as instruments of judgment against a sinning people (e.g., Nebuchadnezzar — see Daniel 4:25; Jeremiah 25:8-12). Even Pharaoh was raised up for the very purpose of allowing God to make His power known (Romans 9:17). In fact, the Scripture says that God "worketh all things after the counsel of His own will" (Ephesians 1:11), and that He makes even "the wrath of man to praise Him" (Psalm 76:10). The real fact of God's absolute sovereignty, however, does not obviate the equally real fact of human responsibility, even though our finite minds cannot completely comprehend this paradox.

for all that are in authority; that we may lead a
quiet and peaceable life in all godliness and
honesty" (I Timothy 2:1,2).

However, the Scripture teaches that it is *the power*
that is ordained of God, not (necessarily) specific men
who wield that power or particular governmental struc-
tures for retaining that power. When any of these
become seriously remiss, then they should be either
corrected or removed by the people of that nation
(believers and unbelievers alike) by peaceful means in
general, but by force if necessary, since the ultimate
authority for the government lies with all the people of
that nation, in accordance with God's primeval commandment to Noah. Furthermore, in event the people of
a particular nation are unable or unwilling to replace an
evil government, then the responsibility still rests on
mankind in general to do so. The key question always
must be: "Is this government implementing the laws of
God, or thwarting them?" If the latter, then "we ought
to obey God rather than men."

There are difficult problems involved here, and
Christians of equally strong commitment to Biblical inerrancy and authority have differed on such questions
as to whether the American colonists were justified in
their war of independence against Great Britain,
whether German Christians should have supported
moves to overthrow Adolph Hitler during World War II,
whether America should aid the people of other nations
in attempting to defeat communism, and similar
questions. Biblical examples include both the case of
the Israelites being instructed by God to overthrow and
destroy the ungodly Canaanites, and Christians being instructed to obey the ungodly Roman government. This
implication of the Noahic covenant in no way justifies
civil disobedience or revolution or war merely because
a group of citizens finds the laws or methods of the
current government objectionable. However, when
governments become vehicles for defying God's laws,
rather than maintaining a stable society within which

God's laws can be obeyed, at least in principle, then Christian citizens (as well as citizens generally) are morally justified in seeking to replace that government with another which will operate within the covenant. It should be emphasized that revolution within a nation or an invasion against another nation would be warranted only upon the most *clearcut* and *extreme* situation of widespread and continuing breaking of the terms of the Noahic covenant by that nation.

Within this general framework, there are no doubt many forms of government that, in different times and places, could and do fulfill these functions effectively. The Noahic covenant was in operation at least a thousand years before the giving of the Mosaic laws, and even the latter applied directly to only one specific nation, so that other legal codes and other forms of government can meet the criteria. Nevertheless, there are certain principles of God's laws recognized by all nations.

> "For when the Gentiles, which have not the law, do by nature the things contained in the law, these, having not the law, are a law unto themselves: Which shew the work of the law written in their hearts, their conscience also bearing witness, and their thoughts the meanwhile accusing or else excusing one another" (Romans 2:14,15).

The ultimate authority, enjoined upon all governments, is of course that for capital punishment.

Thus, the Noahic covenant and its cultural mandate are still very much in effect and applicable to all people. As far as education is concerned, there is ample justification in this fact for using the empirical data acquired in any of the natural sciences or their related technologies and service occupations, whether based on the research or other studies of either Christians or non-Christians. The theoretical analyses and applications of these data are also appropriate to use, provided they do not involve theories of origins or destinies or intrinsic meanings.

The same is true in the social science realm as far as empirical data are concerned, but not where analyses or applications of the data are involved. The facts associated with governmental organization and human behavior, as actually observed and experienced, are valid to use. Their uses in theoretical formulations, sociological applications, psychological interpretations and the like, are very dubious, however, unless guided strictly by Scripture. Problems involving human nature and interpersonal relationships and behavior are bound to be conditioned in large measure by the fact of sin. Such problems cannot really be solved, but only magnified, by measures developed by spiritually-blinded people working either from humanistic or occult premises.

The same sort of contamination affects the humanities and fine arts in even greater measure. These professions cannot even use the empirical data developed by unbelievers, as can be done with the social sciences, because there are practically no empirical data involved in the humanities and fine arts. In this realm, practically everything is based on either human reasonings or emotions, with the exception of the actual mechanical techniques of writing, composing, painting, or performing. But reasonings and emotions come from the mind and heart which, in the unbeliever, are defiled and blinded by sin.

A Christian school, therefore, must be extremely cautious in using the literature or music or art or philosophy developed by non-Christians, even more so than the theories of non-Christian sociologists and psychologists. In the original creation, had sin never entered, the Christian artist and philosopher, poet and musician, would have enjoyed probably the most blessed of all occupations, with their time and talents dedicated solely to the praise of their Creator and His wonderful works of creation. Now, however, with hearts contaminated by sin and minds blinded by false philosophy, their talents become most accessible to Satanic corruption and influence and most dangerous to young minds. The very sensitiveness of their natures and brilliance of their minds make them, when not controlled by God and His Word, the most powerful of all people in influencing people away from God.

But what a difference it makes when a man or woman is converted! The talents which may have made him a good biologist or lawyer or musician can then be used rightly, in accordance with Scripture and to the glory of God. Unlike the animals, man can reason about moral and spiritual things and can experience and convey great emotions, but his reasonings are perverse and his emotions are misdirected until he submits them in repentance and faith to Jesus Christ as Lord and Saviour.

The image of God in which he was created, so marred by sin, can then be restored with all its potentiality for mental brilliance and moral power. Once they have been redeemed through faith in Christ, who died for them and rose again, Christians are enabled and encouraged continually to "put on the new man, which is renewed in knowledge after the image of Him that created Him" (Colossians 3:10).

Of course, the mere fact of spiritual conversion does not automatically convert a humanistic philosopher into a Biblical theologian or a rock musician into a Christian hymnologist, but the potential is there. In every Christian there is a constant battle between the "old man" and the "new man," and the "carnal mind", which characterizes the natural man and is at "enmity against God" (Romans 8:7), may easily continue to dominate the thinking of the Christian's mind (compare I Corinthians 3:1, where "babes in Christ" are said to be "carnal," and Hebrews 5:13, where such "babes" are characterized as those "unskillful in the word of righteousness," still in need of being taught when they themselves should be teachers).

In summary, the question raised at the beginning of this chapter—that is, how much of the data and studies of non-Christians can be properly used in Christian education—can be answered essentially in terms of the following rules.

1. *Natural sciences, with their associated technologies and services:* the empirical data can be used, as well as the theoretical analyses and interpretations, except when this involves questions of origins, meanings, and purposes, in which case they must specifically conform to Scripture.

2. *Social sciences, with their associated technologies and services:* the factual and organizational data, derived by careful studies and experience, can be used, but not the theoretical interpretations or personal or societal applications unless these are in clear harmony with Biblical revelation on these subjects.

3. *Humanities and fine arts:* only the associated skills and techniques can be used; the analyses or compositions produced by these techniques can only be used if they conform to Scriptural principles and thereby glorify God and His works of creation and redemption. This does not imply that only music and art with religious themes should be studied, but merely that their themes should be in accord with Biblical principles, bringing honor to God and blessing to man.

Empirical data, skills, and techniques associated with any field are essentially independent of one's cosmology or personal beliefs and can be discovered and developed by either Christians or non-Christians alike. As far as the spheres of inorganic science and the sciences associated with non-human life are concerned, analyses and applications can also be developed effectively and correctly by believers and unbelievers alike. The same is true with respect to the administrative and organizational aspects even of human societies. All of this is a justifiable conclusion from the intimations of the Noahic covenant and cultural mandate, which are still in effect between God and all mankind.

It is true, of course, that even plain facts and experimental data can be misused, misunderstood, even distorted or denied by men in order to promote particular causes or to resist unwanted conclusions. Consequently, the Christian teacher should not accept even what seem to be factual data and obvious interpretations uncritically. It is always good to check the reporter's methods of acquiring and analyzing the data, particularly the question of whether or not he has been completely objective in reporting *all* the data, rather than only the data supporting his own hypothesis. With this caution in mind, however, and within the limits outlined above, the materials discovered and published even by atheists may be used in Christian schools.

CHRISTIAN RESEARCH AND WRITING

What about books and papers published by Christians? One might think at first that, if we could only limit our teaching materials to those written and published by "born-again" Christians, then all the problems we have been discussing at such length would be solved. The indwelling Holy Spirit in the believer would lead him to discover and publish only true data and true interpretations of the data. The cautions and restrictions listed in the foregoing would no longer be necessary, and we could use such materials confidently and freely.

Unfortunately, while this is potentially and ideally the way it should be, it does not necessarily work that way in today's world. Christian scholars, no less than non-Christian scholars, have several serious obstacles to overcome in attempting to produce truly Christ-centered teaching materials: (1) their own training, particularly at the graduate level, has been largely—often exclusively—from humanistic professors and textbooks; (2) the factor of pride and the desire for academic recognition and prestige is especially strong among intellectuals, including Christian intellectuals, and this factor often leads to compromising positions in their writing and teaching; (3) the demands on time and the difficulty of independent thinking in new directions tend to inhibit qualified Christian scholars from ever undertaking to write genuinely Biblically-based text-books in academic fields; (4) most Christian academics have done little serious Bible study on their own, and so do not really know the implications of a Christ-centered approach to their own academic discipline; (5) even with the best of intentions, there is always a battle between the "old man" and the "new man" in the mind and heart of the believer, with the old nature reasoning in the same manner as unbelievers and with the same results.

Therefore, even textbooks, articles, novels, musical compositions, and other products of the talents and efforts of born-again Christians may well be influenced to greater or lesser degree by evolutionism, humanism, occultism, and other anti-Christian philosophies. If so, they also are unsuitable for use in Christian school curricula.

The fact that a person is a Christian does *not* mean that what he or she writes is divinely inspired and inerrant. The only Christian writers whose writings were divinely inspired, inerrant, and authoritative were those "holy men of God" who "spake as they were moved by the Holy Ghost" (II Peter 1:21). In the final analysis, therefore, the Holy Scriptures provide the norm against which *every* product of man, whether saved or unsaved, must be tested. This is most urgently the situation in those academic disciplines and intellectual pursuits which deal with human, personal, and social relationships (the social sciences) and (even more) those which are largely philosophical, cultural, or emotional (humanities, literature, fine arts). It is also true in the natural sciences wherever they deal with origins or ends or wherever they may appear to contradict specific statements of Scripture.

Restricting the Christian educator in this way does not in any wise prevent him from developing a full and meaningful understanding and presentation of his subject. The Biblical framework, in fact, provides him with the basic information and approach which will ultimately yield the most comprehensive and satisfying treatment of that subject. This must be the case because of the very nature and purpose of the Holy Scriptures.

CHRIST THE TRUE KNOWLEDGE AND WISDOM

Although becoming a Christian does not *automatically* make a person a better scientist or teacher or musician, it *ought* to do so, because it provides him with access to truth and with the potential for developing an understanding of truth which could never have been available to him otherwise. By the same token, every subject taught in school should be clearer and more effective in a Christ-centered framework than it ever could in a humanistic context. The resources accessible to the sincere Christian scholar are literally unlimited and inexhaustible.

As already stressed, true knowledge and true wisdom must both *begin* with "the fear of the Lord" (Proverbs 1:7; 9:10) and be centered in the Lord Jesus Christ, in whom they actually *"dwell"* (Colossians 2:3).

It is reasonable and proper that all wisdom and knowledge should begin with, center on, and glorify the Lord Jesus Christ, because He alone is the Creator, Sustainer, and Redeemer of all things. Note the marvelous summation of His past, present, and future work with respect to the whole universe as expounded by Paul:

"For by Him were all things created, that are
in heaven, and that are in earth, visible and invisible, whether they be thrones, or dominions,
or principalities, or powers: all things were
created by Him, and for Him: And He is before
all things, and by Him all things consist [literal-
ly, 'are sustained']. And He is the head of the
body, the church: who is the beginning, the first-
born from the dead; that in all things He might
have the preeminence. For it pleased the Father
that in Him should all fulness dwell; And having
made peace through the blood of His cross, by
Him to reconcile all things unto Himself; by
Him, I say, whether they be things in earth, or
things in heaven" (Colossians 1:16-20).

He "created all things," "sustains all things," and
"reconciles all things." It is obvious, therefore, that
everything in the cosmos derives its real meaning only
from Him, so it is impossible really to understand
anything apart from Him. All fulness dwells in Him,
and it is appropriate that He should have preeminence
in all things.

Another remarkable assessment of God's knowledge
and wisdom by the Apostle Paul testifies that their
magnitude and variety can never be exhausted. There is
surely no need to fear that students will somehow be
deprived or slighted by not including the philosophies of
the world in their education!

"O the depth of the riches both of the wisdom
and knowledge of God! how unsearchable are
His judgments, and His ways past finding out!
For who hath known the mind of the Lord? or
who hath been His counsellor? Or who hath first
given to Him, and it shall be recompensed unto
Him again? For of Him, and through Him, and
to Him, are all things: to whom be glory for
ever. Amen" (Romans 11:33-36).

Such Biblical testimonies as these certainly point up
the fact that there is no dichotomy between religious

knowledge and secular knowledge. All facts of knowledge and all true wisdom in understanding and utilizing such facts are comprehended in the knowledge and wisdom of God. As we traverse the Scriptures, it seems that everywhere we keep encountering names and attributes of Christ which emphasize this fact.

He is the "Word of God" (John 1:1,14; Revelation 19:13). He is "the Truth" (John 14:6). Christ is both "the power of God, and the wisdom of God" (I Corinthians 1:24). He is "the true Light, which lighteth every man that cometh into the world" (John 1:9). He is "the fulness of Him that filleth all in all" (Ephesians 1:23). In the "Wisdom Message" in Proverbs, wisdom is actually personified in a marvelous prophetic portrait of Christ (Proverbs 8:1—9:10), climaxing in the testimony that "the knowledge of the holy is understanding."

As noted below, the Christian teacher has distinct advantages over one who is not a Christian. Through his creationist perspective, his access to the Scriptures, and the indwelling Holy Spirit, he has both superior insights for understanding and superior resources for applying all of God's truth.

(1) *Superior Insights in the Natural Sciences.* Although non-Christian scientists are capable, under the cultural mandate, of discovering and utilizing data in the physical and biological sciences, Christians do have through the Scriptures certain powerful additional insights into these sciences which evolutionary scientists cannot see. That is, the physical processes in nature continually speak of the power and nature of God, and biological processes continually bear witness of His grace and redeeming love.

This testimony of the physical sciences is stressed in the first chapter of Romans:

> "For the invisible things of Him from the creation of the world are clearly seen, being understood by the things that are made, even His

eternal power and Godhead; so that they are
without excuse" (Romans 1:20).

The power and Godhead of God are clearly seen in the
creation, according to this important verse. The term
"Godhead" means the "God*hood*" of God—that is, the
nature or structure of God, as He is known through
revelation. According to Scripture, God is one God, yet
in three persons—Father, Son, and Holy Spirit. Thus,
this passage states in effect that God is revealed in the
physical creation to be both the omnipotent Creator of
all its processes and the tri-une Designer of its nature
and character. This testimony is so clear that those who
reject God are without excuse.

We have already seen that the two basic laws which
govern all physical processes are the first and second
laws of thermodynamics ("heat power"). The first
states the conservation of power as to total quantity;
the second speaks of the deterioration of power as to its
availability. Since the available power decreases as
time goes on, the primeval cause of that power must be
outside of time. It cannot be temporal power—it must
be *eternal* power! Exactly as Romans 1:20 states,
every process and every event continually bear witness
to His eternal power.

Furthermore, all processes take place in a universe
which is a dimensional continuum of space, time, and
matter (or energy). The universe is a tri-universe, thus
reflecting the tri-une nature of its Creator. Note that
the universe is not a "triad" (that is, a system con-
sisting of three distinct components) but is a true trinity
(that is, a system in which *each* of its three components pervades and comprises the entire system).
Similarly, space is a true trinity of three dimensions,
time is a true trinity of future and present and past
time, and matter is a true trinity in which unseen
energy continually generates motion which is experienced as sense-phenomena (e.g., light energy
generates light waves which are experienced in the seeing of light). The physical creation, thus, is a marvelous

trinity of trinities, always and everywhere bearing witness of the nature of its Creator.[1] The teacher of the physical sciences can emphasize beautifully to his class God's eternal power and Godhead through every system and process which they study, while also noting the remarkable scientific insights in Romans 1:20 and other Scriptures.

In the biological sciences, still more insights are found concerning the loving and gracious character of God.

> "But ask now the beasts, and they shall teach thee; and the fowls of the air, and they shall tell thee; Or speak to the earth, and it shall teach thee: and the fishes of the sea shall declare unto thee. Who knoweth not in all these that the hand of the Lord hath wrought this? In whose hand is the soul of every living thing, and the breath of all mankind" (Job 12:7-10).

> ". . . the living God, which made heaven, and earth, and the sea, and all things that are therein. . . . left not Himself without witness, in that He did good, and gave us rain from heaven, and fruitful seasons, filling our hearts with food and gladness" (Acts 14:15,17).

Every living organism is a marvel of complex interacting systems, and, the more closely one studies them, the more amazed he becomes at the One who could plan and design such systems. Furthermore, every animal exhibits behavior which corresponds in one way or another to instructive attributes of human behavior, providing beautiful object lessons for the teaching of the young. The industrious ant (Proverbs 6:6-8) and the courageous horse (Job 39:19-25) are two examples out of many in the Scriptures, and no doubt every other animal can serve in similar fashion for fruitful learning.

---

[1]For a more detailed discussion and analysis of this remarkable "triuneness" of the physical creation, see the author's book *Many Infallible Proofs* (San Diego, Creation-Life Publishers, 1974), 387 pp.

The very fact of birth and life is itself a beautiful picture of the new birth and eternal life. Although sin and death have come into the world, and God's curse is upon the earth, nevertheless He provides "rain from heaven and fruitful seasons," so that life is renewed day by day and year after year. And always, when a new life begins in the animal kingdom, it is preceded by a time of travail—and perhaps death—on the part of the mother, speaking over and over again of Him who "should taste death for every man" in order to bring forth "many sons into glory" (Hebrews 2:9,10).

Not only do these broad principles of the inorganic sciences and the life sciences serve perpetually as beautiful models and types of eternal spiritual truths, but the Scriptures also contain numerous examples of specific scientific data and processes, always given with perfect accuracy and often in anticipation of later scientific discoveries. The sphericity of the earth (Isaiah 40:22) and the hydrologic cycle (Ecclesiastes 1:7) are two well-known examples, among scores of others. The Bible is a rich mine of scientific principles and insights, as well as object lessons and guidelines for further discovery. The Christian school is certainly under no handicap when it rejects the evolutionary philosophy as a framework of scientific interpretation, for the Biblical and creationist approach opens wide doors of understanding and beauty which could never be glimpsed otherwise. The scientific discussions in this section are very brief, of course, but can be studied in greater fullness of treatment elsewhere.[1]

(2) *Superior Resources in the Social Sciences and Humanities.* The social sciences and humanities, except for the empirical data and mechanical skills associated with them, are almost closed to effective study and treatment by the humanistically-oriented educator, because sin has blinded his mind and heart when dealing with moral and spiritual values. The

---

[1]For example, in *Many Infallible Proofs,* by Henry M. Morris (San Diego, Creation-Life Publishers, 1974) pp. 100-113, 228-248.

Christian, however, at least in principle and in potential, has infinitely greater resources on which to draw as he attempts to solve human problems and to express human feelings toward God and His creation. The social sciences and humanities have been most seriously distorted and perverted by ungodly scholars and teachers, but they provide the greatest challenge and potential for Biblically-instructed Christians.

Not only do Christians have the Bible to guide them concerning human relations and values, but they have the tremendous resources of the mind of Christ (I Corinthians 2:16), if they would only avail themselves thereof. The following list summarizes briefly some of the advantages and potentialities of the Christian mind:

(1) His mental resources are the gift of Christ.

"And we know that the Son of God is come, and hath given us an understanding, that we may know Him that is true" (I John 5:20).

(2) His mind, once blind, can be renewed by the Holy Spirit.

"And be not conformed to this world: but be ye transformed by the renewing of your mind" (Romans 12:2).

(3) The image of God, marred by sin, can be renewed in knowledge.

"Lie not one to another, seeing that ye have put off the old man with his deeds; And have put on the new man, which is renewed in knowledge after the image of Him that created him" (Colossians 3:9,10).

(4) The Christian has been given a sound mind and is now able to think with true rationality when he deals with spiritual matters, an ability which non-Christians do not have.

"For God hath not given us the spirit of fear, but of power, and of love, and of a sound mind. Be not thou therefore ashamed of the testimony of our Lord" (II Timothy 1:7,8).

(5) The Christian mind is capable of realizing all truth as the Holy Spirit undertakes to teach him.

> "Howbeit when He, the Spirit of truth, is come, He will guide you into all truth" (John 16:13).

(6) Christians may actually experience the very "mind of Christ," and it was that mind that planned and designed the entire cosmos.

> "For who hath known the mind of the Lord that he may instruct Him? But we have the mind of Christ" (I Corinthians 2:16).

(7) True reason based on true facts does not contradict the exercise of saving faith, but is in perfect harmony with it.

> ". . . and be ready always to give an answer [literally, 'an apologetic'] to every man that asketh you a reason of the hope that is in you with meekness and fear" (I Peter 3:15).

With both the inspired Word of God and the unlimited resources of a mind renewed in Christ, the potential for great contributions in the social sciences and the humanities (as well as in Biblical exegesis and theology) on the part of Christian scholars is outstanding. It is the ministry of true Christian education to prepare modern Christian young people to realize this potential.

The mere possession of a Christian mind, however, does not guarantee its full and proper use. The Scriptures give us a number of extremely important guidelines that must be followed (and which Christian teachers must emphasize) if the potential is ever to be fulfilled. Some of these are listed in the following:

(1) The Christian mind must be motivated by nothing less and nothing else than love for God.

> "Jesus said unto him, 'Thou shalt love the Lord thy God with all thy heart, and with all thy soul, and with all thy mind' " (Matthew 22:37).

(2) The Christian mind needs to be a *disciplined* mind!

"Wherefore gird up the loins of your mind, be
sober, and hope to the end for the grace that is to
be brought unto you at the revelation of Jesus
Christ" (I Peter 1:13).

(3) At the same time, it needs to be an active and
energetic mind, saturated with the words of both the
Old Testament and New Testament Scriptures.

". . . stir up your pure minds by way of
remembrance; That ye may be mindful of the
words which were spoken before by the holy
prophets, and of the commandment of us the
apostles of the Lord and Saviour" (II Peter
3:1,2).

(4) The Christian should have an informed and
mature mind.

"When I was a child, I spake as a child, I understood as a child: but when I became a man, I
put away childish things. . . . Brethren, be not
children in understanding: howbeit in malice be
ye children, but in understanding be men" (I
Corinthians 13:11; 14:20).

(5) Despite its tremendous capacity, a Christian's
mind must be humble.

"Put on therefore, as the elect of God, holy
and beloved, . . . humbleness of mind . . .
(Colossians 3:12).

(6) Although it should be active and inquiring, requiring sound evidence and logic, it must be a mind of simple faith when it comes to the Word of God.

". . . neither be ye of doubtful mind" (Luke
12:29).

The Christian scholar and researcher, therefore,
should conscientiously seek to develop by God's help,
these positive attributes in his own thinking. The Christian teacher, likewise, must try to inculcate these attributes in the minds of his students, both by precept
and example. The Christian in educational administration—whether college, preparatory school, or

Sunday School, should plan the curriculum and methodology with these attributes as a goal.

SPIRITUAL STANDARDS
IN THE CURRICULUM

We shall conclude this chapter by calling attention to certain important Biblical principles that are applicable to any Christian school curriculum. If the program is to be truly Christ-centered, then the Bible must definitely be used to guide and judge every course and every activity in the school. A religious veneer on a secular program will not do; neither will specific courses in Bible added onto a secular program. The following Scriptural admonitions apply to all courses, but are most urgently needed in those which deal less with facts and skills, and are occupied more with cultural and philosophical emphases.

In the first place, the curriculum should be positive and must be centered on truth. False philosophies and unwholesome moral and spiritual attitudes should not be given any place in a Christian curriculum, regardless of whether or not corresponding secular schools do so. It is not our concern to conform in any respect to secular education, only to be true to the Biblical doctrine of education. And the Bible teaches that we should not even *think* about false or harmful ideas, let alone teach them to our students.

> "Finally, brethren, whatsoever things are true, whatsoever things are honest, whatsoever things are just, whatsoever things are pure, whatsoever things are lovely, whatsoever things are of good report, if there be any virtue, and if there be any praise, think on these things" (Philippians 4:8).

In contrast to such positive thinking about positive things, the Scriptures teach that false or harmful things should be avoided.

> "But shun profane and vain babblings: for
> they will increase unto more ungodliness. And
> their word will eat as doth a canker: of whom is
> Hymenaeus and Philetus; who concerning the
> truth have erred, saying that the resurrection is
> past already; and overthrow the faith of some"
> (II Timothy 2:16-18).

This passage makes it clear that *not* shunning
profane and vain babblings (that is, ungodly and empty
speculative philosophies) will have disastrous consequences for those who entertain them. An example is
given—namely, the teaching that the promised
resurrection of the dead (like other divine interventions
in history) is to be interpreted allegorically, referring
only to some experience of, say, spiritual encounter.

It may also be significant that the Apostle recorded
the names of two men responsible for introducing such
ideas into the church of his day. The name Hymenaeus
probably means "the singing one" and Philetus "the
loving one." Whether or not these names have any
typological significance, it is sadly true that Christian
schools and churches in great numbers have been in-
filtrated and led into apostasy during all of the Christian
era, through the introduction of pantheistic and
naturalistic philosophies into their programs. More
often than not these ideas were implanted by men who
were gracious, eloquent, brilliant men, whose attrac-
tiveness disarmed those who should have been alert to
the subtle introduction of false doctrine. As a matter of
fact, this very danger was long ago foreseen
prophetically.

> ". . . there shall be false teachers among you,
> who privily shall bring in damnable [or 'destruc-
> tive'] heresies, even denying the Lord that
> bought them, ... And many shall follow their
> pernicious ways; by reason of whom the way of
> truth shall be evil spoken of. And through
> covetousness shall they with feigned [literally,

'plastic'] words make merchandise of you" (II
Peter 2:1-3).
These heresies were, it should be noted, to be brought in
"privily" through "plastic words," investing Biblical
terminology with non-Biblical meanings. Their high-
sounding writings and lectures are also called "good
words and fair speeches" which "deceive the hearts of
the simple" (Romans -16:18), and "great swelling
words, having men's persons in admiration because of
advantage" (Jude 16).
   Now, if the bringing of anti-Biblical philosophies and
practices into churches and theological training institutions is condemned in scathing terms by the Apostles,
how much more serious is the sin of subjecting children
and young people to these ideas under the guise of "progressive education," "education for life," or similar
high-sounding titles!
      "But whoso shall offend one of these little
   ones which believe in me, it were better for him
   that a millstone were hanged about his neck, and
   that he were drowned in the depth of the sea.
   Woe unto the world because of offences! for it
   must needs be that offences come, but woe to
   that man by whom the offence cometh!"
   (Matthew 18:6,7).
The ways become especially "pernicious" when they
proceed onward from teaching their heretical
philosophies to the direct teaching of disobedience to
parents, rebellion against authority, questioning God's
Word, unrestricted sexual freedom, and all the other
ugly fruits of the bitter roots of curricular compromise.
The warnings in the Holy Scriptures against being identified in any way with such teachings are more than
plain.
      "But fornication, and all uncleanness, or
   covetousness, let it not be once named among
   you, as becometh saints; Neither filthiness, nor
   foolish talking, nor jesting, which are not convenient: but rather giving of thanks . . . . Let no

> man deceive you with vain words: for because
> of these things cometh the wrath of God upon
> the children of disobedience. Be not ye therefore
> partakers with them" (Ephesians 5:3-4, 6-7).

> "But chiefly them that walk after the flesh in
> the lust of uncleanness, and despise govern-
> ment. Presumptuous are they, self-willed, they
> are not afraid to speak evil of dignities" (II
> Peter 2:10).

> "While they promise them liberty, they
> themselves are the servants of corruption" (II
> Peter 2:19).

And lest anyone protest that such ideas must be allowed
in Christian schools on the grounds of dialogue, or
awareness, or accreditation, or for whatever reason,
note that Scripture makes no allowance for such compromise.

> "And have no fellowship with the unfruitful
> works of darkness, but rather reprove them. For
> it is a shame even to speak of those things which
> are done of them in secret" (Ephesians 5:11,12).

There are, of course, situations where ungodly
philosophies (evolution, communism, etc.) need to be
included in the curricular subject matter, since these
beliefs are so powerful in the modern world which
students will face after graduation. They need to be
armed against them, however, not merely conditioned
to understand them.

Note the emphasis in Ephesians 5:11, quoted above.
"Have no fellowship" with them, but "rather, reprove
them!" Students need to be well equipped to "give an
answer" (I Peter 3:15) when confronted with anti-
Biblical ideas and practices. They should never be exposed to such things in their formal education unless
they are simultaneously shown, from Scripture and
sound logic and experience, why they are both false and
harmful. Furthermore, unless there is really a viable
need for them to have such preparation, it is better

usually for them not even to be exposed to such things at all, as the limited time available in classroom and outside study could be better spent in teaching the positive truths about God and His world.

In summary, true education must be built on, centered in, and continually judged by Christ and the Scriptures. Scientific data from the physical and biological sciences may be used and taught, whether obtained from Christian or non-Christian sources, provided they are taught under those standards. The same criteria apply to empirical and organizational data, as well as the acquisition of mechanical skills, associated with the social sciences, humanities, and the fine arts. The philosophical formulations and cultural expressions of these disciplines, however, are especially dangerous when coming from non-Christian sources (or even from Christians whose purpose is compromise or accommodation with pagan systems). These must be taught, if they are necessary at all, only with extreme caution, with clear warning to students, and with adequate refutation from both Scripture and experience. Secular humanistic philosophies, attitudes, and practices are easily acquired outside the classroom, so that formal Christian instruction must guard against, rather than aid, this acquisition.

Chapter 5

The Teaching and the Teacher

The purpose of this book does not include discussion of the problems associated with the founding, financing, and day-to-day operation of a Christian school or college. These are important matters, but are beyond the scope of this book. We are occupied here more with the basic Biblical doctrine of education, its nature and importance. Of special concern is the subject material included in the curriculum and the over-all Biblical perspective of the school. In the next two chapters we wish to look in more detail at the curricular structure and the principles for its development, the necessary qualifications of the teachers who must implement it, and the most effective methods for implementing it. Not even in these areas, however, are we attempting to produce a "how-to-do-it" manual, with detailed curricula and course syllabi, but simply to formulate broad principles, based on Scripture, which can serve as a framework within which the complete structure can be developed in accordance with the local needs and goals of individual institutions.

To some extent, thse later chapters will review and codify the material introduced in previous chapters, while simultaneously amplifying important principles and methods for their best implementation in this great ministry of true education.

PRINCIPLES OF CURRICULUM CONSTRUCTION

One of the great dangers in a Christian school is the temptation to conform its courses to those of the secular school. Many denominational colleges, for example, are today so secularized that it is hard to tell the difference between a private religious school and a private nonreligious school. In fact, many great universities today (Harvard, Dartmouth, Yale, and others) were founded by Christians to provide Christian education, but have long since lost their Christian orientation and are now completely humanistic. Others (Notre Dame, Baylor, Southern Methodist, etc.) still have a nominal religious and denominational flavor but have become altogether dominated by evolutionism and religious liberalism.

Even evangelical schools (especially those in the "neo-evangelical" movement) have compromised with evolutionary, humanistic, and liberal philosophies to an entirely unwarranted degree, from the perspective of the Biblical doctrine of education. On the other hand, many Bible colleges and similar institutions have tended to concentrate almost exclusively on evangelism, Bible exegesis, and the spiritual life, largely ignoring the wide range of subject areas embraced within God's original mandate of terrestrial stewardship.

It is not sufficient insofar as the Biblical doctrine of education is concerned, merely to provide a Christian environment (e.g., chapel services, behavior rules, annual spiritual emphasis week) for what amounts to a secular curriculum. Neither is it adequate to add a specified number of courses in Bible and religion to an otherwise secular curriculum. It is not even enough to require students and faculty to agree to a "statement of faith," to open classes with prayer, and to weave occasional illustrative Scripture texts into the class lectures.

All of the above practices are important, but they are not enough. They have not prevented institutions that once practiced them from eventually becoming apostate. In fact, some schools still have many of these exercises in effect, but are essentially secularized nonetheless. The chapel services are dull and poorly attended, the Bible courses are taught from a liberal perspective, the statement of faith is signed with tongue-in-cheek and generally ignored.

The *Biblical* norm, on the other hand, requires that every course not only be based on Scripture and integrated with Scripture, but that it stand *under* the Scripture, being judged and corrected by Scripture continually. This standard is far more difficult to accomplish and maintain, but far more important, than all the religious services and spiritual emphases on the campus, valuable as they may be.

Furthermore, the Biblical doctrine requires that high standards of discipline and academic integrity be maintained in every course. We should *"do* the truth" (I John 1:6) as well as teach the truth. The Christian is commanded to: "Study to shew thyself approved unto God, a workman that needeth not to be ashamed, rightly dividing the word of truth" (II Timothy 2:15). The word for "study" is a very strong word, meaning "exercise all diligence." Our English word "speed" is derived from the Greek here. A student is a "workman," and the work to which God has called him for the present is that of preparing for the future work to which God will call him later. It is his responsibility to study with all diligence to that end. By the same token, it is the school's responsibility to provide the necessary environment, encouragement, and discipline conducive to such study.

The Christian is commanded to "redeem the time" (Ephesians 5:16; Colossians 4:5) but he will be unlikely to keep this commandment as an adult unless he has learned to do so when young. Note also that Paul's advice to the Thessalonians is very appropriate for a classroom.

> ". . . study to be quiet, and to do your own
> business, and to work with your own hands, ...
> That ye may walk honestly toward them that are
> without, and that ye may have lack of nothing"
> (I Thessalonians 4:11,12).

A classroom should be a quiet place, conducive to diligent study, and the students (who will soon be grown citizens) should be responsible and honest in their work, first as students, later as responsible citizens and Christian witnesses. It is the duty of the school and its teachers to establish these conditions and attributes.

Other things being equal, a Christian student should be a better student than he could ever have become without Christ. A Christian teacher should be a better teacher, each course a better course, and a Christian school a better school. These are obvious implications from the fact of the greater personal and spiritual resources of the Christian, as well as the greater scope and meaning of cosmic truth to the Christian.

As far as the construction of a formal curriculum is concerned, this obviously depends on the type of school (elementary school, high school, college, etc.) as well as the background of the students and any particular goals of the school (vocational school, seminary, etc.). The traditional "three-R's," of course, must be basic in everything, because of the all-importance of communication and order in human society.

Beyond this, the Christian school must certainly emphasize history (to provide perspective on God's

plan and program for man and the world in which he
lives), natural science (to provide an understanding and
appreciation of God's creation and the cultural
mandate), the factual aspects of the social sciences—especially geography and government (to provide knowledge
of the nations of the world under God and His Noahic
covenant), and (most important of all) the Bible. Some
amount of formal study in practical apologetics and
Christian evidences is expecially vital if the Christian student is to be adequately prepared to meet the challenges
of today's world.[1] Other general interest courses
(literature, music, foreign language, speech, etc.), are
desirable if resources permit, but are less essential.

The innumerable professional and vocational
specialties (engineering, medicine, law, theology,
agriculture, accounting, journalism, manufacturing,
retailing, etc.) can be added as needed and where
economically feasible. These should all, of course, be in
addition to (not in place of) the general educational background courses taught for all Christian students.

The selection of specific courses and construction of a
curriculum should also be oriented toward two broad
needs: (1) the need to optimize the Christian character
and witness of all students; (2) the need to optimize the
implementation of Christ's Great Commission.
Economic factors obviously have to play a part in these
decisions, particularly those courses that involve expen-
sive equipment and specialized teachers. Basic to these
and all other decisions, of course, is the most important
factor of all—God's leading in response to believing
prayer.

LIMITATIONS ON COURSE CONTENT

Once the over-all curriculum has been established,
then individual courses have to be designed. Rules
guiding the type of subject matter to include have
already been discussed at some length in previous

---

[1] See Chapter 8 for elaboration of this point.

chapters. All courses should be taught in a strong
creationist and Biblical context, as far as the underlying premises and basic outlook are concerned, being
careful that nothing in the course conflicts with either
the letter or the spirit of the Word of God.

All humanistic, evolutionary, or anti-Biblical subject
matter should be deleted, even when such material is
standard in the corresponding courses taught in secular
schools. When it is really *necessary* to include topics
of this sort in a course (and this question should be
closely studied first), the teacher must then be sure to
emphasize that it is anti-Biblical, giving the class
cogent and persuasive reasons for rejecting it.

Any material of a pornographic nature, or even of an
erotically suggestive or titillating nature, must especially be avoided. Young people have a hard time
resisting this type of temptation as it is, without having
to confront it in their Christian classroom, of all places!
Note again, in this connection, the warning of the Apostle Paul:

> "But fornication, and all uncleanness, or
> covetousness, let it not be once named among
> you, as becometh saints; Neither filthiness, nor
> foolish talking, nor jesting, which are not con-
> venient: but rather giving of thanks. For this ye
> know, that no whoremonger, nor unclean per-
> son, nor covetous man, who is an idolater, hath
> any inheritance in the kingdom of Christ and of
> God. Let no man deceive you with vain words:
> for because of these things cometh the wrath of
> God upon the children of disobedience"
> (Ephesians 5:3-6).

This particular problem arises especially in courses
in literature and, to a lesser degree, psychology and
sociology (the latter category including courses in so-
called "sex education"). Not only textbooks, but also
outside reading assignments frequently contain
material of this type. Even so-called "classics"

(Chaucer, Shakespeare, etc.) often include vulgar or suggestive passages, and the problem is almost endemic in modern literature. Psychology classes in courtship and marriage, Freudian counselling principles, etc., also frequently are offensive in this way.

There is no clear reason, however, why such materials need to be included in a Christian curriculum at all. There is an abundance of Christian literature available, of all types and periods, most of which the Christian never even hears of. Principles of writing and literature could certainly be taught just as effectively with these as with the works of Byron and Steinbeck and other such authors. Similarly, only Biblical principles need be taught in psychology and sociology courses. The standard objection raised against having a curriculum from which all anti-Christian philosophies and writings are deleted is that this somehow deprives the student of a real education. He needs, it is said, to study Plato and Kant and Shakespeare and Marx to have a true liberal arts education and to appreciate his cultural heritage. He must study Sartre and Henry Miller and Aldous Huxley to understand the nuances of modern thought. He must study tribal music and nude art because these are true art forms expressing certain cultural concepts which all should appreciate. And so on.

Christian intellectuals often add another argument to that of general cultural awareness. They argue that a Christian's effectiveness in witnessing is increased by his having a first-hand understanding of the various philosophies and attitudes of the unbeliever. He needs to have a good knowledge of existentialism, for example, before he can effectively witness to an existentialist and be well grounded in Marxist thought before he can deal with the spiritual needs of a communist.

There seems to be a certain amount of merit in this argument, but it is not too different from contending that a Christian should subscribe to *Playboy* and attend X-rated movies in order to witness more effectively to swingers and call girls. The basic argument is that

a Christian should subject his mind and emotions to ungodly teachings and influences in order to become a
more empathetic and productive witness. In other
words, the end justifies the means, and the situation
determines the ethics. But this is a specious type of
argumentation, as far as God is concerned.

> "For what if some did not believe? shall their
> unbelief make the faith of God without effect?
> God forbid: yea, let God be true, but every man
> a liar; . . . . But if our unrighteousness commend
> the righteousness of God, what shall we say? Is
> God unrighteous who taketh vengeance? (I
> speak as a man) God forbid: for then how shall
> God judge the world? For if the truth of God
> hath more abounded through my lie unto His
> glory; why yet am I also judged as a sinner? And
> not rather (as we be slanderously reported, and
> as some affirm that we say,) Let us do evil, that
> good may come? whose damnation is just"
> (Romans 3:3-8).

God has made it plain in His Word that His people are
not to compromise with the "profane and vain
babblings" of humanistic or occultist philosophers or
with the "unfruitful works of darkness" practiced by
the "children of disobedience" (II Timothy 2:16;
Ephesians 5:6,11). That being so, they certainly should
not teach them to others, even if it *were* true that this
might eventually result in some people in these
categories being won to Christ (a result which is much
less probable than that they shall "overthrow the faith
of some"). It is *not* right to do evil, that good may
come!

We do recognize that evolutionist, humanist, occult,
or even pornographic materials may be suitable for formal study in a Christian school provided three conditions are met: (1) the material be taught only to those
who have a genuine need to know it, in order to be able
to meet situations which they can really be expected to
encounter in their Christian life and ministry; (2) they

are sufficiently mature and have a solid background of training in the Word sufficient to assure they will not be confused or sidetracked spiritually by such teachings; (3) they are simultaneously given adequate Biblical and scientific evidence to demonstrate that these materials are false and harmful and should be rejected. In most cases, such spiritually dangerous materials would only be appropriate, under the above criteria, for upper level college students or graduate students, who have previously had sound courses in Biblical doctrines and Christian evidences. The tragedy is that most Christian schools have been very lax at this point, with sad results in the lives of many Christians and, eventually, of the schools themselves.

QUALIFICATIONS OF TEACHERS

The curriculum and course content are all-important in Christian education, but so is the faculty which must teach it. Although every Christian vocation is honorable, if it is followed in accordance with God's will, surely the profession of teaching is one of the most vital of all in the divine economy. There is very little distinction in the Scriptures between the ministries of the pastor and teacher (in fact, the two are essentially the same in the important passage on the Spirit's gifts in Ephesians 4:11), especially when one recalls that there is no real dichotomy between religious truth and secular truth. All truth is God's truth and is to be conveyed through the ministry of teaching from each generation to the next, all within the interpretive framework of the Scriptures. Whether one is teaching, say, Biblical ecclesiology in a Sunday School class or trigonometry to a section of college freshmen is basically irrelevant as far as the ministry of teaching and the qualifications of the teacher are concerned. All should meet the same Biblical standards.

Our discussion will center first on the spiritual

qualifications of the teacher and then on the professional qualifications. These are really not distinct and are both important, but it is convenient to categorize them for discussion purposes.

(1) *Spiritual Qualifications.* The essential spiritual qualifications may be recognized as very similar to those for the "bishops" or "pastors" or "elders" (all of which terms are used essentially synonymously in the Scriptures), keeping in mind the fact that a true Christian teacher has essentially the same type of ministry and responsibility as a pastor. It is instructive and legitimate to paraphrase the passage in Timothy which sets forth a bishop's qualifications with this in mind.

> ". . . If a man desire the office of a [teacher], he desireth a good work. A [teacher] then must be blameless, the husband of one wife, vigilant, sober, of good behaviour, given to hospitality, apt to teach; Not given to wine, no striker, not greedy of filthy lucre; but patient, not a brawler, not covetous; One that ruleth well his own house, having his children in subjection with all gravity; (For if a man know not how to rule his own house, how shall he take care of the [class he teaches in the] church of God?) Not a novice, lest being lifted up with pride he fall into the condemnation of the devil. Moreover he must have a good report of them which are without; lest he fall into reproach and the snare of the devil" (I Timothy 3:1-7).

And doing the same with the corresponding passage in Titus:

> "For a [teacher] must be blameless, as the steward of God; not self-willed, not soon angry, . . . a lover of good men, sober, just, holy, temperate; Holding fast the faithful word as he hath been taught, that he may be able by sound teaching both to exhort and to convince the gainsayers" (Titus 1:7-9).

It should go without saying (but does need to be said,

in view of the careless practices of some Christian schools, which regard educational background as more important than these spiritual qualifications) that every teacher should be a born-again, Spirit-filled Christian. How can an unsaved teacher instruct either children or college students in any subject and impart the true Christian perspective concerning that subject?

> "Can the blind lead the blind? shall they not both fall into the ditch? The disciple is not above his master: but everyone that is perfect shall be as his master. . . . For a good tree bringeth not forth corrupt fruit; neither doth a corrupt tree bring forth good fruit, ... For of thorns men do not gather figs, nor of a bramble bush gather they grapes" (Luke 6:39-40, 43, 44).

> "Thou therefore which teachest another, teachest thou not thyself?" (Romans 2:21).

Every teacher has a tremendous responsibility before God, and surely needs to examine himself, his spiritual convictions, and his own motives carefully before presuming to assume authority as a teacher of any kind of class. It is not sufficient that he be a Christian; he must be "filled with the Spirit" (Ephesians 5:18) and "an example of the believers" (I Timothy 4:12,13).

It is noteworthy that the filling of the Spirit is needed even for a teacher of mechanical skills. Concerning the man who was placed in charge of constructing the Old Testament tabernacle, God said:

> "I have filled him with the Spirit of God, in wisdom, and in understanding, and in knowledge, and in all manner of workmanship, To devise cunning works, to work in gold, and in silver, and in brass, And in cutting of stones, to set them, and in carving of timber, to work in all manner of workmanship" (Exodus 31:3-5).

In addition to being a Christian filled with God's Spirit and obedient to God's Word, a teacher of course must be capable of the actual work and art of teaching. This is *not* merely a matter of being trained in teaching methods and knowing the subject. It is an actual "gift" of the Holy Spirit.

As noted in Chapter I, there are three New Testament listings of the gifts of the Spirit (Romans 12:4-8; I Corinthians 12:4-11, 27-28; Ephesians 4:7-11), and these all differ from each other, the point being that no one of the three is meant to be complete, but only representative. It is significant that only the gift of prophecy and the gift of teaching are listed in all three, thus emphasizing the relative importance of these two gifts. Furthermore, the gift of prophecy (that is, receiving and conveying special divine revelation) was to "vanish away" (I Corinthians 13:8) once there was no more need for it, when all of God's permanent revelation had been inscripturated for the guidance of all Christians until Christ's return. It would then be completely superseded by the ministry of *teaching* — teaching the completed Biblical truth as well as God's truth in His completed creation.

How does one know, then, whether he has this gift of teaching, and how do parents and school administrators know whether a prospective teacher has such a gift. The answer is: "By their fruits ye shall know them" (Matthew 7:20).

A God-called, Spirit-filled teacher will be recognized, both by himself and others, on the basis of the characteristics listed above, as applied from I Timothy 3:1-7 and Titus 1:7-9. Note again some of these: blameless, married to one wife, vigilant, sober, well-behaved, hospitable, patient, content with limited income, effective parent, of good community reputation, amicable, unselfish, temperate, holy.

Especially important is the requirement that he "hold fast the faithful word as he hath been taught." This implies that, before he is himself a teacher, he must have been taught "the faithful word." He must know the Scriptures, as well as the subject matter of his own discipline and hold them firm in his own mind and in his teaching.

Note also the requirement that he be "apt to teach." He must have proved out as a good teacher, effective at instructing and inspiring his students. This attribute is further amplified in the following:

"And the servant of the Lord must not strive; but be gentle unto all, apt to teach, patient, In meekness instructing those that oppose themselves; if God peradventure will give them repentance to the acknowledging of the truth" (II Timothy 2:24,25).

Further, he must be willing to accept his responsibility of caring for those in his class *en loco parentis* ("in the place of their parents"). He must remember that the ministry of teaching is *primarily* the responsibility of parents, according to the plan and order of God. The teacher is an agent of the parents, a steward, performing a function which they would if they could, and for which they are responsible before God. He has no right to teach the students in his class *anything* contrary to the parents' convictions, unless (and he must be very sure) the Scriptures themselves teach otherwise ("we must obey God rather than men").

This role of the teacher and the school *en loco parentis* also implies responsibility for the behavior and discipline of the student while at the school, as well as for his intellectual training. Unfortunately many schools today have essentially abdicated this responsibility, especially at the college level. It is definitely a Scriptural responsibility, however, and ability in this regard is a component of the gift of teaching. Note again the qualification of a bishop (or "pastor" or "teacher") that he be "one that ruleth well his own house"; otherwise, he cannot take care of the church of God (or a school of God).

No wonder, with such sobering and demanding responsibilities, the Apostle James issues such a sharp warning.

"My brethren, be not many of you teachers,

knowing that we shall receive the greater condemnation" (James 3:1).

(2) *Professional Qualifications.* Assuming that teachers can be found with the right spiritual qualifications, it is necessary also to select men and women with the best professional qualifications, those having to do with competence in the subjects being taught. In a very real sense, these professional qualifications are also spiritual qualifications, since the subjects being taught are part of God's truth, but it is convenient to discuss them separately.

Professional qualifications can be further subdivided into training and experience. A teacher's training, in turn, involves three main areas: (1) general education; (2) education in a major academic discipline; (3) education in the necessary associated mechanical skills and techniques. This same division applies to the training for any other profession or vocation, of course, as well as that of teaching. Depending on the discipline, one or another of these three categories may occupy the major part of the curriculum.

The term "general education" is used more or less synonymously with the term "liberal education" or "liberal arts education." It comprises courses which are considered of general interest, knowledge important for people in any profession. As used today, the term usually includes courses in the natural sciences (especially biology, geology, chemistry, physics, and mathematics), the social sciences (especially history, economics, geography, psychology, and sociology), the humanities (especially rhetoric, literature, foreign language, and philosophy), and the fine arts (music, art, drama). At least some of these are included in almost every type of curriculum. Those who advocate a strong component of liberal arts courses or even an exclusively liberal arts program feel that it is more important for schools to produce well-rounded people of culture and sensitivity than narrow specialists.

Whatever merit there may have been in this contention at one time, it is complicated now for Christian
education by the fact that these liberal arts areas have
been almost completely taken over by evolutionists and
humanists. The very term "liberal education," in its
origin and basic meaning, was understood to be
"liberating education," setting one free from the
limitations of a mundane existence and the constraints
of a narrow and legalistic outlook on life. As it is now,
however, the "liberation" is actually from a theistic
and Christian world view in favor of naturalism and
humanism. The constraints removed are those of
Biblical morality and personal reponsibility before God.

In contrast to humanistic liberal education, the Bible
teaches that real freedom is found only in Christ.

> "Then said Jesus, ... If ye continue in my
> word, then are ye my disciples indeed; And ye
> shall know the truth, and the truth shall make
> you free. . . . Whosoever committeth sin is the
> servant of sin. . . . If the Son therefore shall
> make you free, ye shall be free indeed" (John
> 8:31,32,34,36).

Since freedom is found only in Christ and His Word,
genuine "liberating" education is education which sets
a person free from his bondage to sin and death, and
such education must be Christ-centered. Therefore *real*
liberal education is education founded and centered on
the Holy Scriptures. As discussed previously, in Christian schools, not only should there be formal courses
required in Bible, but *all* courses should be developed
within a Biblical framework and continually guided
by Biblical constraints.

In addition to a general education centered in Christ
and the Word of God, as required for all students, the
teacher should have thorough training in his own
academic specialty, in fact the very best he can obtain.
Other things being equal, a Christian mathematician,
for example, should be a better mathematician than he

could ever have become as a non-Christian, which means that he should have at least as complete a training in mathematics as he could have acquired as a non-Christian. The same applies to all fields to which the terms of the cultural mandate and Noahic covenant are applicable.

The prophet Daniel is a good example. He was one who was "skilful in all wisdom, and cunning in knowledge, and understanding science" (Daniel 1:4). As he and his friends were given, as it were, specialized graduate training in the Babylonian royal academy, they remained faithful to God and His Word. As a result, "God gave them knowledge and skill in all learning and wisdom" (Daniel 1:17) and used them greatly.

Note, however, that this was through a three-year period of intensive study and discipline (Daniel 1:5). Similarly, in spite of having already acquired the best education available in his day, the Apostle Paul had to spend three long years (Galatians 1:15-18) in Arabia and Damascus, where he evidently received specialized education through "the revelation of Jesus Christ" Himself (Galatians 1:12).

While graduate degrees are not more significant than the spiritual qualifications, they are nevertheless very important for Christian teachers in that they represent two important attributes: (1) intensive study and understanding of the field in which they are to be a teacher; (2) discipline and dedication to serious and persistent study. Both of these are highly valuable assets for a Christian educator (or researcher or designer, for that matter). Many would-be Christian teachers seem to think that, if they are not capable or industrious enough to acquire a good position in a secular school, they can still teach in a Christian school, where their spiritual orientation may compensate for a lack of scholarly achievement.

But this is not true. Demands of scholarship and

academic contributions ought to be higher in Christian schools than in secular schools, because Christians have truer goals, greater resources, and fuller access to all truth than do non-Christians.

It is interesting to note in passing that the very titles used today to denote holders of advanced degrees (e.g., "Master" and "Doctor") are synonymous in the New Testament with the word "Teacher." All three are translations of the same Greek word, *didaskalos*. In Ephesians 4:11, for example, it is rendered "teachers," in James 3:1 "Masters," and in Luke 2:46 "doctors." A real teacher should be a master of his field of expertise and a doctor capable of fully "in-*doctor*-inating" his students with all relevant truths.

There is an obvious danger, of course, in taking such graduate degrees. Practically all graduate schools today are dominated by evolutionary humanists. It is extremely difficult for young Christians to be subjected to this type of philosophy intensively for three or more years without being injured spiritually by it. There is an urgent need for Christians to establish schools at all levels, including graduate schools.

As it is now, this is impossible in practically every field[1] except Biblical studies—and even there it is difficult. Nevertheless, it is still important for Christian teachers to obtain advanced degrees, in order to have a real mastery of all the relevant factual data and skills in their fields. The Lord is able to help them sort out the true facts from the false theories, provided they have had a solid-background training in Bible and Apologetics and provided they stay close to the Lord and deep in His Word during the time they are getting their graduate training. It should be understood, however, that whenever possible, the Christian should

---

[1]The Institute for Creation Research has offered creationist M.S. degree programs in the key sciences since 1981. A few other graduate programs (e.g., in education) are offered at certain schools.

take his training, both graduate and undergraduate, at institutions that are thoroughly true to the Word. It is dangerous and presumptuous for one deliberately to subject himself to indoctrination by a humanistic or compromising teacher when he could get the equivalent training elsewhere from the true Biblical perspective.

(3) *Biblical Maturity.* In fact, real in-depth study in the Bible is the most essential part of the educational preparation of any Christian teacher, for he cannot conform his courses to the doctrines of Scripture unless he knows the doctrines of Scripture.

> "For when for the time ye ought to be teachers, ye have need that one teach you again which be the first principles of the oracles of God; and are become such as have need of milk, and not of strong meat. For every one that useth milk is unskilful in the word of righteousness: for he is a babe. But strong meat belongeth to them that are of full age, even those who by reason of use have their senses exercised to discern both good and evil" (Hebrews 5:12-14).

Among other things, this passage points out that those who "ought to be teachers" will be unable to "discern the evil" in the literature and philosophy of the subject they would teach unless they are mature enough in the Word of God to be feeding on its "strong meat," and not merely its "first principles."

The tremendous passage on the Scriptures written by Paul to the young pastor and teacher Timothy is most appropriate here.

> "All scripture is given by inspiration of God, and is profitable for doctrine, for reproof, for correction, for instruction in righteousness: That the man of God may be perfect, throughly furnished unto all good works. . . . Preach the word; be instant in season, out of season; reprove, rebuke, exhort with all longsuffering and doctrine—For the time will come when they

will not endure sound doctrine; but after their
own lusts shall they heap to themselves
teachers, having itching ears, And they shall
turn away their ears from the truth, and shall be
turned unto fables. But watch thou in all things,
endure afflictions, do the work of an evangelist,
make full proof of thy ministry" (II Timothy
3:16-17; 4:2-5).

This passage stresses, among other things, that the
teacher must constantly be on guard against the entrance of false doctrine into his teaching. Students often
have "itching ears," flocking to those teachers who will
amuse them and excuse them in their ungodly tenden-
cies, but he must constantly use the Word of God to
rebuke and exhort them, even doing the work of an
evangelist, leading them to Christ and the truth. To be
perfectly effective in this good work, making full proof
of his ministry, he must be a student of "*all* Scripture,"
which is both completely inspired and comprehensively
profitable.

We are accustomed to limiting such Scriptures as
these to those who are full-time pastors or Bible
teachers, and so teachers of other subjects often fail to
realize the tremendous responsibility that is theirs. We
merely repeat what has been shown before. All truth is
God's truth and should be taught by God-called teachers
in God's way. Every subject should be structured in a
Scriptural framework and guided and controlled by Bible doctrine. These Biblical instructions *do* apply to
every teacher!

(4) *Experience and Wisdom.* In addition to
thorough training, both in general education (especially
the Bible) and in a professional specialty, the teacher
should be a man or woman of true wisdom, which can be
gained only through experience. The experience may
be either in actual teaching, as an apprentice to an experienced teacher, or in the practice of his or her
profession. It should also include some years of experience as a practicing Christian.

The practice has become all too common at the college level of appointing young people to faculty positions fresh from completing their education, but without any practical experience. There may be occasions when this is justified, but it should be the exception and not the rule, especially for teachers of the upper-level professional courses. How can a man teach pastoral counselling, for example, if he has had no experience as a pastor, or geophysical exploration methods if he has never had experience as a working geophysicist?

> "For if a man think himself to be something, when he is nothing, he deceiveth himself. But let every man prove [or 'test'] his own work, and then shall he have rejoicing in himself alone, and not in another" (Galatians 6:3-4).

The warning in I Timothy 3:6 that a bishop (and this word simply means "one who oversees," thus clearly including anyone in a position of authority in either church or classroom) should be "not a novice" is very much in point here.

The teaching ministry of women teachers should be primarily one to other women or to children or young people, not to men (I Timothy 2:12), except under such unusual circumstances as required Priscilla (Acts 18:26) or other Bible women to assume such authority on a temporary basis. This reservation is not because of any imagined "lack of ability," but solely because of Biblical precept and example.

The combination of good training and relevant experience will, hopefully, produce the quality of true wisdom which is so important in a Christian teacher. As we have already shown at some length, this wisdom is not the foolish "wisdom of this world" (I Corinthians 3:19) or the "love of wisdom" for its own sake that comprises the philosophy of the world (Colossians 2:8), but is rather the true "wisdom of God" (I Corinthians 2:7) centered in the world's Creator, the Lord Jesus Christ.

The contrast in the practical outworking of these opposing concepts of wisdom is strikingly pictured by James:

"Who is a wise man and endued with knowledge among you? let him show out of a good conversation his works with meekness of wisdom. But if ye have bitter envying and strife in your hearts, glory not, and lie not against the truth. This wisdom descendeth not from above, but is earthly, sensual, devilish. For where envying and strife is, there is confusion and every evil work. But the wisdom that is from above is first pure, then peaceable, gentle, and easy to be intreated, full of mercy and good fruits, without partiality, and without hypocrisy" (James 3:13-17).

The above description of worldly wisdom is an incisive and realistic commentary on the typical faculty of a secular university (as the writer can unreservedly testify after 28 years' experience on such faculties!). On the other hand, the faculty of a truly Christian school should be characterized by "the wisdom that is from above."

Chapter 6

The Implementation of Christian Education

The two most important components in the implementation of true Christian education are the curriculum and the faculty. If these are good, then the education will probably be good, regardless of what teaching methods are used. Nevertheless, the teaching methods *are* important and it is reasonable to expect that, if the Scriptures are so clear on the questions of curriculum content and teacher qualifications, they would provide guidance on the matter of methodology as well.

There is no Biblical passage, however, which says in so many words just what teaching method should be employed, so the question is evidently left open. It is evidently appropriate to adapt various methods to the changing circumstances of time and place, so long as optimum transmission of knowledge from teacher to students is accomplished.

TEACHING AND INDOCTRINATION

Nevertheless, although the Bible does not specify a particular method, certain principles are indicated which should help in ascertaining the best teaching methods. For example, it must be remembered that teaching is essentially *indoctrination* in fixed truth, not *discovery* of new truth. The two words "teaching" and "doctrine," in the Bible, are actually the same Greek word, *didaskalia*. Thus the teaching method should be designed for the purpose of most complete and effective transmission of knowledge from teacher to students. The principle is implied in the 78th Psalm, though in a slightly different context.

"We will not hide them from their children, shewing to the generation to come the praises of the Lord, and His strength, and His wonderful works that He hath done. For He established a testimony in Jacob, and appointed a law in Israel, which He commanded our fathers, that they make them known to their children: That the generation to come might know them, even the children which should be born; who should arise and declare them to their children: That they might set their hope in God, and not forget the works of God, but keep His commandments" (Psalm 78:4-7).

Although there is certainly a place under the cultural mandate for research and discovery of new truth, the function of *teaching* is indoctrination in truth already known. Truth, once known, should be transmitted to every succeeding generation. With respect to the most important truths, however—those concerning God's works of creation, redemption, and judgment—it does seem that scholars are "ever learning, yet never able to come to the knowledge of the truth" (II Timothy 3:7). The reason, of course, is because such men "resist the truth" and "turn away their ears from the truth" (II

Timothy 3:8; 4:4). This prejudice of educational leaders in the natural realm is, of course, not to be emulated in Christian schools. The ministry of teaching is the ministry of transmitting truth—above all, these great revelational truths.

SCRIPTURAL GUIDANCE ON TEACHING METHODS

Since the basic purpose of teaching is indoctrination, methods should be selected which best accomplish this. The transmission, acquisition, and retention of knowledge normally implies training, drilling, memorizing, testing, etc. The most important principle, however is to recognize the authority of the teacher. The teacher is not merely a counsellor or a guide. Biblically, the teacher is the *"master"* or the *"doctor,"* as we have already pointed out. If really qualified to be a teacher, he or she is a person of thorough training, relevant experience and spiritual wisdom. Students should be required to be attentive, respectful, and obedient. Not only is this the Biblical norm; it has also been practiced in the educational systems of almost every nation in history until modern times.

The progressive education theories of Dewey and his disciples, as well as the so-called "discovery" method and the "open classroom" concept of more recent vintage, for all practical purposes have abandoned this time-proved principle. Students, in these systems, are no longer being taught by an authoritative teacher. In effect, they have become their own teachers, with only low-key and indirect guidance by the instructor and programmed-learning textbooks.

As noted before, research and discovery are legitimate functions under the cultural mandate but they are not usually appropriate as a classroom enterprise. The exception to this evaluation would be when the topic to be learned in the classroom is itself the nature and practice of research and discovery. That is, the student should be taught methods and techniques of research and given practice in applying those techniques, thus helping to develop his inventive and analytical abilities. This is only one topic out of many to be covered, however, and it should not become the very framework of instruction, as it often has in so-called "progressive" schools.

Furthermore, research and discovery projects should only be undertaken when three conditions are satisfied: (1) the student has already been provided with a solid factual foundation upon which he can safely build analyses for his new data; (2) he understands well that all new data and interpretations must be developed within the constraints of Scripture; (3) such projects are to be reviewed and their results either accepted or rejected, as appropriate, by the teacher, who must always be respected as the one in responsible charge of the learning activities in the classroom.

With these general criteria in mind, there are four main types of teaching methods which must be considered. Each may have value under certain circumstances, and our purpose here is to evaluate them insofar as possible on the basis of Biblical precepts and examples. Of special importance is the example set by the Lord Jesus Christ, acknowledged by both Christians and non-Christians to be the greatest Teacher who ever lived. These four types of methods are each discussed briefly below.

(1) *Lecture Method.* The basic method of instruction followed by the Lord Jesus in His human ministry of teaching was what is commonly known as the "lecture method." This is the method in which the teacher simply expounds verbally to his class the subject being studied. An excellent example in Christ's ministry is His so-called "Sermon on the Mount." The emphasis in the actual record is on His teaching, not preaching! The passage begins as follows:

"And seeing the multitudes, He went up into a mountain: and when He was set, His disciples came unto Him: And He opened His mouth and taught them, saying, . . . (Matthew 5:1,2).

Note that this was not a sermon to the multitudes, but rather instruction to His disciples (the Greek word for which means literally "the taught ones"). After beginning the lecture, it continues for three chapters (Matthew 5,6,7) without a break so far as the record goes. At its conclusion, the following significant comment is made:

"And it came to pass, when Jesus had ended these sayings, the people were astonished at His doctrine [or, literally, 'His teachings']: For He taught them as one having authority, and not as the scribes" (Matthew 7:28,29).

Note the contrast between His teaching and that of the scribes of His day. He was the teacher; He knew what He was talking about; He was the authority; therefore He taught (lectured) those things to His disciples, and they learned them from Him. The scribes, on the other hand, taught by citing opinions and interpretations from earlier teachers, often undermining the actual teachings of the Scriptures through their traditions (Matthew 15:3).

The lecture on the Mount is only one example out of many that could be cited[1] in the teaching ministry of Christ. The Apostles followed His example later in their own teaching, practically always using the lecture or sermonic method of teaching.[2]

Closer study of these examples of the teaching ministry of Christ and the Apostles indicates that they did often allow their listeners to ask questions during a lecture (for example, Luke 12:41) or at the end of the lecture (Matthew 13:36). The modern-day teacher who

---

[1]Matthew 4:23; 10:5-42; 13:1-52; 23:1-39; 24:4, 25:46; Luke 12; 15:3-32; John 13:31, 17:26; etc.

[2]Acts 2:14-40; 13:15-41; etc.

desires to follow as closely as possible the example of the greatest Teacher would, therefore, use the lecture method, with opportunity allowed for questions from the class. Occasionally, though rarely, Christ began a lecture on a certain point by first asking His disciples a leading question (Matthew 16:15).

Sometimes, modern educators suggest that Christ used a dialogue approach, but the examples commonly cited (e.g., the case of Nicodemus in John 3 and the woman at the well in John 4) were *witnessing* situations, not formal teaching sessions. These were cases of one-on-one conversations, with the purpose of winning these people to faith in Christ, and are thus important examples for guidance of the Christian in witnessing and soul-winning. But they are altogether different from formal instruction sessions of groups of learners. Similarly, there are a number of sessions of verbal interchanges between Christ and an audience in which the tone was one of argumentation (e.g., John 8:20-59) but again these are not examples of teaching as such, but rather of witnessing or evangelizing.

So far as the record goes, in every recorded instance of formal group teaching by Christ or the Apostles the lecture method (sometimes supplemented by questions from the hearers) was used. While this fact does not in itself constitute a commandment for present-day teachers to use the lecture method, it does constitute an example to be taken seriously. If there is some better method, it is strange that Christ did not use it!

Use of the lecture method by a teacher today of course presupposes that the teacher is well prepared. As the authority in the classroom, he should have correct information to impart and be able to do it effectively. It is certainly appropriate for him to use visual aids in his lecture (as Christ did when He referred to the lilies of the field in Matthew 6:28,29, for example). The best visual aid is probably a chalkboard or its equivalent, on which the teacher can make helpful sketches and write down important concepts. Aids requiring a darkened room (movies and slides) are occasionally helpful, but make it difficult for students to take notes. Lecture notes for study and review are vital if the student is really to learn and retain what he sees or hears in class, and the teacher should do everything possible to encourage and assist such retention.

In order to optimize the understanding and retention of the subject matter, class lectures normally must be supplemented by correlative reading and homework assignments, the rule-of-thumb (for college students at least) being that such outside work should take from 1.5 to 2.0 hours, including time spent in laboratories, for each hour of class lecture time. This rule corresponds approximately to a 40-hour work week spent by the student on his courses, and should apply to the normal student. Slower students should expect to spend more time in outside study. Proportionately smaller amounts of outside studies should be expected from pre-college level students.

The lecture method may also be modified to include class recitation sessions and skills sessions, depending on the age level and subject matter. Individual consultation should also be provided by the instructor to those students in need of it.

Finally, it is assumed that the lecture method will be accompanied by adequate testing and fair grading on the part of the instructor, but this condition would also apply to any other teaching method too, at least in classes where credits or grades are awarded.

It is obvious that the relative amount of lecture time to question-and-answer time to recitation-and-drill time will vary with the age level and course subject. An elementary school penmanship class may be largely devoted to writing practice supervised by the teacher, whereas a college economics class should consist mostly of a lecture by a gifted economics teacher supplemented by questions from the class. In any case, the key facet in the lecture method is the authority and knowledge of the teacher, with the format of the class session designed for maximum conveyance of his knowledge and skill to the students.

(2) *Class Participation Method.* By this term is meant a teaching format in which the students are encouraged to teach themselves, with only minimal guidance or restraint by the teacher. The class may be a "rap session" in which students and teacher "share" their ideas and suggestions about solutions to various problems or interpretations of various writings. The "discovery" approach may be used, whereby students are given access to library resource materials to work out their own individual or group answers to open-ended questions. In the "progressive education" concepts of Dewey, *et al,* the students are subjected to little or no discipline or learning requirements, each one being allowed to "express himself" in whatever ways he might choose and to learn as much or as little about the course subject matter as he wishes. Such an approach was considered by progressive educationalists to be democratic, good preparation for living in a socialist democracy and welfare state. Students are "passed" regardless of whether or not they have attained any objective standard of performance in the course.

To some extent, these methods have been rejected in recent years even by secular educators, because of their obvious failure to produce graduates with even minimal skills in the three-R's and other basic knowledge. The so-called "open classroom" and "discovery method," however, are still very widely used. The use of teaching machines and programmed-learning textbooks has proliferated widely, with the students largely teaching themselves, each proceeding at his own pace.

It would be presumptuous to say that such methods are always wrong. For highly-motivated students, these experiences may be quite rewarding, particularly if they are carefully planned and controlled by the teacher. They may help in developing skills in research and development, but only if an adequate foundation of indoctrination in basic truths has been laid previously.

Many students, however, are neither highly motivated nor properly prepared. For them, such an approach is a poor use of time at best and often frustrating and discouraging. Rap sessions may appeal to outgoing students who like to talk and vent their opinions, but sensitive students find them embarrassing or even offensive, and serious students desiring to learn find them a futile waste of valuable time. Courses involving transmission of real factual data (e.g., mathematics, history, drafting, etc.) obviously are incapable of effective teaching through group brainstorming sessions. Courses in literature or sociology may be more amenable to such an approach since the proportion of human opinion to factual data is high in such courses, in secular schools. In Christian schools, however, even such courses as these should be developed within the framework of factual data and inspired principles derived from Scripture, and these are *not* matters of opinion or discovery.

Even more questionable is the recent practice of teaching the Bible in this way. Many Sunday School classes, as well as home Bible study classes, and even occasional church services, nowadays are being conducted with a very loose "discover and share" type of format.

Sometimes this approach is presented as the Biblical method, on the basis of the pattern described in the Corinthian church.

> "How is it then, brethren? when ye come together, everyone of you hath a psalm, hath a doctrine, hath a tongue, hath a revelation, hath an interpretation. Let all things be done unto edifying. If any man speak in an unknown tongue, let it be by two, or at the most by three,

and that by course, and let one interpret. But if
there be no interpreter, let him keep silence in
the church; and let him speak to himself, and to
God. Let the prophets speak two or three, and
let the other judge. If any thing be revealed to
another that sitteth by, let the first hold his
peace. For ye may all prophesy one by one, that
all may learn, and all may be comforted. And
the spirits of the prophets are subject to the
prophets. For God is not the author of confusion,
but of peace, as in all churches of the saints. Let
your women keep silence in the churches: for it
is not permitted unto them to speak; but they
are commanded to be under obedience, as also
saith the law. And if they will learn anything, let
them ask their husbands at home: for it is a
shame for women to speak in the church"
(I Corinthians 14:26-35).

This extended quotation has been given in order for
the reader to see the whole context. This type of church
service was obviously quite different from the informal
Bible "studies" as often practiced today, although to
some extent these are patterned after it. The New
Testament was not yet available to these Corinthian
believers and, in the absence of an Apostle or
authoritative teacher such as Paul, the Lord provided
the necessary guidance for a particular local church by
direct supernatural means. Thus, in their worship services, some received a prophecy, some a revelation,
some a message in a tongue, accompanied by someone
who would give its translation and meaning. Apparently
some were also inspired to recite a psalm or a teaching
of the Old Testament Scriptures when these were
applicable to their needs.

Even though such group study and worship was led
by the Holy Spirit, speaking through one believer
after another, it was easily subject to abuse.

People could "feel" led to speak, either by their own desire to be heard or even by evil spirits, who were not really being led by the Holy Spirit. Hence, Paul had to place the various restrictions which he outlined in this epistle.

In any case, the condition which justified this type of session in the early church is no longer applicable today. We *do* have the complete New Testament, as well as the Old Testament, for the guidance of every church, so we do not need special localized revelations anymore. Churches do need, of course, true teachers (possessing qualifications outlined previously) to teach and apply the Scriptures, but the Lord will provide such for each true church that will heed them.

Many modern-day Bible classes and worship services are conducted with this format. In such classes, a certain Bible passage or theme is agreed on for discussion and then each person is encouraged to "share" with the class what it means to him or her.

Such meetings may have real value as testimony meetings or times of Christian fellowship, but they have little value as far as learning the Bible is concerned. A Bible passage does not "mean" one thing to one person and have another meaning for someone else. What it *means* is what the writer (and the Holy Spirit who inspired him) intended it to mean, and this is to be determined by sound Biblical exegesis only, not by vague feelings or subjective opinions. Thus if such sessions are intended for learning the Bible, they are essentially a waste of time. People who have not *studied* the Bible cannot teach the Bible. Such "sharing sessions" become merely sessions of "shared opinion."

Imagine trying to learn calculus by having the class members share what this equation and that axiom and such-and-such a function means to them! The Bible is far more accurate and Biblical exegesis a much more demanding discipline than mathematics. If a properly-prepared and gifted teacher is necessary for the

teaching of calculus, such a teacher is far more
necessary for the effective teaching of the Bible.

(3) *Directed Study Method*. Many courses today
are taken by correspondence or by programmed-
learning procedures. In college, a course may occasionally be taken by a single student, with special
assignments and regular consultation with the instructor taking the place of formal classroom lectures. This
expedient is used either when the student cannot
schedule the class at its regular time, when there are
not enough students to justify setting up a regular section, or when the instructor desires to try out a new
course in this way prior to offering it on a regular basis.

Depending on the student, the course content, and the
advisor, this may or may not work satisfactorily. To be
effective, it must be closely guided and supervised, and
the student must have a good background in prerequi-
site courses and be essentially self-motivating. When
these criteria are met, the directed-study method is not
too much different from the standard lecture method,
except that the writer of the course textbook replaces
the lecturer.

There obviously are situations when this approach
may be meritorious, particularly in enabling a student
to complete his education more rapidly than he could
otherwise. It obviously should be limited to good
students, who will neither take advantage of it, nor be
discouraged and frustrated by it.

As far as that is concerned, many people have simply
taught themselves various subjects without receiving
any kind of formal institutional credit for it. Foreign
languages, music, history, and many other fields have a
wealth of self-help books and study guides available for
this purpose.

The Bible, especially, can and should be studied in
this way by every Christian, whether or not he also has
opportunity for formal Bible training at a college or
seminary. There are many aids to Bible study available
(correspondence courses, commentaries, reference

Bibles, concordances, lexicons, etc.), and a diligent student can learn almost as much this way as he could in regular credit classes.

Two cautions are in order, however. A Bible student (or a student in any field) may acquire much misinformation and incorrect understanding in this way, unless he is very judicious in his choice of study aids. He would do well to keep in close touch with his pastor or other mature and trusted teacher, to be sure he is not going off on a tangent or into a dead end. He needs to guard against the temptation of assuming that a little self-study of this sort is all he needs to become an authority in his field, a temptation to which superficial Bible students seem especially prone.

Secondly, at the very best, a course or subject learned by either directed-study or self-study will miss the inspiration and insights that can be imparted by gifted lecturer-teachers. The student who takes a course in this way should try to find opportunity to attend seminars, conferences, or lectures in the field represented by the course, to obtain this added dimension in some measure.

(4) *Research or Practicum Methods.* By this term is meant the accomplishment of individualized research or practice in a particular field, under the direction of a qualified practitioner. This approach might include such widely-diverse activities as a research paper assigned in a regular lecture course, a semester of practice teaching for a senior college student majoring in education, a medical intern in a hospital, or a doctoral dissertation. In any case, the student is largely on his own, as far as the conduct of his research or practice is concerned, with only very general guidance from his teacher or supervisor but with the prospect of a rigid evaluation at its conclusion.

There is no question that this can be a highly valuable teaching method, provided: (1) the student is properly prepared with adequate indoctrination of factual knowledge and skills on which to build his research or practice; (2) he is adequately directed and evaluated by his advisor; (3) both student and advisor are continually conscious of channeling the research or practice within the framework and constraints of Scripture.

A good example of this method is found in Christ's training of His disciples. After thorough preparation, both through His own lectures and by His own example, He sent them out on their own.

"These twelve Jesus sent forth, and commanded them, saying, Go not into the way of the Gentiles, and into any city of the Samaritans enter ye not:[1] But go rather to the lost sheep of the house of Israel" (Matthew 10:5,6).

The ability and command to discover new truth or applications of old truth and to utilize truth which is known for the benefit of mankind and the glory of God, is of course implied in the Adamic mandate and Noahic covenant. There is, no doubt, much truth yet to be discovered, both in the Scripture and in the world. A legitimate and valuable component of true education, therefore, is the development of this ability in the young. Whereas this teaching method would be calamitous if it were employed exclusively (in effect requiring each student to rediscover all previous truth for himself—thus reducing him essentially to the level of the animals, who are unable to pass learned information to their offspring), it is very valuable as a supplement to the lecture method.

THE PROBLEM OF TEXTBOOKS

One of the most serious obstacles to developing a fully Biblical system of education is the dearth of Christian textbooks. Evolutionism and secular humanism is either explicit or implicit in practically every textbook available today, in many fields. How can a truly Christian course in literature or psychology, for example, be

---

[1]They were apparently not yet ready for these more demanding assignments.

developed when the textbook carries selections promoting atheism and immorality or advocates Freudianism and determinism? Similar textbook problems are encountered in many other courses.

In courses strictly involving factual data or mechanical skills (calculus, engineering, clothing construction, aircraft maintenance, etc.) there are few, if any, problems of this sort. The same criteria apply to selection of textbooks as we have discussed previously for curriculum and course content. Thus, textbooks on chemistry, physics, and geography, for example, may be reasonably acceptable. Textbooks in psychology, social studies, and modern literature, however, almost always contain emphases unacceptable to a Christian. There is a wide spectrum of evolutionary and humanistic indoctrination in the various books and each needs to be carefully examined with this in mind.

It is encouraging that a few publishers are concerned about this problem and are trying gradually to fill the gap.[1] It is a very slow and difficult process, however.

In the meantime, what should a teacher or school do if there is no suitable textbook available? An obvious answer is not to specify any textbook at all, but to teach the course from assigned topical readings from acceptable sources and from handout sheets prepared by the teacher. This is not as unreasonable or difficult a task as might appear at first. The writer has himself taught no less than a dozen different subjects in just this way, in each case using his handout sheets (written originally on a day-to-day basis in preparation for the next lecture) as the eventual basis for seven different textbooks—textbooks which are now used in many other schools as well. It is probable that most other textbooks in use today have been developed in the same way.

Surely this kind of dedication and effort is not too much to ask of God-called Christian teachers. If enough of them would take this need seriously, the great lack of

[1]Hefley, James C., *Textbooks on Trial* (Wheaton, Illinois, Victor Books, 1976) pp. 198, 212.

Christian and Biblically-sound textbooks could be
remedied in a very few years.

Many Christian teachers, however, will defend the
use of objectionable textbooks on the ground that their
students should read the material firsthand. The
teacher then can give the alternate and correct view in
class, explaining directly what is wrong with the textbook.

The problem with this procedure, however, is that
students forget very quickly most of what they hear in
class, whereas their textbooks are always available for
quick reference any time in the future. In addition, most
people believe what they read in a publication much more
readily than anything they hear from a teacher. Furthermore, parents and friends of the students, not having
heard the counter-explanations of the teacher, will tend
to judge the school by the textbook it specified. The
disadvantages of using such books clearly overbalance
any nebulous advantages.

If there is no alternative to using such a textbook (and
this is doubtful), the instructor should at least prepare
printed or mimeographed hand-outs critically analyzing
and correcting the objectionable sections in the textbook,
so that these sheets can be inserted at the appropriate
places in the books. In the writer's judgment, however, it
is better for all concerned (except, perhaps, for the instructor of whom the extra work is required) to use no
textbook at all until a suitable one can be compiled. If
enough Christian teachers would make this decision, it
would not be very many years before good textbooks
would become available.

SIZE OF CLASSES

One of the most common questions among educators
is that of optimum class size. Classes of various kinds
and circumstances have ranged all the way from one
person (the writer remembers teaching one of his first
lecture classes, forty years ago, to a single engineering

student) up to a thousand or more in large freshmen university classes or church auditorium Sunday School classes. Televised classes may reach tremendous numbers.

In general, however, teachers for a hundred generations have argued that a class size of about 25 was best. Larger classes become too large for individual counselling and adequate grading by the teacher; smaller classes may be uneconomical in relation to costs.

These limitations can be overcome, however, under some conditions. Teachers of large classes can be provided with assistants if necessary. Small classes can be offered if students are willing to pay larger tuition or if financing can be arranged in some other way. There are many types of classes, of course, where the teacher is a volunteer worker and receives no compensation. Consequently there are no firm restrictions on class size in either direction. The question is—are there any Biblical guidelines on this practical and important matter of class size?

Obviously there is no Scripture that answers this question directly. There are certain general principles, however, that are worth applying here.

The most important factor in effective teaching, of course, is the teacher, and the basic method of teaching is the lecture method, as already shown from the New Testament examples. If a teacher is qualified, meeting the Biblical and other qualifications outlined previously, there is every reason to allow his class to become as large as the demand warrants and facilities allow, especially for adult or college classes. If the class does become much larger than the traditional 25 to 30 students, then the need for individual student counseling and evaluation can be met through the provision of assistants or apprentice teachers to work with smaller groups within the class.

Large classes are typical of college freshman and sophomore courses, the "general education" courses that are taken by students from many different majors. For these classes it is essential that the best teachers be provided. The foundation of a student's education is vitally important if an effective superstructure of higher education and life career is to be erected. The individual abilities and interests of different teachers must be taken into account when making teaching assignments, of course, but teachers of the larger freshman and sophomore classes should, if possible, be the most knowledgeable in their fields, the most capable lecturers, and those with the most sincere concern for their student's spiritual growth.

If possible, of course, similarly well-qualified teachers should be assigned to the smaller upper-level classes as well, but this is not as critical as for the larger lower-level classes. Not only do the latter affect a larger number, but they also tend to make a more lasting impression, younger minds being more impressionable, so that it is vital for this influence to be a right influence.

It is noteworthy that the greatest Teacher taught classes of various sizes. When He taught beginners, it was commonly a large multitude (e.g., Luke 6:17), though He also taught individuals (John 3:1,2) when occasion permitted. He also had a more "advanced class" of seventy (Luke 10:1-24) whom He had taught in depth before sending them out on a field assignment. The "senior class," which He taught intensively for three years, however, had only twelve students. It appears that these are not unlike what today would be a large freshman class, an intermediate-sized upper-level class and a small graduate class.

A different type of situation is found in the typical Sunday School. Here the teachers are mostly unpaid so that cost is a minor factor and classes can be small, at least if the church has an educational building with many classrooms. In this case, the tendency has been opposite to that in the university. Instead of more large classes, the Sunday School tends in many churches to proliferate into many small classes, each with a relatively inexperienced and inadequately-trained teacher. This arrangement tends to be counter-productive as far as real teaching of the Bible is concerned, especially for adults at college age or above.

It should be remembered that the purpose of Bible classes is to teach the Bible, not social fellowship or rap sessions about life situations. For this purpose a truly God-called and qualified teacher is essential—not someone who merely wants to be heard or someone who consents to teach just because the pastor or superintendent urged him to do so.

In other words, the class size depends on the number of qualified teachers. It is better to have one class of a thousand studying under a good teacher than a hundred classes of ten students each if their teachers are not God-called, Spirit-filled, and knowledgeable in the real meat of the Word.

Fellowship with others in one's peer group and age group is important, and so is study concerning social problems and personal counselling. Provision may be made in the church for such things, but these should not usurp the place of serious Bible study for *all* its communicants. God has given His teachers to the church for this purpose (Ephesians 4:11), and they must be allowed to teach the Word in such a way that quality Bible teaching reaches all its members, if the church is to prosper spiritually.

Chapter 7

Christian Rules for Christian Schools

A vitally important component of Christian education, is character training. It has already been noted that real educaton teaches the student—as well as the subject. A Christian needs to *do* the truth as well as *know* the truth.

In today's amoral "anything-goes" society, it has become very difficult to maintain high standards of conduct and discipline in any school, even in a Christian school. Many public schools, especially those in large cities, are little more than "blackboard jungles," where teachers have to be almost as concerned with physical survival as with teaching. The stultifying mental and moral effects of television on younger children, as well as the effects of drugs, alcohol, and movies (saturated with violence and sex) on teenagers, have all but devastated real learning in many such schools. Permissive parents, broken homes, administrative restraints against punishment of unruly students, emphasis on "relevance" instead of content in curriculum, advancement of unqualified students to higher grades, teacher strikes, grade "inflation" to enhance teacher popularity and college admission of graduates, and many other such factors have all played a part in the dessication of public education. At the college level, the student riots of the Sixties and the utter amoralism of the Seventies have become a national cancer.

The two factors of humanistic curriculum and destructive moral environment have persuaded multitudes of Christian parents in recent years to send their children and young people to Christian schools and colleges. The amazing growth of the private Christian school has been one of the phenomenal movements of modern times, with estimates running as high as three new Christian schools being started every day! In no sense are these schools mere "segregation academies," as their enemies allege; practically all of them are completely nondiscriminatory as far as race is concerned, and they are convinced that nondiscrimination is the clear teaching of Scripture. Curriculum and conduct—*these* are the reasons for widespread loss of confidence in public schools and establishment of Christian schools. Furthermore, these are such serious problems that great numbers of even non-Christian families are now patronizing Christian schools (though whether this is advisable as far as the Christian schools themselves are concerned is debatable).

Mere transfer to a Christian school, however, is not necessarily the solution to all problems. As emphasized throughout this book, Christian schools also are beset with many problems, and few of them have been able to achieve a fully Biblical, truly Christian, system of education. Compromises with secular educational systems (via textbooks, teacher training, accreditation, financial support, etc.) have been many and serious.

The question of student conduct, discipline, and punishment is also a very real problem in Christian schools, though not nearly as severe as in public schools. Many students are unsaved, many come from non-Christian homes, and many more are still babes in Christ, easily swayed by the many non-Christian pressures to which they are constantly subjected in today's world. It is vital, therefore, that a thorough set of Biblical standards of conduct be developed and enforced if the Christian school is to achieve its goals.

BIBLICAL CONSIDERATIONS IN FORMULATING STANDARDS OF CONDUCT

Any school or college which seeks to base all its courses and curricula on the principles of Scripture should, by the same token, try also to base the standards of behavior for its faculty and students on the principles of Scripture. It is not right merely to follow tradition or to copy other schools or to adjust to the prevailing culture. We want to "do the truth" (I John 1:6), as well as teach the truth, and the principles of truth in all things are to be found only in the inspired Scriptures (II Timothy 3:16, 17; John 17:17).

Any kind of organized, functioning group in society must operate within some system of rules if it is to function in an orderly manner. "Order" presupposes "law." A society which attempts to operate with unrestrained freedom become chaotic; liberty becomes license, and soon anarchy and violence prevail. This actually happened in the antediluvian world. Man had been created in God's image, in complete fellowship with God and, therefore, with other men, so there was at first no need for any restraining rules or laws. When sin came in, however, it was not long before "the earth was filled with violence" (Genesis 6:13) and had to be cleansed with a global washing in the Deluge.

There are now three basic institutions among men which God has established for the maintenance of order and the accomplishment of His purposes in the world.

These are, in chronological order: (1) the family (Genesis 1:26-28; 2:18-23); (2) the nation (Genesis 9:1-6; 10:32; Acts 17:24-27); and (3) the church (Matthew 16:18; 18:15-17; I Corinthians 6:1-4).

It is very significant that the school, as such, is not a separate divinely-established institution. It is also significant that there is nothing in Scripture to indicate that schools are to be organized and operated by the nation and its governing structure. On the contrary, the Bible everywhere teaches that the function of education belongs primarily to the family, especially the father (Genesis 18:19; Ephesians 6:4), and secondarily to the church (Matthew 28:18-20; I Timothy 3:15; Ephesians 4:11-15).

Unfortunately, Christian families and churches have, largely by default, let governments take over the work of education. The Christian school movement is a belated, but still necessary, effort by Christian parents and their churches to fulfill their responsibilities in the education of their families.

The true school, therefore, is not an arm of the government. Neither is it an autonomous creation of some individual or group. Its purpose is not the same as that of government (which should be primarily the maintenance of order in the nation and defense against other nations, protecting the life, liberty, and property of its citizens). The purpose of any school should be to implement the teaching goals of the families and churches which sponsor or support it.

Consequently, the rules of order and behavior established by a school are not the same as the laws of the nation, although they must not conflict with such laws (note I Peter 2:13-17) unless they in turn contradict God's laws (note Acts 5:29). Rather, school standards must partake essentially of the rules established in the home and church for the accomplishment of *their* purposes.

The tabulation on the next page summarizes the Biblical principles which delineate the rule structure for each of these four basic institutions.

Institution	People Subject To Its Rules	Purpose of Its Rules	Penalties for Breaking Its Rules
State	All Citizens	Protection of Life, Liberty & Property (Gen. 9:6; I Pet. 2:13-15; Mt. 22:21; I Tim. 2:1,2)	1. Taking property (e.g., fines) 2. Taking liberty (e.g., prison) 3. Taking life (e.g., capital punishment) (Rom. 13:1-7; I Peter 4:15)
Church (Local)	Members of Church	Protection of Testimony & Accomplishment of Purpose of Church (I Pet. 2:11, 12; Phil. 2:15; I Tim. 6:1; I Thess. 4:1-12)	1. Public Rebuke (I Tim. 5:20) 2. Expulsion from Membership (Mt. 18:15-17; Titus 3:10; I Cor. 5:1,2, 11-13; 6:9-11)
Home	Members of Family	Training in all aspects of life & godliness (Gen. 18:19; Eph. 6:4; I Tim. 5:8; I Thess. 2:11, 12; Heb. 12:11)	Chastening (Heb. 12:7) a. Withholding rewards & privileges b. Verbal rebuke c. Corporal punishment (Prov. 22:15; 23:13, 14)
School	Members of Student Body	Extension & Combination or Purposes of Rules in Home & Church. School is (a) *en loco parentis* (b) *en loco ecclesiae*	Judicious Combination of Equivalent Penalties in Home & Church (not as in state). a. chastening for minor infractions b. expulsion for major infractions

One reason why a school must have rules is so that its overall ministry and that of its supporting churches will be protected from destruction or compromise by the actions of its students, in the same way that churches must have similar rules protecting them from the consequences of flagrant sins by their members. The penalty of expulsion must be involved in such cases as blatant immorality, heresy, etc., as noted in the Scriptures cited in the tabulation (I Corinthians 5:11-13, etc.). Of course, neither the church nor the school can justifiably invoke the type of penalties for law-breaking used by the state (e.g., fines, imprisonment, capital punishment).

Another reason for school rules is so that the school can perform its proper function of training the student *en loco parentis* ("in the place of the parents"). The parents entrust their children to the school and its faculty in order for them to be properly prepared for a fruitful Christian life and ministry. They are away at school almost as much as they are at home, even in elementary school. In college, they may be away from home for months at a time. A true Christian school, therefore, must establish and enforce the same kinds of rules for its students that godly and concerned Christian parents would expect them to follow at home, and that their churches would maintain in their church lives.

Since individual homes and their practices may vary considerably, even among Christian homes (the same is true of churches, of course), and since the school must obviously establish the same standards for *all* its students, the school administration must decide on a body of regulations which will represent, insofar as possible, the optimum standards of all its constituents and which will, at the same time, safeguard its own ministry. Most importantly of all, however, these standards should conform as completely as we can make them do so to *Biblical* standards.

In the first place, there are many specific rules or divine laws set forth directly in the Bible (e.g., the Ten Commandments). When the Bible speaks plainly and unequivocally on a certain matter, then that should settle any question, as far as the individual or the school is concerned.

Secondly, there are many broad principles in the Bible which can be applied in making decisions concerning a wide range of human activities not specifically mentioned in the Bible. These principles enable us to ascertain whether certain behaviors are morally and ethically appropriate for a Christian school student or staff member.

Finally, there are many school activities which may have no moral connotation at all (e.g., registration procedures), but which must be subject to administrative regulation. Even these, however, can be established in a context of Biblical order and equity.

The following sections set forth a set of possible school rules developed from the implications of, first, the Ten Commandments and then, second, from certain key New Testament principles which might be called Ten Commitments. These were originally developed several years ago for use in the student manual at Christian Heritage College and have served effectively in this capacity since. This particular formulation is only one of many possible formats in which such rules could be developed and is not intended as anything more than an example of how it might be done. The important point is that, whatever framework is used, the school's code of conduct should be based, insofar as possible, on Biblical principles, rather than arbitrary human judgment.

BIBLICAL MORAL CHARACTER: GOD'S ETERNAL LAW

Basic and foundational to orderly human life are certain fundamental divine standards which make up God's eternal moral law. The most important of these laws are the Ten Commandments (Exodus 20:1-17). Of course, neither the Ten Commandments nor any other statement of God's eternal moral law are able to produce either salvation or spirituality in an individual. Only the saving work of the Lord Jesus Christ can accomplish this, as received by grace through faith. Nevertheless, they do reflect the character of God and thus serve as a basic standard of righteous behavior and conduct. They have, in fact, provided the underlying foundation of the laws of our nation.

Jesus summed up the Mosaic Law by condensing it to two laws, " 'Thou shalt love the Lord thy God with all thy heart, and with all thy soul, and with all thy mind.' This is the first and great commandment. And the second is like unto it, Thou shalt love thy neighbor as thyself.' " Matthew 22:37-39. The following ten groups of suggested regulations are arranged in these two broad categories, as applied especially in the New Testament. Rules dealing with our relationship to God and our neighbors form the first category of Standards of Conduct.

1. Relationship to God.
   (1) Devotion to God (Exodus 20:3)
       (a) Both students and teachers[1] should be expected to love God and give Him first priority in all aspects of their lives. This principle that only the one true God should be worshipped and served abides forever (James 2:19; I Tim. 2:5).
       (b) Students are expected to obey the clear teachings of God's word without question (I John 5:3).
   (2) No Idolatry (Exodus 20:4,5)
       (a) An idol is anything that is a substitute for God (I John 5:21).
       (b) Christians are not to employ objects of any sort, especially statues or pictures, as devices of prayer or worship or other spiritual exercises (John 4:24).
       (c) Since idolatry is associated with demonism and paganism (I Cor. 10:19-21) and these in turn with ritualistic incantations (Matthew 6:7), all must avoid any religious exercises which seek to induce religious feelings or experiences by means of unthinking recitations or repetitive physical movements.
       (d) Other occultic practices in religion (astrology, fortune telling, spiritism, witchcraft, Zen, transcendental meditation, yoga, Buddhism, illuminism, etc.) are all associated in some degree with idolatry and spiritism and so must be completely avoided by Christians (Eph. 5:11, I Cor. 8:1-10: Acts 15:29).

[1]Although the rules are stated normally in terms of student behavior, it is implied that the teachers and staff of the school will also be expected to abide by the same (or higher) standards.

(3) No Irreverent Use of God's Name (Exodus 20:7)

   (a) As children of the King of Kings each student must use His name only in a reverent and worthy manner, never in a trivial or joking way. To take His name "in vain" literally means "in a useless manner" (James 5:12).

   (b) One must never seek to emphasize a statement or claim by invoking God's name (Matthew 5:34; James 5:12).

   (c) Insofar as possible even the so-called "minced oaths" should be avoided, since these are merely corruptions of one of the names of God (Matthew 5:37; 12:36).

(4) Regular Worship (Exodus 20:8-11)

   (a) Coupled with the preceding Biblical principles is the admonition for worshipping God and resting on one day in seven. The Christian rest day is also normally the Lord's day on which we commemorate the finishing of God's work of redemption, as well as that of creation (Gen. 2:1; John 19:30; I Cor. 16:2; Acts 20:7).

   (b) All students should regularly attend church services on the Lord's day, seeking also throughout the day to make it a day of rest and worship, to enjoy fellowship with other Christians, for study and exhortation (Heb. 10:25), and through prayer and Bible reading to concentrate their thoughts especially on fellowship with Christ (I John 1:3-7). Exceptions may be justified on the basis of illness or other emergency, on the basis of duty requirements, or on the basis of other spiritual priorities in the Lord's work.

2. Relationship to One's Neighbors.

   (5) Respect for Parents (Exodus 20:12)

   (a) Though their parents are not at school or on campus, students should obey their instructions as though they were (not applicable to married students unless they are still supported by their parents), always behaving in a way that reflects well on them and always speaking of them to others in a respectful way (Eph. 6:2,3; Col. 3:20). If home standards are more rigorous than college standards in a given situation then the student should continue to obey the rules of his or her parent.

(b) Since the college is functioning *en loco parentis,* students must also give the same honor, respect, and obedience to the teachers and officials at the college that the Scriptures require for one's parents (I Tim. 4:1,2; Eph. 6:1-9).

(6) No Murder or Hatred (Exodus 20:13)

In addition to the obvious command against murder, a crime which would require that any such guilty student be turned over to the civil authorities and possible capital punishment (Gen. 9:6), the New Testament emphasizes that this commandment applies also to hatred, which, if unrestrained might lead to actual bloodshed (Matt. 5:21-22). Thus, a Christian should not manifest hatred toward anyone, especially a fellow Christian (I John 3:15) nor engage in fighting (James 4:1-3) except in self-defense or in the defense of others in danger.

(7) Moral Purity (Exodus 20:14).

(a) Adultery is a term referring explicitly to unfaithfulness to one's husband or wife. The Lord Jesus Christ made it clear that it also refers to sexual lust, whether or not it culminates in actual adultery (Matt. 5:27, 28).

(b) Christians are not to engage in any sexual relations outside of marriage. These include premarital sex, homosexual relations, incest, adultery, etc. (Gal. 5:19-21; I Cor. 6:9, 10).

(c) Young people are to flee youthful lusts (II Tim. 2:22) which might, if allowed to grow, eventually lead to unlawful sex actions; this means that one should not have erotic

materials in his possession nor subject himself
to their influence. They must also be cir-
cumspect in their conversations and activities,
avoiding temptation in this sensitive aspect of
campus life.

(8) Respect for Property (Exodus 20:15)
   (a) Students must respect the property of others.
       Not only outright theft, but also failing to take
       care of borrowed property (Eph. 4:28),
       carelessness which results in damage to some-
       one else's property, unfair business practices,
       failure to provide adequate work for one's
       wages (I Thess. 4:11-12) and other such prac-
       tices (e.g. "goofing off" on jobs for which
       one is paid), are all forms of stealing and must
       be scrupulously avoided by Christians.
   (b) Perhaps the worst form of stealing is to steal
       from God by failing to bring Him tithes and
       offerings from the material blessings provided
       us by Him. (II Cor. 9:6-15).

(9) No Lying (Exodus 20:16)
   (a) Christians must maintain a reputation for
       honesty and integrity in all things, especially in
       matters affecting the reputation of other peo-
       ple (Eph. 4:25).
   (b) Students must refrain from gossip and hearsay
       testimony (II Thes. 3:11; I Tim. 5:13) as well
       as from giving the impression of possessing
       knowledge which they do not possess (e.g.,
       cheating on exams, receiving unauthorized
       help in preparing class assignments,
       plagiarism).

(10) No Covetousness (Exodus 20:17)
   (a) Covetousness is actually a form of idolatry
       (Eph. 5:5; Col. 3:5), a worshiping of mammon
       (Matt. 6:24), and is thus extremely subtle and
       dangerous. It may manifest itself as the break-
       ing of one of the other commandments (steal-
       ing, murder, adultery, etc.), but even when it

does not lead to flagrant lawbreaking, it eats at the heart and life (I Tim. 6:6-11). Even though covetousness is a sin of the mind it is easily visible in one's attitude toward material and fleshly possessions—either a selfish pride in what he owns or an inordinate craving for what is not his. Christians must avoid such an attitude by all means. God's promises are far better (Heb. 13:5; Phil. 4:19) than any material possession we have or may seek to acquire.

The organization of these standards in a format based on the Ten Commandments does not mean that the Mosaic law (which was given explicitly to Israel on Mount Sinai) is definitive for the Christian life, which both begins and grows by grace, through the Holy Spirit. However, an organized society (whether a nation, church, or school) must have rules to maintain order and to accomplish its purpose, and these commandments are the best means to that end, reflecting as they do the eternal character and moral law of God.

CHRISTIAN CHOICES: BASIC COMMITMENTS

When the Bible speaks unequivocally on matters of conduct, as in the Ten Commandments, there can be no question as to one's course of action, if he believes the Scriptures. But there are innumerable questions not treated explicitly in the Bible (e.g., smoking, automobiles, movies), and the right decision on these must depend on the application of general Biblical principles.

There are many such principles provided by God in His Word. If these are intelligently and sincerely applied, they are more than adequate for guidance on any particular problem. The list below is somewhat arbitrary and could be extended, but is ample for most needs. Ten principles are listed, after the example of the Ten Commandments. However, they should be regarded as "ten commitments"—that is, the commitments by the school

on behalf of its testimony and commitments by the
students and staff in the best interest of their Christian
growth and future ministry. Each of these leads to the
establishment of specific guides of conduct in modern-
day Christian living. These Biblical commitments will
help one to appropriate and follow "all things that per-
tain unto life and godliness, through the knowledge of
Him that hath called us to glory and virtue" (II Peter
1:3). The principles and the rules based on them are listed
and discussed in the following pages.

1. The Example of Christ (I Peter 2:21; I John 2:6)
    The first commitment is this: "We will seek to follow
    the example of the Lord Jesus in all things." For
    instance:
    (1) The Christian student should willingly submit to
        the authority of those higher in the chain of com-
        mand, even when their decisions seem arbitrary
        and unfair (I Peter 2:23).
    (2) He or she should be obedient to the revealed will
        of God, even when it entails personal sacrifice
        (Phil. 2:8; Heb. 5:8).
    (3) One should seek to develop a spirit of humility
        (Matt. 11:29) rather than an attitude of arrogance.
    (4) One will be willing to perform humble tasks as
        needed (John 13:13-17).
    (5) Each Christian should seek to develop a real con-
        cern for souls of lost people (Luke 19:10).

2. The Temple of the Holy Spirit (I Cor. 6:19, 20; 3:16)
    "We must regard our physical bodies as temples of
    God, dedicated to Him." Not only is this true of the
    individual Christian, but also of each assembly of
    Christians in an organized local church. This principle
    requires that each temple be kept holy; otherwise there
    is danger of destruction of the one causing its defile-
    ment (I Cor. 3:17). In consequence of this sobering
    truth:
    (1) Christian students must maintain their bodies in a
        state of purity, not only with relation to fornica-
        tion (I Cor. 6:18) but also by refraining from

actions (e.g., petting, close physical contact) which might lead to sexual sin.

(2) Insofar as possible, they should try to maintain their bodies in a sound state of health and service, through proper habits of eating, rest, and exercise, avoiding unnecessary exposure to injury through pranks, rough play, dangerous sports, and useless foolhardiness (I Cor. 13:11).

(3) They should not allow their bodies to participate in sensuous or suggestive dancing, "choreography," or similar actions which might cause sexual stimulation in themselves or in others. They will not frequent locations where such activities are practiced.

3. The Danger of Addiction (I Corinthians 6:12)

"We will not partake of anything that could lead to addiction." The believer should be controlled by the Holy Spirit (Ephesians 5:18), not by alcohol or anything else which might gain inordinate control over his will.

(1) Christian students must not use either alcohol or tobacco, recognizing that these substances have acquired control over the bodies and wills of multitudes.

(2) The even more dangerous drugs—marijuana, cocaine, and other such poisonous or hallucinatory substances—must be utterly shunned.

(3) The practice of gambling may well be addictive and even destructive to many, and Christian concern and caution therefore require its rejection by dedicated servants of Christ.

(4) Other recreational and leisure activities can become semi-addictive if not carefully self-monitored for moderation (e.g., television, snacking), and one must be cautious and temperate in all such activities.

4. Avoidance of Temptation (Matthew 6:13)

"We will avoid deliberate confrontations with temptation." In this present evil world, there are temptations everywhere, but the Lord taught us to pray not to be led into temptation and to be delivered from evil. We are tempted through our own lusts (James 1:14) and these begin in the mind. Christians should therefore seek to think with the mind of Christ (Philippians 2:5), permitting only those thoughts which are "true, honest, just, pure, lovely, and of good report" (Philippians 4:8).

(1) Christian students are, therefore, not to read pornographic or erotic literature or to listen to music whose beat or words are sensually stimulating or suggestive.

(2) Young people should attend commercial movies only by special permission in the case of certain "G" or "PG" movies adjudged to have positive educational or spiritual benefits.

(3) Young people likewise should watch only those television programs that are consistent with Biblical standards.

5. Abstinence from Evil Associations or Appearances (I Thessalonians 5:22)

"We will avoid those things which might even appear to be evil." For the sake of maintaining an unquestioned clear-cut testimony for Christian righteousness, the Christian should be willing to be different from the world (Romans 12:2) and to forego his Christian liberty (Galatians 3:13), even though the rights which he relinquishes may involve actions which are quite innocent in themselves. For example:

(1) If unmarried couples go on unchaperoned dates, they must be especially careful not to subject themselves to temptation or to any questionable situations or appearances. Single students should never visit the off-campus residence of an unmarried person of the opposite sex without a chaperon.

(2) Male clothing and hair styles are not acceptable for females, nor female clothing and hair styles and lengths for men (note Deuteronomy 22:5; I Co-

rinthians 11:5-7, 13-15).

(3) Because of the common association of scraggly beards and odd patterns of facial hair with the rebellious and amoral attitudes of young men in motorcycle gangs and other anti-Christian groups, male students are expected either to be clean shaven or to keep facial hair neat and well trimmed at all times.

(4) Both male and female students and staff members must dress modestly and neatly at all times (I Timothy 2:9; 4:12).

The above regulations may seem arbitrary, but have been suggested with the purpose of maintaining a good and wholesome appearance and testimony to the unsaved men, women, and young people around us, "adorning the doctrine of God our Savior in all things" (Titus 2:10), in order "that the word of God be not blasphemed," and so "that he that is of the contrary part may be ashamed, having no evil thing to say of you" (Titus 2:5,8).

6. Avoidance of Offense (I Corinthians 10:31-33)

Christians are commanded to "give none offense, neither to the Jews, nor to the Gentiles, nor to the church of God." Therefore, a sixth commitment is this: "We will avoid activities that are offensive to others, even though they may be harmless otherwise."

(1) Christians should be willing to forego any activity in the presence of another Christian, which he or she believes to be wrong. Even in their absence, if participation in such an activity will "wound their weak conscience," the Scripture teaches that "Ye sin against Christ" (I Corinthians 8:12).

(2) Older, stronger Christians must be especially careful not to do or say anything which might cause a younger, weaker Christian brother or sister to harbor doubts about Christianity or to "stumble" in their Christian walk (Romans 14:13, 21; I Corinthians 8:8-13; Romans 15:1-3).

(3) The same consideration should be given to non-

Christians, and Christians should be careful to respect their own convictions and cultural differences (Romans 15:1-3), seeking to change them (if they are contrary to Scripture) only by careful and loving persuasion through Christ.

7. Non-Conformity to World (Romans 12:2; I John 2:15-17)
The Christian is called to be a "good soldier of Jesus Christ" and thus must not "entangle himself with the affairs of this life" (II Timothy 2:3,4). Worldliness involves the attitude of covetousness and pride and we are commanded to "be *not* conformed to this world." The seventh commitment, therefore, is: "We will not base our life-style on current worldly standards, but only on that which honors Christ and His Word."
   (1) Students should never seek to justify any belief or any action by the contention that "everyone is doing it," but only by means of Biblical principles soundly applied.
   (2) Similarly, "peer pressure" must be consciously resisted if that pressure is in the direction of lower spiritual or moral standards.

8. Redeeming the Time (Ephesians 5:15; Colossians 4:5)
"We will be careful to make the best use of the time available." Activities which waste time are in disobedience to God's command to "redeem the time." Even idle conversation will one day be judged (Matthew 12:36). Christian students are engaged in serious training for serious work in the kingdom of God, and time is brief and precious.
   (1) Recreational activities, properly chosen and limited, have positive value, but must not be allowed to interfere with scholastic or spiritual responsibilities.
   (2) Social and fellowship activities should be planned for optimum use of the time involved, with evangelistic or educational goals whenever feasible, not merely as time fillers or for selfish purposes. Times of rest and relaxation are also of

spiritual value, but these also need to be controlled by this motive.

(3) Students should be careful to provide time daily for prayer and Bible study, foregoing leisure and recreational activities if necessary.

9. The Criterion of the Positive (I Corinthians 10:23; I Thessalonians 5:21)

The common question, "But why can't I do it?" should be replaced with "What good purpose will be served by it?" The Apostle notes that, while all things may be lawful for the believer, not all things are edifying. He commands us to "prove [that is, 'examine carefully' or 'test'] all things" and then to "hold fast that which is good." The ninth commitment, therefore, is: "We will engage only in activities which are of positive benefit."

(1) Students should refrain from practical jokes (Proverbs 26:18, 19) or pranks that are dangerous or destructive.

(2) Young people should select and plan their recreational and leisure activities with the goal of positive improvement in their Christian growth and witness thereby.

(3) They should always consider the needs of others in carrying out their own activities, giving particular attention to maintaining quiet and wholesome conditions in the dormitories, lounges, libraries, and other common areas.

(4) In the classroom, students should do everything possible to assist the learning environment, dressing neatly, not talking or passing notes, asking questions courteously and only if they are relevant to the needs of the class as a whole, paying close attention to the lecture and speaking only when called on by the instructor. Personal questions or complaints should be voiced only after class, to the instructor alone.

(5) Students should not criticize other students or staff members or complain about administrative

policies and decisions, remembering the Biblical injunction to "do all things without murmurings and disputings [literally, 'griping and questioning']" (Philippians 4:15). There are channels for conveying such questions, and any suggestion offered in a spirit of helpful understanding will always be considered in the same spirit.

(6) Students should only speak factually and positively about any aspect of their school to outsiders, as criticism of the school to outsiders can only harm and hinder its ministry and future development. Any criticism should be directed internally through the proper channels.

10. Honoring Christ (Colossians 3:17)

One final commitment, which might well summarize all the others and embrace any concept not yet covered, is: "We will do only those things which we know honor the Lord Jesus Christ." To the sincere Christian, "to live is Christ" (Philippians 1:21).

(1) Any decision or questionable activity can usually be evaluated by the test of praying for Christ's blessing on it. If this can conscientiously be done "in the name of the Lord Jesus, giving thanks," then it is probably safe to proceed. If asking His blessing on the matter comes hard, then this is a good sign it is wrong and should be abandoned. " . . . for whatsoever is not of faith is sin" (Romans 14:23).

ADMINISTRATIVE ARRANGEMENTS AND REQUIREMENTS

The regulations and requirements that would be set up under this category are not necessarily derived from specific Biblical principles, but are necessary for the efficient and orderly functioning of the school, as well as to assure equitable treatment of all students in all situations, to as great an extent as possible. Although specific rules in this section can not always be based on specific Scripture texts, there is certainly an adequate Biblical basis for developing such a body of rules, in accordance with the experience and Spirit-led judgment of the administration of the school.

The Scriptures teach that it is the responsibility of the people of God to do "all things decently and in order" (I Corinthians 14:40). Further, all Christians are taught to "obey them that have the rule over you, and submit your souls, as they that must give account, that they may do it with joy, and not with grief; for that is unprofitable for you" (Hebrews 13:17). These two principles, which are amplified many times throughout the Bible, require the administrative staff of each Christian school to develop such "rules and regulations" as will promote order, and the students to follow those directions willingly. The spirit of administrative officials in making the rules is tempered by the knowledge that "they must give account." The spirit of students in obeying the rules should be guided by the knowledge that grudging and rebellious attitudes will be "unprofitable for you." The detailed regulations will depend on the type of school and the local circumstances. They would include a wide variety of procedures regarding registration, dormitory housekeeping, athletic policies, use of automobiles, off-campus dating, study hours, financial aid, use of library, and a host of other miscellaneous items.

PRINCIPLES AND RULES OF ENFORCEMENT

Since schools are essentially extensions of the home and church, their systems for establishing and maintaining the order necessary for the accomplishment of their mission must combine the appropriate enforcement methods of home and church. Although governments have often set up educational systems, the Bible does not give human government this authority. Neither does the Bible indicate that a school should be formed by any arbitrary combination of individuals or extra-church organizations. Parents and/or churches are responsible under God for education. Specialized schools which are beyond the abilities of parent-church groups to organize and operate should nevertheless recognize this principle and require their boards and personnel to have sound doctrine and to be members of sound churches.

The school should seek to base all its programs and methods on the Word of God, and this is true not only of the standards of conduct expected of its students and staff, but also of its provisions for maintaining those standards. It should seek to be responsive to the standards of all those homes and churches from which its students come. Insofar as possible, it should remain free of governmental control, not accepting funds for its facilities or programs from government grants or loans (individual students may have access to such funds, but not the school as such).

As pointed out earlier, governments can enforce their laws by the taking of either property or liberty or life from those citizens who break them. However, neither the home nor the church is authorized either by the Bible or the government to use these measures (fines, p ison, capital punishment) in enforcing their rules. Instead, parents discipline their children by three methods:

- a. Verbal correction (private) (Hebrews 12:9; Proverbs 3:12; 15:5).
- b. Withholding family rewards and privileges (Luke 15:19; 11:13).
- c. Corrective (but not injurious) physical chastisement or other punishments (Proverbs 13:24; 18:18; 23:13; 29:15).

Similarly, churches discipline their members by three methods:

- a. Verbal correction
  1. Private (Galations 6:1; Matthew 18:15,16)
  2. Public (Matthew 18:17; I Timothy 5:19,20)
- b. Withholding church rewards and privileges (I Corinthians 5:11; Titus 3:10)
- c. Expulsion from membership (Matthew 18:17; I Corinthians 5:2,13).

These systems are similar, except that parents cannot

"expel" a child from family membership and churches cannot employ corporal punishment on their members (that is, these things cannot be done with Biblical sanction). Schools, as agents of Christian homes and churches, therefore, should employ four methods of rule enforcement:

a. Verbal correction—preferably in private, but publicly if necessary.
b. Withholding school rewards and privileges.
c. Chastisement or other punishments, when acting *en loco parentis*.
d. Expulsion, when acting *en loco ecclesiae*.

Corporal punishment can be employed by school officials on younger children, when needed, just as conscientious parents would do. This procedure, however, is necessarily limited to elementary and secondary schools at most. College students cannot (or at least should not) be subjected to this type of punishment, for this would not be used by their parents. The ultimate discipline for college students, consequently, must be that of dismissal, either temporary (suspension) or permanent. Other lesser punishments can be used as appropriate.

It is on the basis of such principles that each school is responsible for enforcing its standards of character and behavior, as well as its administrative regulation. The code of standards is three-tiered, in order of relative Biblical emphasis, and, therefore, the disciplinary enforcement must likewise be three-tiered in order of relative severity. This division is summarized in the table on the following page.

The disciplinary procedures as outlined are intended only as guidelines and are understood to be flexible, permitting adjustment as needed for individual circumstances. Each of the three major categories of offenses is discussed briefly below, with comments on the corrective measures appropriate in each case.

1. *Failure in Christian Character*

The most serious problem arising in a student's Christian life involves willful disobedience to the explicit

Category of Offenses	Nature of Disciplinary Procedures
Failure in Christian Character Responsibilities (e.g., as under the "ten commandments," pages 188-193)	Possible immediate suspension, followed by counseling and appropriate remedial measures, including possible expulsion.
Engaging in Conduct Unbecoming to Christians (e.g., as under the "ten commitments," pages 193-200)	Counseling, followed by appropriate measures and suspension if behavior problems persist.
Breaking Administrative Regulations	Official notice of infraction, followed by appropriate measures and then by counseling and possible suspension if uncorrected.

commandments of Scripture. Some of the implications of these commandments for student life have been codified on pages 188-193. This is not an exhaustive list, however, and it should be understood that any action which constitutes a willful infraction of any clear and applicable commandment of the Bible may result in such disciplinary procedures as outlined in this section.

A deliberate breaking of such a commandment must be regarded as rebellion against God, so the possible ultimate penalty of dismissal from school must be seriously considered. If such is warranted in the judgment of the administration, an immediate suspension may be imposed, pending establishment of guilt and consideration of possible mitigating circumstances. An immediate investigation by a school disciplinary committee should follow any suspension. At the same time, the student involved should receive appropriate counseling by a qualified person. The committee action may range from complete exoneration or forgiveness (in event of innocence or sincere repentance and restitution) to various measures as judged appropriate (e.g., public apology, restriction from campus activities, reprimand on permanent records, reduction of grade in course, etc., depending on circumstances and other persons affected) and possible dismissal from school.

Offenses under this category should be considered as extremely serious, involving as they do such matters as theft, cheating, false witness against a teacher or fellow student, fornication, etc., and should occur very rarely, if at all, among sincere Christians. If any student is tempted to break one of these standards, however, he or she is urged to realize that such an action must have serious consequences, quite possibly including the penalty of expulsion. There are also offenses in this category (e.g., rape, murder, burglary) which are defined as crimes by the government and would have to be dealt with accordingly.

With serious charges such as these involved, the establishment of degree of guilt or innocence is, of course, extremely important, and the investigative committee must take its responsibility seriously. The person making the original charge must be willing to explain and justify the basis of the charge to the committee.

The school should not necessarily require any student to "inform" on another student or faculty member, leaving this to his or her own best judgment and conscience. The student should take into consideration the consequences to the school, to fellow students, and to the cause of Christ if he elects to do so or not to do so. The source of any such information should be kept confidential insofar as possible, except that the one reporting the situation must be willing to repeat and support the charges if they are denied, at such time and place as the disciplinary committee deems necessary. If the offense has been committed directly against an individual (e.g., false witness, theft), then that person should first go to the individual, as instructed in Matthew 18:15, with the hope of repentance, restitution, and resultant forgiveness.

If at all possible the staff and faculty of the school will seek to help and restore any student involved in this type of problem. Evidence of sincere repentance and willingness to make adequate restitution are obviously key factors in any possible restoration (II Corinthians 2:6-8). At the same time, the testimony of the school and its students as a whole to the Christian community and to the unsaved world must be given greater weight than personal feelings.

2. *Conduct Unbecoming to a Christian*
A number of additional standards of expected conduct (see pages 193-200) have been derived from the general principles of Christian behavior outlined in Scripture and summarized herein as "Ten Commitments." Since these standards are not explicit com-

mandments of the Bible and normally do not entail consequences as serious as those which follow actual law-breaking, we need not regard this category of offenses with quite the same concern as those in the first category. Nevertheless, these standards *are* based on Biblical principles and are, therefore, important in the development of each student to his highest potential in Christian service, as well as in maintaining the strongest witness of the school as a whole. The list of specific standards is not exhaustive, but representative. Any attitude or behavior which is inconsistent with basic Biblical principles of conduct is understood to be covered by this section. In many cases, these standards govern attitudes, rather than overt actions. In such cases, the student must, for the most part, be his or her own monitor and judge. It is only when wrong attitudes generate objectionable actions that school enforcement may become involved.

When a student is guilty of failing in one of these standards, he should be informed of that fact by a school official and receive any appropriate counseling. A notation concerning the offense should be kept on record, together with a record of the student's attitude. If the same offense is repeated, he or she is then subject to possible suspension and essentially the same procedural sequence as described under Category 1.

3. *Breaking Administrative Regulations*

The third category of behavior standards is less obviously related to Biblical precepts, but is necessary to maintain order and equity in the operation of the school as a whole. They are, therefore, also quite important and students must abide by these as well. Such regulations may be changed from time to time, or new regulations established and announced.

If a student breaks an administrative regulation, he should be apprised of the offense verbally by an appropriate official. A second infraction of the same standard should result in a written citation and warning. A third infraction may (depending on attitude and other circumstances) be considered as a moral infraction and the procedure of counseling and possible suspension inaugurated as described in the previous section. Other penalties (e.g., special work assignments, restriction to campus) may be ordered as appropriate.

4. *Appeals*

The procedures described for disciplinary enforcement of the standards of conduct in each of the three categories involve a careful and equitable series of evaluations and remedies, and the decision normally will be final. If the student believes that he or she has been unfairly judged or that the penalty is too severe, an appeal can be made to the disciplinary committee, which will then carefully review the case. This request should be in writing, with substantiating documentation. The decision of the disciplinary committee should be final.

Finally, if the student believes any administrative policy or regulation is itself contrary to Scripture, or otherwise unfair in some way, he should be able to present his reasons to the administration, either verbally or in writing, preferably the latter. Until such time as the school actually revises the section with which he disagrees, however, he must be expected to abide by its stipulations.

In the case of strong disagreement, it is conceivable that a student might elect to withdraw from school rather than submit to the policy in question. Since the school should recognize its ultimate responsibility to the Christian home and church, there is one further appeal he may wish to make. His parents and/or home church should be always welcome to discuss any school policy with any school official.

Chapter 8

The Need for Biblical Certitude

EDUCATION AND THE EVIDENCES
OF CHRISTIANITY

The reader will certainly be aware by this time that the basic premise throughout this book is that of absolute Biblical authority. The teachings of the Bible, rather than human experience and philosophy, constitute the basis of what we have called the Christian doctrine of true education. Many recommendations in this book may seem contrary to conventional wisdom in educational matters, and many of them will be difficult to implement, but they seem clearly warranted by Biblical constraints and criteria, as we have tried to show throughout.

But they all depend on the assumption that the Bible indeed is the very Word of God, completely without error and absolutely authoritative on every subject with which it deals. If the Bible is *not* the Word of God, or if it only has authority in "religious" matters, then this book is a futile exercise, with its conclusions and recommendations all based on a fallacious premise. But, of course, the Bible *is* the Word of God!

This fact of Biblical certitude is critically important. The development of a genuine Biblical doctrine of education is squarely dependent on the strength of our confidence in Biblical authority. A prospective administrator or teacher who harbors any doubts on this question should never be appointed to the staff of any Christian school, regardless of his or her other qualifications.

This absolute confidence in the inerrancy and authority of the Bible must also be instilled in the students. If they are going to cooperate in a system of teaching and standards of behavior which are radically different from those in the public schools and state universities, the students—no less than their teachers—must understand and be satisfied that these matters are all decided on the basis of God-revealed criteria in His Word.

Now the question is, how is this confidence to be established? Children of elementary school age may believe the Bible on the say-so of their parents or teachers, but most older students need more than that. They will quickly learn that most educational and scientific authorities reject the Bible and they will—quite understandably—want real answers, not mere pronouncements, on these questions.

It is especially vital to establish a solid conviction in the minds and hearts of the students that there really is overwhelming evidence of the existence of a personal transcendent Creator of all things, the one who made them and by whom they will ultimately be judged. They must also be shown, through sound reasoning, that the Bible is truly the written Word of God, divinely inspired, inerrant, and authoritative. They must be satisfied that Jesus Christ is the Son of God, that He died for their sins, that He rose from the dead, and He is coming again. These must all be sound convictions, of the intelligence as well as the emotions, if they are to stand against the attacks of the wicked one in this unbelieving age. Finally, if the students are not yet saved, they must by all means be won to personal saving faith in the Lord Jesus Christ as early in their school experience as possible. All of this means that the subjects of Biblical apologetics and Christian evidences need to have a prominent place in the curriculum, especially at the college level.

WHAT IS THE GOSPEL?

One of the essential purposes of a true Christian school is to indoctrinate its students in the truth of the Gospel of Jesus Christ. While it is good to encourage them in an ongoing "search for truth," equipping them to do research in both the Word that God said and the world that God made, this can never take priority over understanding and propagating truth already known. The latter must provide the foundation and framework for truths yet to be discovered; otherwise, the student becomes highly vulnerable, easily "tossed to and fro, and carried about with every wind of doctrine" (Ephesians 4:14). It is only the humanist school system that is "ever learning, and never able to come to the knowledge of the truth" (II Timothy 3:7).

The vital question, therefore, is: "What is truth?" (John 18:38). The answer is that Jesus Christ Himself is truth incarnated (John 14:6), the Word of God is truth inscripturated (John 17:17), and the Spirit of God is the indispensable Guide into all truth (John 16:13).

The Lord Jesus Christ is the Creator of all things, the Sustainer of all things, and the Reconciler of all things (Colossians 1:16, 17, 20). "Of Him, and through Him, and to Him, are all things" (Romans 11:36). He is Alpha and Omega, from eternity to eternity. Thus it is that the Gospel of Jesus Christ, which we are commanded to preach (Mark 16:15), embraces *all* truth. The Gospel is the "good news" about Christ—His person and His work—and "all things" are "gathered together" in Him (Ephesians 1:10). The Gospel begins with the creation of the universe (Revelation 14:6, 7), centers in the cross and empty tomb (I Corinthians 15:1-4), and culminates in His everlasting kingdom (Matthew 4:23). Without the creation, the Gospel has no foundation; without the final reconciliation, the Gospel is devoid of hope; without the atoning death and justifying resurrection, it has no power.

It is such a Gospel, embracing all that is true, excluding all that is false, presenting our Creator and Savior in all His beauty throughout His great creation, that constitutes the commission of true Christian education.

THE DEFENSE OF THE GOSPEL

It is vital that the proclamation of the Gospel be also undergirded by a defense that confirms its truth and relevance. A merely emotional faith, based only on subjective personal needs, is a credulous faith, a leap into the unknown, easily undermined and immobilized.

There have always been many "enemies of the cross" (Philippians 3:18), false teachers who shall cause the "way of truth" to be blasphemed (II Peter 2:1-2), and these must be opposed and answered, for they turn many away from Christ. Their "mouths must be stopped" (Titus 1:11), not by force but by truth. We must "convince the gainsayers" (Titus 1:9).

Even though many say the Gospel needs no defense, the Apostle Paul was not among them. He said to the Philippians: " . . . in the defence and confirmation of the Gospel, ye all are partakers of my grace" (Philippians 1:7). Again he said, "I am set for the defence of the Gospel" (Philippians 1:17).

The word translated "defence" is the Greek *apologia,* and it is the source of our English word "apologetics." In substance, the Apostle Paul is saying: "I am set to give an apologetic for the Gospel, to defend it against the attacks and charges of its adversaries, in the same manner as in a formal courtroom defense, in a way systematic and scientific, persuasive in evidence and logic."

WHY TEACH APOLOGETICS?

The basic reason that a Christian school should include apologetics in its curriculum is because of its vital place in the life and witness of every Christian, if he is to be both stable and fruitful in his Christian service. It is an integral part of his "general education," every bit as important as English or history or science or any of the other basic subjects that provide the tools of background knowledge needed for effective ministry in the modern world.

Christ's parable of the seed is instructive in this connection. The seed which fell on stony ground sprang up quickly, but the roots were shallow and the weak plants soon withered away in the heat of the sun. The teaching of the parable was this: "But he that received the seed into stony places, the same is he that heareth the word, and anon with joy receiveth it: yet hath he not root in himself, but dureth for a while; for when tribulation or persecution ariseth because of the word, by and by he is offended" (Matthew 13:20, 21). Luke 8:13 adds that he "falls away."

Here is the all-too-common case of a quick emotional acceptance of the Gospel; the seed was sown carelessly, on shallow soil. Thus the only "root" that the young believer had was his own personal experience, and this could not stand the withering blasts of opposition which quickly bore down on him, not because of his subjective experience but "because of the word." The shallow ground could have become "good ground" if the stones had been first removed; then "he that receiveth seed into the good ground is he that heareth the word, and understandeth it; which also beareth fruit" (Matthew 13:23).

The witnessing Christian, in fact, is actually *commanded* to use Biblical apologetics in his witness to the world. "But sanctify the Lord God in your hearts; and be ready always to give an answer to every man that asketh you a reason of the hope that is in you with meekness and fear" (I Peter 3:15).

In this well-known admonition of the Apostle, the

word "answer," once again is *apologia,* and the word "reason" is *logos,* related to our English word "logic." Thus Peter says, in effect: "Be ready always to give an apologetic to every man, a logical word appropriate to each question he asks, validating to him externally the hope you possess internally."

This apologetic is not to be rendered in high-sounding philosophical argumentation, however, but to be given meekly and reverently, in the presence and power of the indwelling Christ. The Christian witness must be neither ignorant nor arrogant! (Note also II Timothy 2:15-18, 23-26).

Such a commandment presupposes that there actually is an apologetic which can be given. The Christian faith is not a credulous leap into the dark, but is based on a great abundance of solid, objective evidence. It is, indeed, a *faith,* but it is a reasonable faith.

In contrast, the unbeliever is the one who is blindly credulous. The Apostle Paul says: "For the invisible things of Him from the creation of the world are clearly seen, being understood by the things that are made, even His eternal power and Godhead; so that they are without excuse" (Romans 1:20). The word "excuse" is none other than the same word *apologia* again. The evidence concerning the existence and character of the God of the Bible is so clear, even in the realm of nature, that the one who rejects Him is left "without an apologetic." He has no basis and no reason for his faith in evolutionary pantheistic humanism (which system constitutes the essence of all anti-Biblical or extra-Biblical religions and philosophies).

The Christian has access to a powerful apologetic, though most Christians rarely use it and often are unaware of it. The non-Christian has *no* apologetic, yet he somehow entertains the common delusion that science and reason actually support him in his unbelief. This anomalous and tragic situation has been fostered by false teachers for over a hundred years, and it is high time for our Christian schools, at least, to set about correcting it.

Wherever possible, even the public schools and secular universities should be persuaded at least to incorporate a "two-model approach" (theistic creationism as an alternative to evolutionary humanism) in their curricula. This, in fact, is one of the main goals of our Institute for Creation Research, and these efforts are meeting both with the expected opposition on the one hand and with increasing acceptance and enthusiasm on the other hand.

Christian schools and colleges should go far beyond this neutral approach, of course, developing *all* courses and curricula in accord with the full Biblical perspective on truth. And for this to be truly effective, students should be taught not only *what* is true, but also *why* it is true. The curriculum should not only include formal courses in apologetics, but also should structure all other courses in an apologetics framework, either implicit or explicit. The years just ahead are dangerous years, with atheistic communism already enslaving much of the world and with evolutionary humanism and bureaucratic socialism dominating even the free world. Christian young people nurtured only on religious emotionalism or compromising intellectualism will never "be able to withstand in the evil day" (Ephesians 6:13) which may soon be coming, without the "whole armour of God" (Ephesians 6:11).

The admonition of Jude is appropriate for the Christian school today. When he, like most modern evangelicals, was minded to write in comforting terms merely of our "common salvation," he was suddenly constrained by the Holy Spirit to write in an entirely different vein. "It was needful for me to write unto you, and exhort you that ye should earnestly contend for the faith which was once delivered unto the saints" (Jude 3).

IS APOLOGETICS EFFECTIVE IN EVANGELISM?

We not only want to keep Christians from falling away from the faith, of course, although this is an urgent need in these days of widespread intellectual unbelief. We want also to win men to salvation in Jesus Christ, and to such "steadfast faith in Christ" that they will never fall, "rooted and built up in Him, and stablished in the faith, as ye have been taught" (Colossians 2:5,6).

Many well-meaning Christian workers would warn us against *substituting* apologetic argumentation for straightforward Gospel proclamation, noting that for every argument for Christianity, the skeptic can mount an objection and counterargument. Even if he is unable to answer the Biblical argument, he can never be convinced to believe what he doesn't *want* to believe. No amount of evidence or logic can convince a person against his will. The only recourse in such a case is to pray that the Holy Spirit will somehow change his will, making him at least willing to believe the truth when it is accurately presented to him.

But not everyone is a hardened skeptic who simply chooses not to believe. There are multitudes of people, especially young people, who would be easily accessible to the Gospel if they had not been brainwashed against it through years of humanist indoctrination in the schools and other media of instruction and influence.

Actually, therefore, the question of apologetics *or* evangelism is a false dichotomy. True evangelism *includes* apologetics. It is not a case of either evangelism *or* apologetics, but of evangelism *using* apologetics, judiciously and prayerfully and Scripturally.

The best example of this is in the witness of the Apostles themselves, as they went forth preaching the Word in the first century, following Christ's great commission. They continually used what we today would call Christian evidences, or apologetics, in their preaching and witnessing. They repeatedly called attention to the bodily resurrection of Christ (e.g., Acts 2:32), to fulfilled prophecy (e.g., Acts 2:22), to their own miracles (e.g., Acts 4:9, 10), to the uniquely holy life of Jesus (e.g., Acts 10:38, 39), and to the evidence of their own personal regeneration (e.g., Acts 26:9-11, 22), among other things. Their preaching and personal witnessing were always warm and evangelistic, yet always thoughtful and logical, adapted to their particular audiences. When the apostles were witnessing to people who were already familiar with the Scriptures and believed the Scriptures, then they *used* the Scriptures, to demonstrate and vindicate the claims of Christ (e.g., Acts 17:1, 2, 10, 11). Moreover, they *reasoned* with them out of the Scriptures! However, when they encountered pagans who neither knew nor believed the Bible at all, they began their testimony with that which they *did* understand, namely the evidence of God in the creation (e.g., Acts 14:15-17; 17:23-31).

With both the example of the early church and the direct commands of Scripture to guide us, it is clear that effective Christian witnessing and preaching should incorporate whatever level of apologetic data is appropriate to each situation, to make it as sure as possible that the one who *hears* the Gospel also *understands* the Gospel and *why* he should believe it.

That such an approach is still fruitful today has been verified time after time. The campus witness of Probe Ministries and other similar student-oriented organizations, as well as the campaigns of Josh McDowell and others who stress a strongly Biblical apologetic witness, have been more fruitful than any other student evangelistic movement in generations. Our own Institute for Creation Research has an abundance of similar data. A questionnaire sent to the ICR mailing list several years ago elicited a strong sample of 2,000 returns. Of these, over 120 testified that they had been won to Christ directly through the creationist literature or lectures of ICR scientists. Nearly 1,000 testified that they had been enabled to win one or more others to stable faith in Christ as Savior through the use of these creationist materials (some told of leading almost entire classes to Christ in this way). At least 1,500 told how their own faith had been confirmed and their spiritual life strengthened through the ICR ministry. Similar testimonies come to us daily in the mail and in the various creation seminars and Bible conferences. We are convinced that a real revival of Scriptural apologetic emphasis along with a warm Gospel

presentation, if adopted by Christian evangelists and individual witnesses everywhere, would lead to the most
widespread expansion of true Biblical Christianity in
generations.

THE CONTENT OF APOLOGETICS

The Christian *apologia* should demonstrate and defend
at least the following basic truths: (1) the Fact of God;
(2) the Character of God; (3) the Son of God; (4) the
Word of God; (5) the Plan of God. Most individual
evidences and problems are aspects of one or more of
these. For the average student, the content of an
apologetics course (or the apologetics content in some
other course) should be in terms of practical Christian
evidences rather than philosophy (the seminary is the
proper place for philosophical apologetics). The most
fundamental of all truths is the fact of a transcendent
personal God who created all things and who, therefore,
is the Fountain of all other truths. The existence of the
triune God follows directly from all the evidence of creation and causality. That God is righteous, despite all the
obvious sin and suffering in the world, also follows from
causal reasoning (if cause-and-effect is not a valid process
for determining truth, then there is no meaning in the
world, and all reasoning about anything is futile). The
principle of causality can be applied very simply and
powerfully as an evidence of the existence and nature of
God.

The revelation of Christ as the unique Son of God is
demonstrated conclusively by His resurrection. The written Word of God validates its own claims through the
testimony of Christ. The centrality of the Gospel as the
plan of God is evident both in Scripture and in all experience. A careful examination of all real evidence does,
indeed, warrant a full, reasoned belief (faith *is* required,
but it is a faith based on fact, not fancy) that the triune
God is the one true God, that He is both holy and
gracious, as well as omnipotent and eternal, that Christ is
the Son of God, the Bible is the Word of God, and the

Gospel is the Plan of God.[1]

Formal instruction in this array of evidence may, of course, be given in various ways. At Christian Heritage College, for example, every new student took at least six semester hours of course work in "Practical Christian Evidences," in which he studied the evidences for all the five basic truths outlined above, being equipped also with sound answers to all the major objections to them. This course included also a grounding in the Biblical doctrine of true education, as well as a good introduction to the vital field of scientific creationism.

In addition to this basic sequence in apologetics, they took an additional six semester hours of formal course work in "Scientific Creationism." Finally, all other courses were structured in a Biblical, apologetic context, so that the student would, hopefully, not only know the facts associated with each subject, but also the Biblical principles for interpreting and utilizing them and the reasons and evidences for defending and propagating them.

With such a foundation, young men and women should be equipped for a solid and fruitful service for Christ in the most strategic fields during the coming years.

THE SEARCH FOR TRUTH

Many colleges and universities (the University of Minnesota, where the writer did his own graduate study, among them) have adopted as one of their mottoes the words of Christ in John 8:32: "And ye shall know the truth, and the truth shall make you free." The scholars at these institutions are ostensibly marching forth in a devoted search for truth, exploring all avenues and examining all data, in confidence that all the bits and pieces of truth so discovered will contribute to the liberation of the minds and hearts of men. This liberating search for truth is believed by many to be the very definition of a

---

[1]See the writer's book *Many Infallible Proofs* (San Diego, Creation-Life Publishers, 1974, 381 pp.) for the type of apologetics material recommended for this purpose.

"liberal arts" education.

This may be well and good, but how do they recognize the truth when it is found? How is real truth to be distinguished from untruth? Or is truth only relative—can one generation's truth be rejected as error by the next generation?

One important and widely used device for evaluating any "would-be-truth," especially in connection with the phenomena of natural science, is the so-called *scientific method*.

> Science seeks to discover patterns of relations among empirical facts and to advance hypotheses or theories that explain why the facts are as observed. A hypothesis is empirical or scientific only if it can be tested by experience . . . . A hypothesis or theory which cannot be, at least in principle, falsified by empirical observations and experiments does not belong to the realm of science.[1]

Such sentiments and goals are noble, but scientists are human and often let their own emotions and prejudices influence their interpretations. The "theory" of evolution, for example, is promoted as scientific fact by many scientists, even though they are well aware that it cannot even be tested, let alone proved, by the scientific method! A few evolutionary scientists are beginning to acknowledge this anomalous situation.

> I argue that the theory of evolution does not make predictions, so far as ecology is concerned, but is instead a logical formula which can be used to classify empiricisms.[2]

> I know geologists who regard the whole of Darwin's theory and the present-day synthetic theory of evolution (which do in fact have weak spots) as a type of religion, but we may readily imagine the

---

[1]Francisco Ayala, "Biological Evolution: Natural Selection or Random Walk?" *American Scientist,* Vol. 62, Nov. 1974, p. 700.

[2]R. H. Peters, "Tautology in Evolution and Ecology," *American Naturalist,* Vol. 110, No. 1, 1976, p. 1.

chaos that would face us in geology were the
evolutionary concept to become a myth . . . .[1]

The natural sciences, once highly revered, are increasingly being questioned today for other reasons also.
Many people hold scientists responsible for such social
problems as environmental pollution, the danger of
nuclear warfare, the development of urban slums, and
other evils. Furthermore, the scientific method seems in-
competent to solve real human problems. A leading
philosopher comments as follows:

> Many people have come to believe that science
> and clear rational thought cannot save us and
> that, indeed nothing that human beings can col-
> lectively do can save us. There is, many think, no
> rational hope for changing society and, indeed,
> we would not even know how to change it if we
> would.[2]

In recent decades, a sort of conflict has arisen between
what some call the "two cultures," the scientific approach and the humanities approach, and many voices
call for increased attention to the fine arts and the world
of literature, with less trust in science, thinking this may
somehow lead to truth and liberation. However, a prominent scholar working at the interface between the sciences
and the humanities (as a historian of science, speaking to
a joint meeting of the American Association for Advancement of Science and Phi Beta Kappa) has shown
that this solution is also unsatisfactory:

> In the effort to humanize ourselves, to enhance
> our ethical and moral sensibilities, people have
> often appealed to the humanities to do it for us,
> almost as to an ideology. The redemptive power
> of the humanities to produce an enlarged con-
> sciousness, to make us aware of the reality of the
> human predicament, and to enlarge our sym-

---

[1] B. B. Sokolov, "The Current Problems of Paleontology and Some Aspects of Its Future," *Paleontological Journal,* Vol. 9, No. 2, 1975, p. 137.

[2] Kai Nielsen, "Religiosity and Powerlessness," *The Humanist,* Vol. IIIVII, May-June 1977, p. 137.

pathies has been an important theme in Wordsworth, in Shelley, and in many twentieth-century writers. I am skeptical about this assumption. People can be extraordinarily sensitive to music and poetry and not necessarily apply this sensitivity to their daily lives. George Steiner . . . has reminded us that people returned from a day's work as guards in the concentration camps and then put Mozart on their gramophones . . . . the people who went to the Globe Theatre and saw Shakespeare's marvelous dramas, with their rich poetry and their human understanding, would at the same place in the same afternoon, watch a monkey tied to the back of a horse being chased by dogs who slowly bit it to death . . . . I think, too, that we must not delude ourselves into believing that words and university courses are a substitute for human hearts and human action.[1]

If neither the sciences nor the humanities can lead us to the truth, can we expect "education" to do it? As a matter of fact, modern education increasingly seems committed to the sad prospect that *real truth* does not even exist. Everything is relative and everything is changing. Students are encouraged to "inquire" and to "discover," but it is really only important that they become adjusted to the current consensus.

It was not always thus in American education. There was once a time when a search for truth could lead to truth!

The American nation had been founded by intellectuals who had accepted a world view that was based upon Biblical authority as well as Newtonian science. They had assumed that God created the earth and all life upon it at the time of creation and had continued without change thereafter. Adam and Eve were God's final crea-

---

[1] June Goodfield, "Humanity in Science," *Key Reporter,* Summer 1977, p. 3.

tions, and all of mankind had descended from them.[1]

This meant, of course, that there were absolutes to be discovered, in both science and Scripture, and that man's duty was to find and teach the truth in both. The very enterprise of science was, as Newton and other great scientists had expressed it, merely "thinking God's thoughts after Him."

All of that changed gradually, not only because of the capitulation to evolutionism, but also through the influence of the public-school advocate, Unitarian Horace Mann and, even more, of John Dewey. The latter was the most influential leader in the development of so-called "progressive education" in America and throughout the world. Dewey was an evolutionary pantheistic humanist, rejecting all absolutes and, especially, any belief in divinely ordained purposes in the world.

> In general the concept of education from kindergarten to graduate school was reoriented from the teaching of a fixed body of knowledge to the teaching of methods of inquiry to be applied to the continually changing facts of existence.[2]

Thus, human experience and opinion, expressed democratically through the state, became the ultimate arbiter of "truth."

Sad to say, human experience is even more fallible than the scientific method as a criterion of truth. Truth is not definable as merely a show of hands!

The *reductio ad absurdum* of the modern intellectual's frustrating search for truth was his descent into the cult of meaninglessness and the almost unbelievable trip into the never-never land of hallucination taken by sad multitudes of lost young people during the past two decades. The "liberal arts" ideal (the term means, ostensibly, the "liberating arts") of the academic world

[1] Gilbert M. Ostrander, *The Evolutionary Outlook, 1900-1975,* (Clio, Michigan, Marston Press, 1971), p. 1.
[2] *Ibid.,* p. 2.

had produced an imprisoning chaos that it neither intended nor anticipated.

Somehow it seemed not inappropriate that one of the
first great prophets of what came to be known as the drug
culture was the great literary figure Aldous Huxley, with
his *Brave New World,* grandson and brother, respectively, of Thomas Huxley and Julian Huxley, the chief prop-
agandists for evolution in the 19th and 20th centuries in
turn. In one of the most revealing testimonials ever written, his "Confession of a Professed Atheist," Aldous
Huxley discusses "liberation" as follows:

> I had motives for not wanting the world to have
> meaning; consequently assumed it had none, and
> was able without difficulty to find satisfying
> reasons for the assumption . . . . The philos-
> opher who finds no meaning in the world is not
> concerned exclusively with a problem in pure
> metaphysics, he is also concerned to prove there is
> no valid reason why he personally should not do
> as he wants to do . . . . For myself, as no doubt
> for most of my contemporaries, the philosophy of
> meaninglessness was essentially an instrument of
> liberation. The liberation we desired was simul-
> taneously liberation from a certain political and
> economic system and liberation from a certain
> system of morality. We objected to the morality
> because it interfered with our sexual freedom.[1]

This is certainly not the liberation that Christ had in
mind when He promised that the truth would make us
free. This, however, is the predictable outcome of the
open-ended "search for truth" advocated by academic
liberals in recent generations.

The problem is that this wonderful promise of the Lord
Jesus Christ is almost always taken out of context by
those educators who like to quote it. The preceding verse
(John 8:31) lays down the indispensable condition for

---

[1]Aldous Huxley, in "Confession of a Professed Atheist," *Report: Perspective on the News,* Vol. 3, June 1966, p. 19.

knowing the truth which truly sets one free. "If ye continué in my word, then are ye my disciples indeed." *Continue in my word!* This is the open secret in a successful search for truth. "I am the Truth" (John 14:6). "Thy word is truth" (John 17:7).

Neither the sciences nor the humanities have proven able to meet the real needs of mankind, though both have undoubtedly discerned many *elements* of truth. Neither the humanistic educator (in the tradition of John Dewey) nor the existentialist philosopher (*a la* Aldous Huxley) has found the truth. The one thinks that it is continually changing, the other that it doesn't exist at all. Today, the ideal of a wistful search for truth by a community of scholars operating in academic freedom has an air of unreality, to put it mildly, or futility, to put it bluntly.

Inescapably, the prophecy of the Apostle Paul comes to mind: "This know also, that in the last days perilous times shall come, for men shall be . . . ever learning, and never able to come to the knowledge of the truth" (II Timothy 3:1, 4). Despite our almost ubiquitous educational media and institutions, and a perpetual search for truth by teachers and researchers without number, the truth seems always retreating.

The same passage which contains this gloomy (but fulfilled) prophecy also gives the precise reason why such men and women cannot find the truth. They "resist the truth" (II Timothy 3:8), and "turn away their ears from the truth" (II Timothy 2:4).

As a matter of fact, real truth *does* exist, and it does *not* change. It can, indeed, be discovered and extolled and applied for the benefit of mankind. The search for truth is a legitimate and noble calling, with unending opportunities and challenges.

But it must be based on a sound premise. The world of reality is not the product of random evolutionary processes, but is the creation of God. Therefore, real truth is a part of God's creation and can be understood only in this light. Men are created in God's image and therefore must either think God's thoughts after him or else they will become "vain in their imaginations" (Romans 1:21).

GOD'S MANDATE AND EDUCATION

God actually has, in effect, commanded man to engage in a search for truth. Immediately after the completion of His creation, He gave to the first man and woman a stewardship over the creation. They were, under God, to "have dominion . . . over all the earth," and to "subdue the earth" (Genesis 1:26, 28).

This primeval commission has never been withdrawn and contains implicit authorization for all the following basic human enterprises:

(1) Discovery of truth (e.g., science, research, exploration)

(2) Application of truth (e.g., technology, agriculture, medicine)

(3) Implementation of truth (e.g., commerce, transportation, government)

(4) Interpretation of truth (e.g., fine arts, literature, theology)

(5) Transmission of truth (e.g., education, communication, homemaking)

In its primary role, education is concerned not with the discovery of truth, but with the transmission of truth already discovered. However, the entire range of legitimate human activities as outlined above—the discovery of truth, as well as its true interpretation and right methods for its application and implementation in human life—is properly incorporated in the educational process. But it should be stressed that true education is responsible under God for the transmission of truth—*not the transmission of untruth!* True education is *conservative,* conserving for other peoples and for future generations all that is good and true and winnowing out all that is false and harmful.

Too many "liberal educators, on the other hand, believe in propagating all concepts indiscriminately (all except those consistent with Scripture, that is—against these they practice systematic discrimination!). They argue that exposing their students to the whole spectrum of academic opinion will somehow "liberate" them and aid in their ongoing search for truth. The sad failure of such teaching seems more obvious with each generation.

In our Christian schools, of course, there is no justification for wasting valuable time and resources on anything but truth. It may be necessary, in some cases, to include enough instruction in the false philosophies of men (e.g., evolutionism) to arm students with the true facts refuting them and thereby enabling Christian students to "give an answer" (I Peter 3:15), but it is never necessary to leave students in doubt concerning truth and untruth or to have them repeat the errors of others in arriving at the truth. There is far too much truth awaiting discovery for such inertial wheel-spinning as that.

Lest anyone misunderstand or distort this principle, however, it should be stressed that such constraints in no way inhibit the Christian teacher or student from doing all the research and analysis and discovering all the knowledge of which he is capable. He has the whole scope of God's marvelous creation to explore, and the opportunities are boundless. Since *true* truth is infinite, he is not harmed by not having access to untruth. Eve already had knowledge of good and was happy and whole therein, but she became lost and sorrowful when she yielded to the desire for knowledge of good *and evil*. And how do we discern what is true and what is false? "To the law and to the testimony: if they speak not according to this word, it is because there is no light in them" (Isaiah 8:20). God's created world can never be at variance with His revealed Word.

The Christian scholar can use and should use the scientific method and all the relevant data of human thought and experience, but he also has the inestimable advantage of being able to evaluate all his analyses, methods, and results in terms of the principles revealed in God's infallible Word! He can look forward not only to a *lifetime,* but also an *eternity* of "ever learning and ever coming to the knowledge of more and more of God's infinite truth."

THE GLORY OF THE WORD

I will worship toward thy holy temple, and
praise thy name for thy lovingkindness and for
thy truth: for thou hast magnified thy word above
all thy name (Psalm 138:2).

It is impossible to place the Word of God on too high a
pedestal, or to rely too fully on its absolute authority.
Liberals may worry about bibliolatry and maintain that
we should worship God rather than the Scriptures, but
the fact is that God Himself is the One Who has invested
His Word with such uniquely high eminence. Furthermore, all we know about His Living Word (Jesus Christ-
—John 1:1,14) is found in His written Word (the Holy
Scriptures—John 5:39).

The writer has been studying the Scriptures daily and
diligently for forty years, and he is more convinced today
than ever before that every single word of the Bible is absolutely true and authoritative. The testimony of the
psalmist in Psalm 119:97 has become more real and experiential each year: "O how love I thy law! It is my
meditation all the day."

It is marvelous to appropriate the great array of figures
which the Bible writers apply to Scripture, and then to
realize that it will meet every need of our lives. Consider
the following examples:

(1) *Conviction:* "For the Word of God is quick and
powerful, and sharper than any two-edged sword,
. . . and is a discerner of the thoughts and intents
of the heart" (Hebrews 4:12).

(2) *Salvation:* "The holy Scriptures are able to make
thee wise unto salvation through faith which is in
Christ Jesus" (II Timothy 3:15).

(3) *Cleansing:* "Wherewithal shall a young man
cleanse his way? by taking heed thereto according
to thy word" (Psalm 119:9).

(4) *Truth:* "Sanctify them through thy truth: thy
word is truth" (John 17:17).

(5) *Righteousness:* "Thy word have I hid in mine

heart, that I might not sin against thee" (Psalm 119:11).

(6) *Zeal:* "But His word was in mine heart as a burning fire shut up in my bones, and I was weary with forbearing, and I could not stay" (Jeremiah 20:9).

(7) *Guidance:* "Thy word is a lamp unto my feet, and a light unto my path" (Psalm 119:105).

(8) *Instruction:* "The testimony of the Lord is sure, making wise the simple" (Psalm 19:7).

(9) *Delight:* "Thy testimonies also are my delight and my counsellors" (Psalm 119:24).

(10)*Purity:* "Every word of God is pure . . . . Add thou not unto His words, lest He reprove thee, and thou be found a liar" (Proverbs 30:5, 6).

(11)*Certainty:* "We have also a more sure word of prophecy: whereunto ye do well that ye take heed, as unto a light that shineth in a dark place" (II Peter 1:19).

(12)*Light:* "For the commandment is a lamp; and the law is light; and reproofs of instruction are the way of life" (Proverbs 6:25).

(13)*Restoration:* "The law of the Lord is perfect, converting [literally 'restoring'] the soul" (Psalm 19:7).

(14)*Joy:* "Thy words were found, and I did eat them; and thy word was unto me the joy and rejoicing of mine heart" (Jeremiah 15:16).

(15)*Peace:* "Great peace have they which love thy law, and nothing shall offend them" (Psalm 119:165).

(16)*Strength:* "Is not my word, like as a fire? saith the Lord; and like a hammer that breaketh the rock into pieces?" (Jeremiah 23:29).

(17)*Sweetness:* "How sweet are thy words unto my taste! yea, sweeter than honey to my mouth" (Psalm 119:103).

(18)*Blessing:* "But whoso looketh into the perfect law of liberty, and continueth therein, he being not a forgetful hearer, but a doer of the work this man shall be blessed in his deed" (James 1:25).

Such a list could be expanded greatly. In the Bible is an answer to every need, and its instructions are true and righteous altogether (Psalm 19:9). In true Christian education, therefore, all subjects and all courses must be founded on God's Word and developed within the constraining, correcting framework of the Holy Scriptures. "Therefore I esteem all thy precepts concerning all things to be right; and I hate every false way" (Psalm 119:128).

There is thus abundant reason to base our entire educational system on the Word of God. The Bible provides absolute truth on every subject with which it deals, principles and justification for discovering new truth about God's creation, and guidance and blessing in every area of life.

Chapter 9

The Christian and the Public School

Does the Bible have anything to say about public education? No, at least not in any direct way. As emphasized repeatedly in this book, the education of the younger generation is the responsibility of the home and church, not the government. There is no dichotomy between secular truth and spiritual truth, since *all truth* is the product of the creative and redemptive works of God, through Jesus Christ. Indoctrination in that truth is the primary function of education, in God's economy, and this requires a curriculum and faculty firmly committed to Biblical authority in all fields. Such a commitment as this could never be achieved by any system of public education, at least not in the present order of things.

The development of sound Christian schools, at all levels and in all fields, is thus urgently important for true education, especially in a world dominated by evolutionism and humanism. Every Christian should support the cause of true Christian education in every way feasible, as this is essential for the future of true Christianity and even for the future of a nation such as ours. Our

country was, after all, founded on Biblical principles and
it possesses a great Christian heritage. These are all being
rapidly undermined by the present humanistic school
system.

NEEDS OF THE PUBLIC SCHOOLS

But this in no way means that Christians should aban-
don and ignore the public schools and colleges of our
country. If nothing else, these institutions constitute a
great mission field, probably the most strategically important mission field in the world. The public schools and
secular colleges of our nation have an enrollment of
millions of young people, and from these will come most
of the nation's future leaders. These young men and
women thus largely control the future of the one nation
which may well be the last great hope of liberty and truth
in the entire world, and they are all now being
systematically brainwashed in evolutionary humanism.
There is urgent, desperate need to reach the students in
these schools with the fact that there *is* a real alter..ative
to this godless philosophy before they become irrevocably
committed to it.

Furthermore, there are still many genuinely Christian
administrators and teachers in the public schools, not to
mention the millions of Christian students and Christian
families who are involved in them. Whether by choice or
circumstance, these Christian people are not yet in Christian schools, and it is especially important that they also,
at least to some degree, be reached, and their testimony
and abilities be used, in the vital cause of true education.

There are many Christian parents who really have no
choice except to send their children to public schools,
since their communities have no Christian schools. Many
do not even have a sound church or any other base on
which such a Christian school could be built. It may be
possible in some instances to opt for private home education, but this is only feasible in the lower grades at best.
In the high school—and especially at the college level
—the special courses required or desired for training in

certain fields (e.g., engineering, computer science, nursing) are scarcely available anywhere in a Christian school context. Yet these are all very important, and people with these specialties are needed to fulfill God's dominion mandate, so they also need to be oriented properly in Biblical education principles. Although the ideal situation would surely be for all Christians to be trained at all levels in all fields in Christian schools, this is not an ideal which can be attained in the near future. And even if it could, there are still the millions of non-Christian young people that need to be reached and wcn. The Christian, therefore, simply must not ignore the public schools and colleges of our country.

CHRISTIAN EDUCATION IN A PUBLIC SCHOOL

Can a Christian young person receive a sound Christian education in a public school and/or a secular university? This may, in many cases, be his only choice. It may even, in some cases, be the *best* choice even if there *is* a Christian school available, since many Christian schools are of poor quality and many others compromise with evolutionary humanism to various degrees. It may, for example, be safer spiritually to go to a secular university where there is a strong Christian student organization and a good campus church than to a prestigious-but-neo-evangelical-Christian college. Each situation needs to be studied carefully and prayerfully on its own merits. Acquiring a true Christian education in a government-school context is certainly not the ideal way, nor the easy way, but it *can* be done. With more concern and effort by the Christian community, much more could be accomplished, even in the public schools.

The writer himself received all his education and three-fourths of his teaching experience in secular schools. Of our own six children, our youngest daughter was able to take just her last two years at a Christian high school, but all the others spent their pre-college years exclusively in public schools. Nevertheless, all six of them are active, witnessing Christians, believing strongly in special creation, Biblical inerrancy, and in all the Biblical principles expounded in this book. Needless to say, in each case a great deal of home Bible instruction and parental prayer was involved, both before and after high school graduation. Also, five of them did get to go to Christian colleges—two to Christian Heritage, two to Bob Jones, one to Columbia Bible. In any case, our own experience demonstrates that it is certainly possible to acquire firm Christian convictions and a fully Biblical/creationist world view even in spite of attending humanistic public schools.

Furthermore, the number of genuinely Christian teachers, administrators, and school board members in the public schools today is probably greater than it has been in the last fifty years. The same applies to the number of Christian professors in secular colleges and universities. The creationist revival of the past two decades, as well as the various campus evangelistic movements and the faculty Christian fellowship groups have all contributed to this encouraging trend. When the writer was a young instructor forty years ago on a secular college faculty, it was all but impossible to find colleagues of similar Biblical, creationist convictions anywhere else in the university world, but now there are many hundreds, at least. One can now find at least some solid, unashamed creationists on just about every faculty, and the number is increasing.

This body of dedicated men and women constitutes a tremendous spiritual resource in our public schools and secular universities. They often face significant opposition, sometimes even academic persecution, by their colleagues, but they are *there!* We need to help and encourage them in every way we can, for their ministry to their own students can often make all the difference in the world to these young people. The Christian students in these schools also need and deserve support, both to conserve *them* for the cause of Christ and to assist them in winning their friends. The same is true for their parents. The problem is, just *what* to do. The public schools obviously cannot be transformed into Christian schools. In the current unfortunate politico/legal/judicial environment, even prayer and Bible reading are banned from the schools, not to mention the teaching of a Biblical/Christian world view in every discipline, such as *true* education would entail. Probably the best we can work and hope for at the present time is that the schools should not be anti-God, anti-Christian, and anti-moral, as too many have already become. A minority of taxpayers are, indeed, anti-God, anti-Christian, and anti-moral, and these people *do* have certain rights in a free society. On the other hand, Bible-believing, practicing Christians also have rights, as do people of other religions and social views, and the public schools should at least be fair and impartial on such matters.

THE TWO-MODEL APPROACH

For well over a decade now, the Institute for Creation Research and other creationist organizations have been advocating a "two-model approach" to the study of origins in public schools. That is, both evolution and creation should be taught as alternatives whenever any topic related to origins is discussed, with the arguments and evidences for each model given as nearly objectively as possible. Similarly, a two-model approach should be followed for all other topics involved in the conflicting values of theism and humanism.

The most fundamental of all questions is that of origins, whether by natural processes or supernatural. Theistic creationism or evolutionary humanism is the great watershed issue which, for the most part, determines what one believes about other key issues of life and meaning. Consequently, it is vital that students somehow learn that there is a real alternative to evolution.

In public schools, however, the creation model must be developed solely on a scientific basis, without using the Bible or theological arguments. Not only is this necessary because of political and legal considerations, but it is also desirable because most public school teachers are neither willing nor able to teach Biblical creationism. As a matter of fact, it is perfectly feasible to teach creation from scientific data only, since all real scientific data support creation better than evolution anyhow. The problem, of course, is convincing school personnel that this can, and should, be done.

The standard objection to the two-model approach, of course, is that evolution is a valid scientific theory while creation is only a religious belief. Even though evolution might be false and creation might be true, they will contend the principle of church-and-state separation requires that only evolution should be incorporated in classroom instruction. This attitude is patently unfair and self-serving, but it is found almost everywhere in the academic world. Furthermore, it has been supported and encouraged by various court decisions, as well as the rejection of proposed two-model ordinances and laws by practically all the school boards and legislatures that have considered them. The writer has contended for over twenty years that creationism can never be mandated in the schools, even on a two-model basis, by any kind of political or judicial process, and that attempts to accomplish this by well-meaning Christians will inevitably be counter-productive. Since it is contrary to Scripture for the government to be involved in education anyhow, it is anachronistic for Christians to seek to use the power of the state to compel government schools to teach Christian doctrine. Even though creationism can certainly be taught strictly from scientific data, with no reference to the Bible, the fact still remains that creation *is* a Christian doctrine. In fact, it is the most foundational and important Christian doctrine of all, since all other doctrines are based on it.

The public schools and state universities on the other hand, are and will continue to be under the dominance of a pervasive humanistic philosophy. It could not be otherwise, since their very existence is based on a humanistic premise.[1] This being the case, it is not only impossible, but wrong, to try to *force* them to teach theism.

However, even though Christians should not try to get creationist instruction *mandated* in the public schools, they should certainly do all they can to *encourage* and *assist* it. In the long run, informed persuasion will accomplish more than coercion. By using every available opportunity (and also by making opportunities) to demonstrate to teachers, school administrators, and others that the two-model approach is better than the present system of humanistic indoctrination, concerned creationists can make a tremendous contribution to the cause of true education, even in the public schools.

First of all, Christians should become well informed on the subject themselves, especially teachers, pastors, parents, and all who are really concerned about education and the future of the young people of our nation. One does not have to be a scientist to understand the essential scientific arguments in favor of theistic creationism, nor does he have to be a lawyer to understand the key legal arguments in favor of the two-model approach, nor even an educator to understand the pedogogical advantages of such an approach. There are books and other materials available, written for the nonspecialist, which will adequately inform anyone willing to take the time to read them.

Furthermore, these and other such materials can be loaned or donated to school libraries, teachers, and other key recipients, with a tactful, gracious request that they be considered and used with an open mind. This may cost money, but few investments could ever be more worthwhile.

As far as the educational advantages of a two-model approach are concerned, for example, one can refer to

[1]The unitarian, socialistic, anti-Christian atheistic background of the development and triumph of the American state school systems, during the first half of the nineteenth century, has been thoroughly demonstrated and documented by Samuel L. Blumenfeld in his fascinating volume *Is Public Education Necessary?* (Old Greenwich, CT, Devin-Adair Co., 1981) 263 pp.

the doctoral thesis[1] of **Richard Bliss, who demonstrated conclusively that students learn and retain more in their science studies under this approach than under the evolution-only approach. Dr. Bliss even showed that these students learned more about evolution itself by the challenge of comparing it with creation as a scientific model of origins.**

The constitutional and legal justification for teaching scientific creation in public schools along with evolution has been compellingly presented by attorney Wendell Bird. [2] Actually, there has never been any genuine legal impediment to a real two-model approach, with both models treated scientifically and objectively. The problem has been only one of education, persuasion, and implementation, not constitutionality

The most controversial question, of course, is whether creation is a valid scientific model. Evolutionists commonly maintain that creation is religious and evolution is scientific. The fact is, however, that creationism can be developed in a purely scientific context, without reference to the Bible or to anything other than actual scientific data. A good part of the work of the Institute for Creation Research, in fact, is to develop and disseminate scientific evidences supporting creation. Some of these evidences have been briefly outlined in Chapter 2, and more detailed expositions are available in various ICR publications.[3] Although Biblical creationism and scien-

---

[1]Richard B. Bliss, *A Comparison of Two Approaches to the Teaching of Origins of Living Things to High School Biology Students in Racine, Wisconsin,* Dissertation ERIC No. ED. 152568, 1978. The results of this dissertation have been summarized in ICR Impact Article 60, "A Comparison of Students Studying the Origin of Life from a Two-Model Approach vs. Those Studying from a Single-Model Approach," June 1978. Available on request from ICR, P.O. Box 2666, El Cajon, California, 92021.

[2]Wendell R. Bird. "Freedom of Religion and Science Instruction in Public Schools," *Yale Law Journal* (Vol. 87, January 1978, pp. 515-570). Reprints can be purchased through Creation-Life Publishers, Box 15666, San Diego, California 92115.

[3]See, for example, *What is Creation Science?* by Henry M. Morris and Gary E. Parker (San Diego, Creation-Life Publishers, 1982, 306 pp.). A complete listing of all ICR creationist publications is available on request.

tific creationism are fully compatible, each one can be taught independently of the other. In general, Biblical creationism should be taught in churches, scientific creationism in public schools, and both in Christian schools.

Although creation can be taught strictly on a scientific basis, it remains true that it can never be proved scientifically. In the final analysis, it must be appropriated by faith, but that faith is a *reasonable* faith, based on sound factual evidence. Evolution, on the other hand, is also based on faith, but evolutionary faith is unreasonable, exercised in spite of all the scientific and other evidences against it.

THE RELIGIOUS ESSENCE OF EVOLUTIONISM

In resisting the establishment of a two-model approach, evolutionists often allege that evolution is a proven fact of science, providing the very framework of scientific interpretation, especially in the biological sciences. This, of course, is nothing but wishful thinking. Evolution is not even a scientific hypothesis, since there is no conceivable way in which it can be tested.

As a matter of fact, many leading evolutionists have recognized the essentially "religious" character of evolutionism. Even though they themselves believe evolution to be true, they acknowledge the fact that they *believe* it! "Science," however, is not supposed to be something one "believes." Science is knowledge—that which can be demonstrated and observed and repeated. Evolution cannot be proved, or even tested; it can only be believed.

For example, two leading evolutionary biologists have described modern neo-Darwinism as "part of an evolutionary dogma accepted by most of us as part of our training."[1] A prominent British biologist, a Fellow of the Royal Society, in the Introduction to the 1971 edition of Darwin's *Origin of Species,* said that "belief in the theory of evolution" was "exactly parallel to belief in special creation," with evolution merely "as satisfactory faith on

---

[1] Paul Ehrlich and L. C. Birch, *Nature,* April 22, 1967, p. 352.

which to base our interpretation of nature."[1] G. W. Harper calls it a "metaphysical belief."[2]

Ernst Mayr, the outstanding Harvard evolutionary biologist, calls evolution "man's world view today."[3] Sir Julian Huxley, probably the outstanding evolutionist of the twentieth century, saw "evolution as a universal and all-pervading process"[4] and, in fact, nothing less than "the whole of reality."[5] A leading evolutionist at the time of his death in 1975, says that Dobzhansky's view of evolution followed that of the notorious Jesuit priest, de Chardin.

The place of biological evolution in human thought was, according to Dobzhansky, best expressed in a passage that he often quoted from Pierre Teilhard de Chardin: "[Evolution] is a general postulate to which all theories, all hypotheses, all systems must henceforward bow and which they must satisfy in order to be thinkable and true. Evolution is a light which illuminates all facts, a trajectory which all lines of thought must follow."[6]

The British physicist, H. S. Lipson, has reached the following conclusion.

In fact, evolution became in a sense a scientific religion; almost all scientists have accepted it and many are prepared to "bend" their observations to fit in with it.[7]

The man whom Dobzhansky called "France's leading zoologist," although himself an evolutionist, said that

---

[1]L. Harrison Matthews, "Introduction" to *Origin of Species* (London, J. M. Dent and Sons, 1971), p. X.

[2]G. W. Harper, "Alternatives to Evolutionism," *School Science* Review (V. 51, Sept. 1979), p. 16.

[3]Ernst Mayr, "Evolution," *Scientific American* (V. 239, Sept. 1978), p. 16.

[4]Julian Huxley, "Evolution and Genetics," Ch. 8 in *What is Science?* (Ed. J. R. Newman, New York, Simon and Schuster, 1955), p. 272.

[5]*Ibid.,* p. 278.

[6]Francisco Ayala, "Nothing in Biology Makes Sense Except in the Light of Evolution: Theodosius Dobzhansky, 1900-1975," *Journal of Heredity,* (V. 68, No. 3, 1977), p. 3.

[7]H. S. Lipson, "A Physicist Looks at Evolution," *Physics Bulletin* (V. 31, n.d. 1980).

scientists should "destroy the myth of evolution" as a simple phenomenon which is "unfolding before us."[1] Dr. Colin Patterson, Senior Paleontologist at the British Museum of Natural History, by any accounting one of the world's top evolutionists today, has recently called evolution "positively anti-knowledge," saying that "all my life I had been duped into taking evolutionism as revealed truth."[2] In another address he called evolution "story telling."[3]

All of the above-cited authorities are (or were) among the world's foremost authorities on evolutionism. Note again the terms which they use in describing evolution.

Evolutionary dogma	A scientific religion
A satisfactory faith	The myth of evolution
Man's world view	Anti-knowledge
All-pervading process	Revealed truth
The whole of reality	An illuminating light
Metaphysical belief	Story-telling

Charles Darwin himself called evolution "this grand view of life." Now such grandiloquent terms as these are not scientific terms! One does not call the law of gravity, for example, "a satisfactory faith," nor speak of the laws of thermodynamics as "dogma." Evolution is, indeed, a grand world view, but it is *not* science. Its very comprehensiveness makes it impossible even to test scientifically. As Ehrlich and Birch have said: "Every conceivable observation can be fitted into it . . . . No one can think of ways in which to test it."[4]

In view of the fundamentally religious nature of evolution, it is not surprising to find that most world religions

---

[1] Pierre P. Grasse, *Evolution of Living Organisms* (New York, Academic Press, 1977), p. 8.

[2] Colin Patterson, "Evolution and Creationism," Transcript of Speech at American Museum of Natural History, Nov. 5, 1981, p. 2.

[3] Colin Patterson, "Cladistics," Interview on BBC Telecast, Peter Franz, Interviewer, Mar. 4, 1982.

[4] Ehrlich and Birch, *op cit.*

are themselves based on evolution. It is certainly unfitting for educators to object to teaching scientific creationism in public schools on the ground that it supports Biblical Christianity when the existing pervasive teaching of evolution is supporting a host of other religions and philosophies.

The concept of evolution did not originate with Charles Darwin. It has been the essential ingredient of all pagan religions and philosophies from time immemorial (e.g., atomism, pantheism, stoicism, gnosticism, and all other humanistic and polytheistic systems). All beliefs which assume the ultimacy of the space/time/matter universe, presupposing that the universe has existed from eternity, are fundamentally evolutionary systems. The cosmos, with its innate laws and forces, is the only ultimate reality. Depending on the sophistication of the system, the forces of the universe may be personified as gods and goddesses who organized the eternal chaotic cosmos into its present form (as in ancient Babylonian and Egyptian religions), or else may themselves be invested with organizing capabilities (as in modern scientific evolutionism). In all such cases, these are merely different varieties of the fundamental evolutionist world view, the essential feature of which is the denial that there is one true God and Creator of all things.

In this perspective, it becomes obvious that most of the great world religions—Buddhism, Confucianism, Taoism, Hinduism, Animism, etc.—are based on evolution. Creationism is the basis of only such systems as Orthodox Judaism, Islam, and Biblical Christianity. The liberal varieties of Judaism, Islam, Catholicism, and Protestantism, as well as most modern pseudo-Christian cults, are all based on evolution.

All of this points up the absurdity of banning creationist teaching from the schools on the basis that it is religious. The schools are already saturated with the teaching of religion in the guise of evolutionary "science." In the modern school, of course, this teaching mostly takes the form of secular humanism, which its own proponents claim to be a "nontheistic religion." It should also be recalled that such philosophies as communism, fascism, socialism, nazism, and anarchism have been claimed by their founders and promoters to be based on what they regarded as scientific evolutionism. If creation is excluded from the schools because it is compatible with Christian "fundamentalism," should not evolution also be banned since it is the basis of communism and nazism?

THE SCIENTIFIC IRRELEVANCE OF EVOLUTION

Some people have deplored the questioning of evolution on the ground that this is attacking science itself. In a recent debate, the evolutionist whom the writer debated did not attempt to give any scientific evidences for evolution, electing instead to spend his time defending such scientific concepts as atomic theory, relativity, gravity, quantum theory, and science in general, stating that attacking evolution was tantamount to attacking science!

The fact is, however, that the elimination of evolutionary interpretations from science would hardly be noticed at all, in terms of real scientific understanding and accomplishment. G. W. Harper comments on this subject as follows:

> It is frequently claimed that Darwinism is central to modern biology. On the contrary, if all references to Darwinism suddenly disappeared, biology would remain substantially unchanged. It would merely have lost a little color. Grandiose doctrines in science are like some occupants of high office; they sound very important but have in fact been promoted to a position of ineffectuality.[1]

The scientific irrelevance of evolutionism has been strikingly (but, no doubt, inadvertently) illustrated in a recent issue of *Science News*. This widely read and highly regarded weekly scientific journal was commemorating its sixtieth anniversary, and this included a listing of what

---

[1] G. W. Harper, *op cit.*, p. 26.

it called the "scientific highlights" of the past sixty years.[1]

Of the sixty important scientific discoveries and accomplishments which were chosen, only six could be regarded as related in any way to evolutionist thought. These six were as follows:

1. 1927. Discovery that radiation increases mutation rates in fruit flies.
2. 1943. Demonstration that nucleic acids carry genetic information.
3. 1948. Enunciation of the "big bang" cosmology.
4. 1953. Discovery of the "double helix" structure of DNA.
5. 1961. First step taken in cracking the genetic code.
6. 1973. Development of procedures for producing recombinant DNA molecules.

Four of these six "highlights" are related to the structure and function of DNA. Even though evolutionists have supposed that these concepts somehow correlate with evolution, the fact is that the remarkable DNA molecule provides strong evidence of original creation (since it is far too complex to have arisen by chance) and of conservation of that creation (since the genetic code acts to guarantee reproduction of the same kind, not evolution of new kinds). One of the two other highlights showed how to increase mutations, but—since all known true mutations are harmful—this contributed nothing whatever to the understanding of evolution. One (the "big bang" concept) was indeed an evolutionary idea, but it is still an idea which has never been proved and today is increasingly being recognized as incompatible with basic physical laws.

Consequently, it is fair to conclude that no truly significant accomplishment of modern science either depends on evolution or supports evolution! There would

---

[1]"Six Decades of Science Highlights," *Science News* (V. 121, March 13, 1982), p. 192.

certainly be no detriment to real scientific learning if creation were incorporated as an alternative to evolution in school curricula. It would, on the other hand, prove a detriment to the pervasive religion of atheistic humanism which now controls our schools.

The two-model approach would enable evolution and creation to be compared scientifically in science courses, but they could also be compared philosophically in a philosophy course. In social science courses, they could be contrasted in terms of their respective sociological, psychological, economic, or political implications. Very effective comparisons could be developed between the two in courses on comparative religion. In fact, going beyond the foundational issue of origins, the two-model approach can be applied incisively to a broad range of issues and problems, in terms of the implications and applications suggested by humanism and theism respectively, the one on the foundation of evolution, the other on the basis of creation, all without reference to the Bible or other religious literature. As long as this is done objectively, rather than dogmatically (on either side), there should be no legitimate objection. Education would be made more effective and stimulating and students would be encouraged and enabled to make an intelligent decision as to which of the two great world views they want to follow.

The key to getting such a two-model approach recognized and implemented is to continue to emphasize, insistently and intelligently, that both evolution and creation (or humanism and theism) are of full equivalence as alternate world views. Creationism is fully as scientific as evolutionism, and evolution at least as "religious" as creation. Furthermore, these are the *only* two world views. Either all things *can* be explained in terms of naturalistic processes in a closed, self-contained universe, or they *cannot*—one or the other! The first is evolutionism, the second is creationism, and both can and should be taught objectively in all tax-supported public institutions.

ANTI-CREATIONIST POLEMICS

Despite the distinct advantages and obvious fairness and reasonableness of the two-model approach, any suggestion that it be adopted in a given school system will probably be resisted with great emotion and intensity, especially by the doctrinaire evolutionists and humanists in the community. Although most people in the community will favor this approach (national polls have shown over 85% on the average), there are always some (including many on the school or college faculty) who are not merely evolutionists, but are anti-creationists, dedicated at all costs to discrediting the creation movement. Unfortunately, such attempts often include a very careless handling of facts, and they need to be corrected before we go further.

A number of these false charges, with brief answers to them are listed below.

1. CHARGE: "The anti-evolutionists have been successful, [William G. Mayer] explains, because they now use a Madison Avenue approach and employ a full-time staff while there is not one scientist who is funded to devote full-time to espousing evolutionary theory." (*Science News,* Jan. 10, 1981, p. 19.)

FACT: There is to our knowledge no one who devotes full time to espousing creationism. The ICR, for example, has a staff of 12 part-time scientists, each of whom has many other duties besides speaking on creation. On the other hand, large numbers of scientists on university faculties spend far more time on evolutionist research and teaching than anything creationists can afford. Creationism is anything but "well-funded" as Mayer charges, having no access to government funding as Dr. Mayer did, when his B.S.C.S. organization expended almost $20,000,000 of federal funds in developing its evolution-based biology textbook series.

2. CHARGE: "The creationist model does not have the same kind of scientific validity as the theory of evolution. This is not to say that it cannot be a true account of

the origin of life. It could be." (*Today's Education,* Apr.-May 1981, p. 58G.)

FACT: The evolutionist's definition of "scientific" is "mechanistic" or "naturalistic," but this is misleading. *Science* means *knowledge,* and the essence of the scientific method is observation and repeatability. Evolution is not "scientific" since macroevolution is neither observable nor repeatable. Evolutionists admit creation may be "true," so it is appropriate—indeed essential—to include it in the educational process if teachers sincerely desire their students to search for truth, as they claim.

3. CHARGE: " . . . creationists tend to be masters of the partial quote." (*Next,* Mar.-Apr. 1981, p. 68.)

FACT: The author cited two alleged out-of-context quotations by creationists, one by Dr. Gary Parker supposedly intimating that Dr. Stephen Gould was "championing creationism," the other by this writer supposedly claiming that two evolutionary geologists had agreed that the strata of the great Lewis "overthrust" were all flat and undisturbed. The fact is that we are always careful not to quote out of context. Such quotations have to be brief, for reasons of space, and so cannot give the full scope of the author's thoughts on the subject, but they do not misrepresent their nature and significance. Out of the many thousands of such references that are included in our writings, critics have to search diligently to find even a handful that they can interpret as misleading. Even in the two that were cited, a careful reading of the *full* context in each case will demonstrate that the reporter was himself guilty of distortion. Dr. Parker made it quite clear that Dr. Gould is a committed evolutionist (in spite of his arguments against certain Darwinian tenets). In the Lewis overthrust discussion, there was ample mention of the physical evidences of disturbances, and the quote (actually appearing only in a minor footnote) certainly did not affect the evidence developed in the particular section against the "overthrust" explanation. In no way did it misrepresent the beliefs of the authors quoted.

4. CHARGE: "[Creationists] have shown a certain

genius for couching their arguments in scientific terms
. . . But their viewpoint remains dogmatically fundamen-
talist and profoundly anti-scientific." (*The Sciences,*
Apr. 1981, p. 18.)

FACT: Whether or not the scientific creation model is
compatible with the Biblical record is irrelevant to the
question of whether the actual scientific data fit the
model. Most creationist scientists do believe that the
tenets of Biblical creationism are compatible with the
tenets of scientific creationism, but it is only the latter
that we believe should be taught in public schools. The
fact that the scientific model of creation can be used to
support Christian theism is parallel to the fact that the
scientific model of evolution can be used to support
Marxist atheism or Religious Humanism or Theological
Liberalism. All this is irrelevant to the fact that creation
and evolution can both be discussed and compared simply as scientific models.

5. CHARGE: "If the world view of fundamental
Christians is presented as science, why not that of the
Hindus or the Buddhists?" (*American School Board
Journal,* Mar. 1980, p. 32.)

FACT: There are only *two* world views, evolution and
creation. Each of these has many variants. Hinduism and
Buddhism are variants of the typical evolutionary world
view, beginning as they do with an eternally self-existing
universe (the same is true of Confucianism, Taoism, and
all the other ancient pagan pantheistic religions). Creationists do not want the Biblical record of creationism
taught in the public schools, but only the general creation
model as a viable scientific alternative to the general
evolution model.

6. CHARGE: "The creationist movement boasts a
number of adherents who have been trained in science.
Significantly, few are biologists. Creationists have done
almost no original research." (*Time,* Mar. 16, 1981, p.
81.)

FACT: There are thousands of well-qualified creationist scientists today, a large percentage of whom are in

the life sciences. Over half of the present and past members of the Board of Directors of the Creation Research Society, for example, are in biological fields. In addition, of the 34 scientists associated directly with ICR (including the 12 staff members, plus trustees, advisory board members, and regional representatives), 17 are in the life sciences. At least 15 scientists in these two groups have regular Ph.D.'s in Biology from leading universities, and the others all have terminal degrees in closely related fields (biochemistry, medicine, etc.). As far as research is concerned, the ICR staff may be typical. These 12 scientists (H. Morris, Gish, Bliss, BArnes, Slusher, Parker, Cumming, J. Morris, Austin, Vardiman, McQueen, and Rybka) have published at least 150 research papers and ten books in their own scientific fields—all in standard scientific refereed journals or through secular book publishers—in addition to hundreds of creationist articles and perhaps 50 books in creationism and related fields.

7. CHARGE: "The basic premise, the basic dogma, is the existence of a divine creator. What they espouse as academic freedom to teach creationism is the academic freedom to teach the flatness of the earth." (*Discover,* Oct. 1980, p. 94.)

FACT: No creationist scientist teaches a flat earth nor, for that matter, is such a notion taught in the Bible. The "dogma" of the existence of a divine creator is not one bit more "dogmatic" than the evolutionist's assumption of "no creation" and of the preexistence of matter as the source of this marvelous universe and its infinite array of complex systems.

8. CHARGE: "ICR is apparently well-funded. This money is used to advance their cause through lobbying and publication. They lobby at all levels of government, and have attempted to introduce a bill in the U.S. Congress to obtain money, time, and space equal to that awarded to concepts involving evolution." (*Geotimes,* Jan. 1981, p. 12.)

FACT: Although it is the largest and most influential creationist organization, the ICR is certainly not well-

funded. Its annual budget is less than that of many
university departments of biology, for example. ICR
never has initiated or lobbied for any creation lawsuit or
legislation, believing that education and persuasion are
more appropriate and effective than compulsion. ICR
staff members occasionally serve as expert consultants or
witnesses in such situations, but these actions are wholly
initiated and financed by local groups of concerned
citizens.

9. CHARGE: "The Institute stood to make $2 million
a year in textbook sales, with a contract renewal option,
if HB 690 were enacted. To achieve its ends, it distributes
a kit to creationist lobbies with a sample resolution
drafted by 'Dr.' Henry Morris, who cautions users not to
reveal its source." (*The Humanist,* May/June 1980, p.
59.)

FACT: The above statement was in reference to the
creation bill currently stymied in the Georgia legislature
due to such distortions as this. ICR's sample *resolution*
(not "creation bill") was prepared in response to many
requests from local groups, in order to help keep such actions focused on science and education rather than
religion and social issues. The suggestion that those who
might adapt the resolution for their own uses should try
to keep ICR out of the picture was simply to emphasize
that it was the local group of citizens, not ICR, who were
the sponsors. As far as profits from potential book sales
are concerned, this may well be the reason behind much
of the opposition to bringing creationist literature into
the schools. Evolutionist writers and publishers have for
many years reaped tremendous profits from their
monopolistic control over school-adopted book sales.
Such publishers, in the past, have refused even to examine creationist (or two-model) textbook manuscripts.
Accordingly, some of us had to pool our own very limited
resources in order to get ICR books published. Rather
than being profitable, however, this operation has been at
a significant loss to all its investors, each of the seven
years it has been in existence. If, perchance, school

boards actually should begin to specify a two-model approach in their schools and begin to look for appropriate textbooks, one can be certain that the big publishers would finally begin to publish such books themselves. We would have no objection to this, of course; they have the resources to do it, and, if they treat the subject properly, we will cooperate in every way we can to help them.

There have been many other such charges against not only ICR but creationists and Bible-believing Christians in general. Space does not permit answering all of them here, but all are unjustified.

The *scientific* arguments against creationism are also quite trivial and unwarranted. A typical critique was that of Isaac Asimov, which appeared in hundreds of newspapers in late 1981 and had a wide influence.

The reason for its impact was certainly not its contents, which featured the usual evolutionary distortions and pseudologic. However, the author was Dr. Isaac Asimov, the most prolific and widely read science writer of our generation, and this fact assured a wide audience for his opinions. He is the author of over 230 books on all kinds of scientific subjects, including even a few books on the Bible, and many people consider him an authority on anything about which he chooses to write.

Asimov does, indeed have impressive academic credentials and is a brilliant writer. It is, however, impossible for any scientist to be a real "authority" on anything outside his own limited field of special study and research (which, in Isaac Asimov's case, consists of certain aspects of enzyme chemistry), so that he owes his reputation more to his exceptional ability in the techniques of exposition than to his accomplishments in scientific research.

Furthermore, Dr. Asimov has his own religious axe to grind. He was one of the signers of the infamous *Humanist Manifesto II,* promulgated by the American Humanist Association in 1973. Among other statements, this Manifesto includes the following anti-theistic affirmations:

As in 1933, humanists still believe that traditional theism, especially faith in the prayer-hearing God, assumed to love and care for persons, to hear and understand their prayers, and to be able to do something about them, is an unproved and outmoded faith.

As nontheists, we begin with humans not God, nature not deity.

No deity will save us; we must save ourselves.

Asimov and other humanists decry the teaching of creationism as "religious" while, at the same time, their Manifesto proclaims their own set of beliefs to be "a living and growing faith."

The quasi-scientific basis of their humanistic faith, of course, is evolution. *Humanist Manifesto I* (published first in 1933) made this clear. Its first four tenets were as follows:

First: Religious humanists regard the universe as self-existing and not created.

Second: Humanism believes that man is a part of nature and that he has emerged as the result of a continuous process.

Third: Holding an organic view of life, humanists find that the traditional dualism of mind and body must be rejected.

Fourth: Humanism recognizes that man's religious culture and civilization, as clearly depicted by anthropology and history, are the product of a gradual development due to his interaction with his natural environment . . . .

It is significant that Asimov, in his anti-creationist harangue, did not attempt to offer even one slight scientific evidence for evolution. Nevertheless he proclaims: "To those who are trained in science, creationism seems like a bad dream, a sudden reliving of a nightmare, a renewed march of an army of the night risen to challenge free thought and enlightenment." Asimov, as a prize-winning writer of science fiction, is a master at the use of emotional rhetoric to intimidate and frighten, and this essay is a skillful masterpiece of alarmist propaganda. He warns about those previous "societies in which the armies of the night have ridden triumphantly over minorities in order to establish a powerful orthodoxy which dictates official thought." He concludes with an Asimovian prophecy: "With creationism in the saddle, American science will wither . . . . We will inevitably recede into the backwater of civilization . . . . " The "prophet" Isaac never mentions the fact that most of the great founding fathers of modern science (e.g., Newton, Pascal, Kelvin, Faraday, Galileo, Kepler, etc.) were theistic creationists, nor that thousands of fully qualified scientists today have repudiated the evolutionary indoctrination of their school days in favor of the much stronger scientific evidences for creation.

Although Asimov gives no arguments or evidences for evolution, he does attempt to identify and refute what he thinks are the seven most important arguments for creation. These he denotes as follows:

1. *The Argument from Analogy.* Since no one would question that the existence of a watch implies an intelligent watchmaker, by analogy the much more intricate and complex universe implies an intelligent universe-maker. Asimov makes no attempt to answer this unanswerable argument, except to say that "to surrender to ignorance and call it God has always been premature." Such an answer is foolishness. The principles of mathematical probability and scientific causality certainly do not constitute a "surrender to ignorance," but provide a compelling demonstration that complex systems do not originate out of chaotic systems by random processes.

2. *The Argument from General Consent.* By this term, Asimov means the widespread belief among all peoples that the world must have been brought into its present form by some god or gods. Asimov maintains that the "Hebrew myths" of creation are no more credible than all these other beliefs and that "such general consent proves nothing." Actually this so-called "argument from general consent" is rarely, if ever, used by creationists. However, it is almost always used by evolutionists to

prove evolution! That is, since they can cite no *scientific* evidences for evolution, they use the argument that "all scientists believe evolution" as the main proof of evolution.

3. *The Argument from Belittlement.* Here Asimov incorrectly accuses creationists of failing to understand scientific terminology and of belittling evolution as "only a scientific theory." As a matter of fact, creationists maintain that real "vertical" evolution is not even a scientific theory, since it is not testable. There is no scientific experiment which, even in imagination, could suffice either to confirm or to falsify either macroevolution or creation. The proper term to use is not "scientific theory" or even "scientific hypothesis," but "scientific model" or "paradigm," or some such title. The creation model can be used far more effectively than the evolution model in predicting and correlating scientific data (the laws of thermodynamics, the character of the fossil record, etc.).

4. *The Argument from Imperfection.* Creationists are often accused of mistaking disagreements among evolutionists as evidence that evolution itself is false. Actually, all creationists are well aware of this distinction, but it does seem odd, if evolution is a sure fact of science, that it is so difficult to describe how it works! How does it happen that, if evolution is such a common process in nature, its mechanices remain so obscure? Yet, as Asimov says: "However much scientists argue their differing beliefs in details of evolutionary theory, or in the interpretation of the necessarily imperfect fossil record, they firmly accept the evolutionary process itself." Evolutionists walk by faith, not by sight!

5. *The Argument from Distorted Science.* One of the main creationist arguments against evolution is its apparent conflict with the second law of thermodynamics, but Asimov says this argument is "distorted science," since it ignores the fact that the earth is an open system. Of course, it does *not* ignore the fact that the earth is an open system; evolutionists such as Asimov seem to have a

THE CHRISTIAN AND THE PUBLIC SCHOOLS

strange blind spot at this point, perversely continuing to ignore the fact that this naive charge has been repeatedly answered and refuted. Asimov should know, as a chemist, that the mere influx of external heat into an open system (such as solar energy entering the earth-system) would *not* increase the order (or "complexity" or "information") in that system, but would actually increase its entropy (or "disorder" or "randomness") more rapidly than if it were a closed system! If "order" or "complexity" is actually to increase in any open system, the latter must first be programmed to utilize the incoming energy in some organizing fashion and then be provided also with a complex energy storage-and-conversion mechanism to transform the raw heat influx into the specific useful work of increasing the organized complexity of the system. Since the imaginary evolutionary process on the earth possesses neither such a directing program nor organizing mechanism, the second law of thermodynamics does indeed conflict with it and, to all intents and purposes, renders it impossible.

Asimov also makes the arrogant charge that creationist scientists "have not made any mark as scientists." The fact is that a cross-section of the records of the scientists on the ICR staff, for example, or of the Creation Research Society, would compare quite favorably with those of most secular colleges and universities (including Asimov's own record).

6. *The Argument from Irrelevance.* This criticism is merely a caricature of the concept of a completed creation, which Asimov thinks would be "deceptive." The fact is that a genuine creation would necessarily require creation of "apparent age," the only alternative being eternal matter and no true creation. There is no deception involved at all. As a matter of fact, the world does not even look old, except to the distorted vision of an evolutionist. The fossil record by its very nature speaks clearly of a recent worldwide cataclysm, and there are far more physical processes which yield a young age for the earth than the handful of processes which, through arbitrary

and unreasonable assumptions, can be forced to yield an old age.

7. *The Argument from Authority*. Asimov insists, as do many other evolutionists, that the only real evidence for creationism is from the book of Genesis. The Bible does, indeed, teach creation and its literal authority was accepted by most of the founding fathers of our country and by our country's first schools. That ought to count for something, especially with those who deliberately chose to come to this country from other countries (Asimov came with his parents as immigrants from Russia in 1923). As a matter of fact, however, creationists are quite content to let the scientific evidence speak for itself in the public schools, with no reference whatever to the Bible. Many of us, in fact, are quite insistent on this point, appalled at the prospect of a humanist teacher such as Asimov teaching the Bible to a class of impressionable young people.

Dr. Asimov opposes creationism in the schools with the following astounding concluding argument: "It is only in school that American youngsters in general are ever likely to hear any reasoned exposition of the evolutionary viewpoint. They might find such a viewpoint in books, magazines, newspapers, or even on occasion, on television. But church and family can easily censor printed matter or television. Only the school is beyond their control."

Unfortunately, his last statement is most correct. Parents have indeed largely yielded control of their tax-supported schools to the educational establishment and its *de facto* religion of evolutionary humanism. However, the increasing incidence of such tirades as this from Dr. Asimov indicates that the creation movement has become a serious threat to this powerful and pervasive system.

In all their polemics, the anti-creationists invariably avoid discussing the actual scientific *evidence* for macro-evolution. If there *were* any such evidence, they could easily settle the whole conflict merely by presenting the evidence! Instead, they seem compelled to resort to bombast, ridicule, defamation, intimidation, and distortion. Surely that great body of working scientists, largely uninvolved so far in the creation/evolution conflict will soon begin to see that a two-model approach to all scientific study is salutary and will persuade their more emotional brethren to open their minds to potential truth wherever it might be found.

THEISTIC EVOLUTIONISM

Another type of anti-creationist is the theistic evolutionist, and sometimes these people make it even more difficult for creationism than the overt humanists do. Such theistic evolutionists often consider themselves to be evangelical Christians, arguing that evolution can be considered as God's "method of creation," and so there is no need to add "special creation" to school curricula.[1] Unfortunately this type of unscriptural compromise, which has been common among certain professing Christians since before the days of Charles Darwin, has had the deadly effect of blunting the true Christian educational witness for generations, easing the way for additional compromises in church after church and school after school. It greatly accelerated the takeover of our American public schools by full-blown humanism and total evolutionism.

Theistic evolutionists (as well as "progressive creation" advocates) should realize that such compromises never satisfy either the scientific evolutionist or the Biblical creationist. Evolution itself is not theistic; it is *atheistic,* since by its very nature it purports to explain all things without God. In his "commentary" on Genesis, the atheist Isaac Asimov has said:

> There, then, is perhaps the most fundamental
> disagreement between the Bible and science. The

---

[1] A recent example of this type of pseudocreationist writing is the book *God Did It, But How?* by Dr. R. B. Fischer, Vice President for Academic Affairs at Biola College (La Mirada, CA, Cal Media, 1981, 113 pp.).

Bible describes a Universe created by God, maintained by him, and intimately and constantly
directed by him, while science describes a universe
in which it is not necessary to postulate the existence of God at all.[1]

Sometimes evolutionists will appear to welcome the
compromises proffered by theistic evolutionists, but this
is only for temporary strategic advantage. Dr. Edward O.
Wilson, the Harvard professor considered to be the
founder and leader of the controversial "science" known
as sociobiology, has made this clear:

Bitter experience has taught us that fundamen-
talist religion, which in its aggressive form is one
of the unmitigated evils of the world, cannot be
quickly replaced by benign skepticism and a purely humanistic world view, even among educated
and well-meaning people . . . . Liberal theology
can serve as a buffer.[2]

Not only is it unnecessary to believe in God if evolution
is the true explanation of all things, it is also inconsistent
and even insulting to charge God with using evolution as
the process to "create" man. According to the Bible,
God is omnipotent, omniscient, and merciful, but evolution is utterly inefficient, wasteful, and cruel. The
atheistic evolutionists understand this, even though many
evangelicals don't seem to.

Unfortunately, the testimony of Design is only
for those who, secure in their beliefs already, are
in no need of confirmation. This is just as well,
for there is no theological comfort in the amplia-
tion of DNA and it is no use looking to evolution:
the balance sheet of evolution has so closely written a debit column of all the blood and pain that
goes into the natural process that not even the

[1] Isaac Asimov, *In the Beginning* (New York, Crown Publishers, Inc. 1981), p.
13.
[2] Edward O. Wilson, "The Relation of Science to Theology," *(Zygon,*
September/December 1980; paper presented at 1979 Star Island Conference,
cosponsored by Institute of Religion on an Age of Science and American
Academy of Arts and Sciences).

smoothest accountancy can make the transaction seem morally solvent according to any standard of morals that humans are accustomed to.[1]

Similarly the humanist Jacques Monod, Nobel-prize-winning biologist who was one of the leading French scientists of our generation, said shortly before his death:

If we believe in a Creator . . . it is basically for moral reasons, in order to see a goal for our own lives. And why would God have to have chosen this extremely complex and difficult mechanism? When, I would say by definition, He was at liberty to choose other mechanisms, why would He have to start with simple molecules? Why not create man right away, as of course classical religions believed?

[Natural] selection is the blindest and most cruel way of evolving new species, and more and more complex and refined organisms . . . . The struggle for life and elimination of the weakest is a horrible process, against which our whole modern ethics revolts. An ideal society is a non-selective society, one where the weak is protected, which is exactly the reverse of the so-called natural law. I am surprised that a Christian would defend the idea that this is the process which God more or less set up in order to have evolution.[2]

A prominent member of Madalyn Murray O'Hair's American Atheist Association has effectively pointed out the incompatibility of evolution with Christian theology.

Christianity has fought, still fights, and will fight science to the desperate end over evolution, because evolution destroys utterly and finally the very reason Jesus' earthly life was supposedly made necessary. Destroy Adam and Eve and the

[1]P. B. Medawar and J. S. Medawar. *The Life Science: Current IDeas of Biology* (New York, Harper and Row, 1977), p. 169,
[2]Jacques Monod. "The Secret of Life." Interview with Laurie John on Australian Broadcasting O., June 10, 1976. Transcribed and printed in *Ex Nihilo,* Vol. 3, No. 2, 1980, p. 19.

original sin, and in the rubble you will find the
sorry remains of the son of god. Take away the
meaning of his death. If Jesus was not the
redeemer who died for our sins, and this is what
evolution means, then Christianity is nothing![1]

Thus, evolution contradicts the wisdom and love of
God, the ethics of Christianity, and the gospel of Christ,
in addition to all the real facts of science. There is abundant justification and need for seeking to have creationism brought back into the public schools, on at least an
objective, scientific two-model basis, as a viable alternative to the evolutionary humanistic philosophy which
now prevails.

OTHER PROBLEMS IN PUBLIC EDUCATION

Our discussion in this chapter thus far has centered on
the creation/evolution issue for the good reason that this
is the foundational problem in the public schools. Christian parents are often concerned more immediately with
other problems, however—problems which may seem at
first to be more immediate and vexing than this. Pornographic reading requirements in literature courses, Marxist teachings in economics and civics courses, distortions of
American history in history courses, promotion of sexual
permissiveness in psychology and sex education courses,
and a general humanistic emphasis in all courses—these
all are matters of great concern.

Also of concern are such extracurricular problems as
the banning of prayer and Bible reading, the widespread
use of drugs and alcohol, the lack of discipline, the increasing incidence of premarital sex, and even crime in
the schools, as well as a host of other social and moral
problems which plague many of our public schools and
which constitute a great burden to Christian parents. Add
to all this the distressingly poor basic education received
by students in so many of our public schools, the pro-
liferation of "frills" courses and facilities, the increasing

[1] G. Richard Bozarth. "The Meaning of Evolution," *(American Atheist,*
September 1978, p. 30).

political power of teachers' unions, and it is not surprising that Christian schools are growing so rapidly all across the country.

An adequate treatment of all these questions is far beyond the scope of this book. However, two important generalizations can be stated. In the first place, it cannot be overemphasized that evolutionary humanism is the real root of all these problems. This fact has been briefly expounded in Chapter 2, but has been developed more fully in other creationist writings.[1]

The relationship is logical, though it may be overlooked in the immediate involvement with one of the "fruits" of these bitter roots. If man is merely the product of random processes operating over long ages in a self-contained universe, as assumed in the evolutionary model, then "God" is redundant. If He exists at all, He is so long ago and far away that we can make all our decisions and plan all our actions just as though He did not exist. God is not needed to make evolution work (in fact, as we have seen, the very essence of evolution contradicts any ideas of divine omnipotence, wisdom, and love). Therefore, God is not relevant in modern life, nor in the training of young people to prepare for modern life. Education should be focused on mankind as the pinnacle of past evolution and the architect of future evolution, with the schools thus becoming essentially agents of social change. Religious concepts and practices (especially those associated with Biblical Christianity) need to be educated *out* of young people as expeditiously as possible, so that we can get on with the goal of a great humanistic world federation of mankind. If one looks and considers carefully, he will discover that all the above-mentioned *problems* associated with public education actually fit in beautifully as methods toward attaining this far-off utopian goal. One should re-read George Orwell's classic *1984* with this in mind. Society may not achieve this goal by 1984, but the teachings and activities in the public

---

[1] For example, see *The Troubled Waters of Evolution,* by Henry M. Morris (Second Ed. San Diego, Creation-Life Publishers), 1982.

schools today are surely moving us in that direction.

Now all this should tell us that fighting Marxist teachings and pornographic literature, not to mention drugs and alcohol, in the public schools, is really dealing only with effects—not causes. These are important, of course, and concerned parents—especially Christian parents—do indeed need to do whatever they can to correct them.

But the root cause is evolutionism, which has been made the pseudoscientific rationale for humanism, atheism, Marxism, racism, behaviorism, hedonism, imperialism, materialism, escapism, and all the other philosophies which are opposing God's purposes in creation and which, therefore, are inflicting grievous wounds on God's creatures everywhere. The most effective remedy—indeed the only *real* remedy—for all these superficial ills is to heal the deadly cancer in the human soul. This cancer is *sin* (not "sins"). The sin is the innate, age-long rebellion against God as Creator and Savior of the world, rejecting His Word and His great purpose in creation, ultimately following Satan in *his* campaign to dethrone God and usurp His kingdom.

As stressed again and again in this book, all true education should be centered in the true God and His true purposes. Government schools, in this context, are an anachronism and can never be what schools *ought* to be, in God's economy. Christians ought to work hard to form and support true Christian schools, in all fields and at all levels, in so far as possible.

Nevertheless, government schools are a reality, and we must also be vitally concerned with the needs of the millions of young people enrolled in them—concerned with evangelizing the non-Christian students and properly training the Christian students. We cannot (and, for that matter, *ought* not) try to make them into Christian schools, since education, Biblically speaking, is not the proper function of government. By the same token, however, they should not be *anti-Christian* schools! Governments are divinely-ordained institutions, and all their citizens are responsible under God for their proper functioning. Above all, they should be *just* in their administration of righteousness (Romans 13:1-4). If governments are going to operate schools at all, they should at the very least be neutral and objective in their teachings, not fostering and supporting a humanistic rebellion against the very God who has given them their authority.

All of which brings us to our second generalization. In the public schools, whenever this great conflict comes up (evolutionary humanism versus theistic creationism)—either in teaching or practice—*both* views should be taught, with all their evidences, implications, and applications, and with a conscientious attempt to be fair and objective. This is what we have been calling a *two-model* approach, and it can be applied not only to the direct scientific question of origins, but also to all these other vexing problems. That is, a two-model approach to the study of American history or sex education or any other subject could be developed, teaching both the humanistic approach and the theistic approach (the latter would not have to be that of Christian fundamentalism only, but a broad concept derived from monotheism in general—that of real divine sovereignty and human responsibility).

If necessary in some instances, this *two-model approach* could become a *two-track approach,* providing separate classes or curricula or social activities for the two groups of students, each of which would have teachers and supervisors who are committed personally to either humanism or theism, in accordance with the track assigned to them. Students would then be assigned to the track elected by them and/or their parents.

One can easily think of many problems in a two-model approach, and even more in a two-track approach. Nevertheless, some such approach is the only *just* way to administer public education at all. The problems could surely be solved in each specific application if the governmental and educational authorities involved would make a conscientious and open-minded effort to do so.

That, of course, is the question. To a large extent the modern professional educational establishment is so pervasively committed to evolutionary humanism and even to drastic social change that they will bitterly oppose any such fair approach. The best hope that this might ever be realized lies at the level of the local school board, whose members are elected by the people in their own communities.

In any case, the goal is a just goal, and is therefore worth trying to reach. The efforts of creationist Christians, Jews, and others who love our country and its godly heritage, and who are concerned about true justice and moral righteousness, should at least be directed to that end.

Chapter 10

True Education— Review and Conclusion

The purpose of this book has been to formulate a truly Biblical doctrine of education, with application not only to the teaching of religious subjects but also of secular subjects. In fact, as we have repeatedly emphasized, there is no dichotomy between these two areas of truth—*all* truth is God's truth and should be taught as such. The public schools and universities have, on the other hand, deteriorated to the point that they teach almost everything from the secular perspective only, while most purportedly religious schools have deteriorated to the point of attempting to divorce religious truth from secular truth, teaching both as compartmentalized segments of reality, one that is outward and factual and another that is inward and spiritual. Very few schools today are making a serious attempt to develop a complete system of education structured within the Biblical framework, but there is a critical need for this to be done.

The Bible-believing Christian needs to be reminded

repeatedly that responsibility for education lies primarily with the parents and secondly with the church. Neither the school nor the state has the right, under God, to usurp this responsibility. Since the school and/or the state *have,* however, usurped this role, it is necessary that parents and churches, working together, establish their own schools, especially for the teaching of children, but also for teaching at least those subjects that have strong theological, philosophical, anthropological, or sociological overtones, to people of all ages.

This does not mean, of course, that the public schools should be abandoned nor their students left to flounder unaided in a sea of evolutionary humanism. These schools have become, in effect, a part of the socio-political structure of the nation, and the government itself is a divinely-ordained institution. When the government becomes anti-Biblical and anti-theistic, it is not only the right but the duty of its citizens, under God, to try to restore it to its proper function. In particular, the people ought to try to bring the schools of the state back to a more nearly Biblical system of education, to the extent this is feasible.

In the present intellectual climate, however, a more realistic objective is to seek to persuade the schools at least to be neutral. If they insist on teaching evolution, they should balance this by also teaching creation, teaching both as viable scientific alternatives, with evidences pro and con for each. If they must teach humanism, they should also teach theism, teaching both as objectively and factually as possible. The teaching of amorality should be balanced by the teaching of moral responsibility. And so on.

With the minds and souls of millions at stake, most of whom, realistically speaking, will never have the slightest opportunity of attending a real Christian school, it is clear that the terms of the Noahic covenant demand that the God-fearing citizens of any nation, whether they are Christians or not, do all they can to reclaim the public schools and colleges of that nation for at least this minimal standard of objectivity in their teachings. A real contribution can be made by godly people—especially by genuinely Biblical Christians—who are willing to work in and with such public educational institutions, serving as teachers, as school administrators, as board members, as professional scientists and other specialists, or simply as concerned parents.

Under the Adamic cultural mandate and Noahic covenant, all men are empowered to search for new truth ("research"), to make application of discovered truth ("development"), and then to indoctrinate such verified research results and useful applications in the minds of members of the next generation ("education"). True "teaching" is synonymous with "indoctrination" in truth, not "discovery" of truth, though the teaching curriculum may well include instruction in proved methods of research and development.

However, such freedom in research and development, as well as academic freedom in teaching, is valid only within the constraints of revealed truth in Scripture. It is particularly limited in the social sciences and humanities because of the deleterious effects of sin in human life and in all human relationships.

It must be continually foremost in the mind and heart of the true Christian educator that *all truth* is founded on the Father and Son as Creator of all things, centered on Christ as Redeemer of all things and guided by the Spirit-inspired Scriptures as Revealer of all things. The Christian teacher should always be sensitive to the fact that the academic and political establishments, on the other hand, have so perverted most modern education that it is founded on evolution, centered on man, and guided by human reasonings and feelings. Modern man, having abandoned Biblical theism, has given himself

over to naturalistic humanism or supernaturalistic occultism.

We have shown that, in a truly Biblical system of
education, all courses and curricula must continually
recognize the importance of special creation as the
foundation of all truth. On this foundation must be
erected a structure of study in all courses which centers
on the Lord Jesus Christ, presenting all the relevant
factual data (as obtained both from the Bible and from
research results under the terms of the cultural mandate), as well as such analyses and correlations as are
guided by Biblical principles and constraints. Only
materials of positive good should be taught as acceptable, materials which glorify God, edify Christians,
and win the lost. Humanistic philosophies and practices
should only be discussed in a context clearly
demonstrating their fallacies and dangers. The same
applies to any material with erotically suggestive or
blasphemous connotations, or teachings tending to
justify any form of evil.

To accomplish such unique, yet vital goals, it is of
supreme importance that the right teachers be obtained. Although teaching methods are important (and
we have shown that the traditional lecture method is
usually the best of these), it is the teacher who is of
primary importance.

The true teacher—not only a Bible teacher, but a
teacher of any subject—should be a God-called man or
woman. The teacher should have the gift of teaching, as
evidenced by the attributes required in Scripture for
pastor-teachers. Such a teacher should also be well
qualified both personally (as a Spirit-filled Christian
holding sound doctrine) and professionally, well
prepared through training and experience to teach the
subject he is called to teach, and to teach it in a
thoroughly Biblical context.

Teachers who are genuinely qualified in this way are
in short supply, but that is no reason for a school to set-

tle for teachers who are not so qualified. God will supply what He demands we use! It is better, indeed, not to offer a course at all (substituting, if necessary, some other course in the student's curriculum) than to offer it through the wrong teacher. Teachers who *want* to be qualified, "desiring earnestly the best gifts," may be helped through special training and study if appropriate. For such God-called teachers Paul's exhortation is appropriate. "And we beseech you, brethren, to know them which labor among you, and are over you in the Lord, and admonish you; And to esteem them very highly in love for their work's sake" (I Thessalonians 5:12,13).

These goals, of course, cannot even be approached in our modern public schools. We come back again, therefore, to the great urgency of establishing sound Biblical Christian schools—and then maintaining, operating, and supporting them. These are desperately needed at all levels and in all fields of education. Whether or not such a truly Christian and Biblical system of education will ever be attained before the Lord returns, it is at least our duty to strive toward such a goal. May Isaiah's great prophecy become our prayer and passion:

And all thy children shall be taught of the Lord;
and great shall be the peace of thy children.
(Isaiah 54:13)

Index of Subjects

Cultural mandate, 30, 109-110
Evolution influence, 50
Noahic covenant, 118, 124-125
Superior Christian insights,
130-133
Neo-evangelical schools, 143
Nimrod, 59-60
Noahic covenant,
Establishment after flood, 32,
116-118
Present continuance, 119-122, 266

O

Occultism
Biblical warnings, 88-91, 189
Campus reaction against
humanism, 84-85
Deceptions, 89-91
Demonism, 85-86, 92, 189
Drug culture, 85, 89
Evolution, relation to, 92-93
Human nature, 93-95
Meditation movements, 86-87
Pantheism, 92-93
Paranormal phenomena, 87,
91-92
Offense, avoiding, 197-198
Order in nature, 49

P

Pantheism, 57-58, 93, 242
Pantheon of gods, 56-58
Parents
Control of education, 17, 34-36,
45, 112, 154, 182
Enforcement of rules, 202-204
Obedience of children, 190-191
Paul, training of, 157
Penalties for rule-breaking
See: *Enforcement*
Philosophy
Condemned in Scripture, 97-102,
137-138
Definition, 99
Physical sciences, 30, 33, 50, 131,
133
Pornographic literature
Christian schools, unacceptable
in, 147-148
Criteria for exceptions, 149-150
Positive, emphasis on, 199-200

Power of God in nature, 131
Profanity, 190
Programmed learning, 18, 165, 174
Progressive creation, 48, 70
Prophecy, gift of, 39, 153
Prophets, school for, 38
Public schools
Antiquity, nations of, 37-38
Christian students and teachers,
232-235
Christian, responsibility of,
231-239, 260-267
Evolutionism dominant, 50,
256-257, 262-264
Progressive education, 22-24
Two-model approach, 235-239
Unscriptural, 20

R

Rainbow, 118
Rationalism, 20-21
Redemptive work of Christ, 26-27,
32, 113, 129
Regulations for schools
See: *Rules and regulations*
Religion
Evolution as religion, 220-221,
239-243
Humanism, 254
Influence of evolution, 52-53
Occultism, 189
Pantheism, 86, 241-243
Research
Christian writers, 126-128
Cultural mandate, 30-31, 109-110,
183
Discovery method of teaching,
165-166, 175-176
Skills, 170
Resurrection
Christ's, 100-101
Doctrine of, 137-138
Rules and regulations
Bible principles, 187, 193-200
Church, 186
Commandments, Ten, 188-193
Commitments, Ten, 193-200
Home, 186, 187
Order, required for, 184
Penalties for breaking, 186,
201-208

Index of Names

Index of Scriptures